Well Stressed

How You Can Manage Stress Before It Turns Toxic

by
SONIA LUPIEN

D1264039

John Wiley & Sons Canada, Ltd.

Wiley publishes in a variety of print and electronic formats and by print-on-demand. Some material included with standard print versions of this book may not be included in e-books or in print-on-demand. If this book refers to media such as a CD or DVD that is not included in the version you purchased, you may download this material at http://booksupport.wiley.com. For more information about Wiley products, visit www.wiley.com.

Library and Archives Canada Cataloguing in Publication Data

Lupien, Sonia, 1965-
    Well stressed : how you can manage stress before it turns toxic / Sonia Lupien.

Translation of: Par amour du stress.
Includes bibliographical references and index.
Issued also in electronic format.
ISBN 978-1-118-27360-9

    1. Stress management.   2. Stress (Psychology).
3. Stress (Physiology).   I. Title.

RA785.L8613 2012   616.9'8   C2012-901340-4

978-1-118-27956-4 (ebk); 978-1-118-27955-7 (ebk); 978-1-118-57987-1 (ebk)

Production Credits
Cover design: Adrian So
Typesetting: Thomson Digital
Cover image: Adrian So
Printer: Trigraphik LBF

Editorial Credits
Executive editor: Robert Hickey
Managing editor: Alison Maclean
Production editor: Jeremy Hanson-Finger

John Wiley & Sons Canada, Ltd.
6045 Freemont Blvd.
Mississauga, Ontario
L5R 4J3

Printed in Canada
1 2 3 4 5 LBF TRI 16 15 14 13 12

Well
Stressed

To my father, who taught me to hunt mammoths.
To my husband, who often hunts them for me.
To my children, for whom I would kill a mammoth with
my bare hands.

Contents

Acknowledgments   ix

Introduction   1

Chapter 1   Do You Know the Meaning of Stress?   4

Chapter 2   Stress Is Really NUTS   9

Chapter 3   Acute Stress to Help Us Survive   23

Chapter 4   The Long and Winding Road to Chronic Stress   31

Chapter 5   Measuring the Weight of Chronic Stress: The Allostatic Load Battery   43

Chapter 6   When Stress Affects Our Memory   49

Chapter 7   Why Are We So Stressed These Days?   65

Chapter 8   Stress to Match Each Personality   72

Chapter 9   Two Sexes, Two Types of Stress?   78

Chapter 10   Your Social Status, Your Stress   89

Chapter 11   Recognizing When You're Stressed   105

Chapter 12   To Kill a Mammoth, You First Have to Know Where to Find It   109

Chapter 13   Addressing NUTS for Adolescents   119

Chapter 14   Addressing NUTS for Adult Workers   126

Chapter 15   Fleeing the Mammoth Can Help Us Control Our Stress   141

Chapter 16   The Power of Others   145

Chapter 17   Your Body Is Your Most Effective Ally   153

Appendix 1: History of the Science of Stress   168
Appendix 2: References   192
Notes   203
Index   207

Acknowledgments

I would like to thank personally all the graduate students who have volunteered their services since the Centre for Studies on Human Stress was founded in 2004 to ensure the center's success:

Alexandra Fiocco, PhD
Nathe François, PhD
Robert Paul Juster, MSc, doctoral candidate
Marie-France Marin, MSc, doctoral candidate
Pierrich Plusquellec, PhD
Tania Schramek, MSc
Shireen Sindi, MSc, doctoral candidate
Lyane Trépanier, BSc
Nathalie Wan, MSc

And I don't want to forget:

Geneviève Arsenault-Lapierre, MSc
Laura Cooper, BSc
Anne Hand, BSc
Benjamin Lai, MSc
Kamala Pilgrim, MSc

Introduction

My publisher was getting impatient as he awaited this book, which it seemed was never going to be finished. I tried to explain all the competing demands on me: my science laboratory where we do research into stress, my teaching at the university, my children, my household and various unexpected events, not to mention the time required for my students. This all leaves me feeling that I'm under heavy time pressure. But even with this pressure, I don't usually feel stressed. On the contrary, I love the feeling of intensity and achievement that goes with getting something done: the conclusion of a major task or the successful completion of a student's doctoral thesis.

Let's keep in mind that I'm the sort of person who talks at a hundred words a minute. I gesticulate constantly and move quickly. I do everything fast, so much so that the people around me conclude (and they don't hesitate to tell me) that I must be operating at maximum stress. However, in the heat of the action, I don't feel stressed at all, although I can easily see that the way I carry on may stress those around me. That's a whole other matter!

One day, one of my research colleagues and I had agreed to have the walls of one of our research laboratories painted bright orange. Most of the people who came by our workplace were quick to tell us that we really did need to do stress research if we didn't know that painting a wall bright orange is not the least bit Zen. Many of them added that this bright orange color would cause stress for everyone, not just the people in the lab but even those just passing by.

My standard answer was that this kind of comment showed a poor understanding of stress. Zen is not a surefire antidote to stress—in fact, an infallible stress antidote simply doesn't exist. You can paint every wall in your house a gloomy beige, but that won't eliminate the stress that may keep you awake at night now and again. I'm utterly convinced of this. Like everyone else, I too experience stress that has me ruminating from 11 p.m. to 3 a.m. and feeling grumpy and impatient the next morning. When this happens, my stress overflows onto my children and husband, sometimes leaving them bewildered by my mood shifts.

Not very long ago, I found myself on a television panel with a well-known doctor who'd written a book maintaining that with the seven or twelve methods he was suggesting, readers could "cure their stress." When the host asked for my view on this, I answered with what 20 years of scientific research had taught me: stress is not an illness, and hence cannot be cured. Stress is a necessary reaction by the body, one that enables us to survive. Therefore, if you eliminate stress from your life, you end up dead. I also added that my colleagues and I, working in the field of stress, have increasingly come to recognize that all those self-help books on stress that promise to cure it, eradicate it or even wipe it out forever through all sorts of outlandish methods may, in fact, have a very harmful effect on your ability to control your stress. Indeed, the popularity of these books may help explain why so many people nowadays are stressed. In short, these supposed cures could just make things worse.

My interactions with the people I've tested in my scientific experiments have led me to understand that stress is the great unknown of our time. No matter how it's dressed up, stress has become the black sheep of our society, something that has to be made to go away. It's important to remember, though, that our brain's primary role is to detect danger. How would you react if you heard me say that, if we're really so very stressed nowadays, it's because our brain doesn't know that we're living in the twenty-first century and not in prehistoric times? And that because of this it doesn't differentiate between the danger from an enraged mammoth and the threat from an office colleague who constantly questions our ability to do our job properly?

Since your brain's primary role is to save your life, what would you say if I added that by generating a stress response each time you detect a threat, whether real or not, your brain really thinks it's helping you? Or if I said you can help your brain understand that the stressful situation or factor (the stressor) you face isn't a raging mammoth, and that once this is clearly understood by your brain, you'll see a decline in your stress reaction? Finally, would you be surprised to learn that a growing number of researchers in the field of stress are starting to believe seriously that, if our children are so stressed these days, it may be because we're overprotecting them, thereby preventing them from developing "stress resistance"?

All this has led me to develop a very clear message based on 20 years of research on human stress. I've got to make it clear right away that I have no magical recipe to offer you for controlling the stress in your life. Nor do I have any foolproof program consisting of seven or twelve "scientifically proven" approaches to "cure" your stress. There is no "scientifically proven" method that can help absolutely everyone control the stress in their lives, and I strongly doubt that any such method will be found.

On the other hand, I can state confidently that, if you're aware of stress—the real thing—and understand it, you'll be able to tame it or even use it in some situations to optimize your performance or your physical health. This is the only method I can offer you in this book. It represents everything I've learned about human stress in the course of my research. This new knowledge will give you a better understanding of what stress really is and of how to control it in most situations.

So here's what I'm suggesting. I'd like to take you by the hand and bring you with me into the extraordinary world of stress. I'll help you understand, step by step, how people become stressed, and I'll explain why, in some cases, stress can make us sick.

I'll teach you how stress can help or hinder your memory and how your emotions can be both a stress generator and a stress remover. Then I'll explain how people lose control over stress and how you can regain control. At that point, you'll have all the tools you need to develop critical thinking regarding all that's being said about stress.

My goal is simple. By offering you what I know about stress, I'll be giving you the power of knowledge. The only way to take control of your stress is to know all about it. Only then can you make it your ally.

Chapter 1

Do You Know the Meaning of Stress?

One day I suggested to my research team that we venture outside our laboratory to conduct a "field" survey. So on a Saturday afternoon we went to a very busy shopping center with the goal of asking the first 100 people we met three questions and then studying their answers.

The first question asked was, "Do you know what stress is?" Ninety-nine people responded "yes," the hundredth being too busy shopping to answer our question! The second question was, "What is stress?" The 99 individuals told us that stress was "time pressure"—people feel stressed when they do not have time to do all the things they want to do in the time available. The last question was, "Which group do you think is the most stressed: the elderly, children or adults?" The 99 blithely replied, "No question! Adults!"

This answer reflects common sense. If stress is a consequence of time pressure, adults are clearly the most stressed group, given the pressure of schedules, the 100,000 jobs to do, children to take to and from daycare, the work that never ends, children's sports activities in the evenings and on weekends, aging parents who need assistance, and the list goes on!

This reaction reminded me of the early days of my research career, when I was studying stress among the elderly. Many people appeared skeptical when I told them about my PhD thesis. I was told, "Oh great! You're working on the stress of the elderly. Not exactly a thrilling research project. You would do better to study us, the adults, with our crazy jobs, our lives as stressed-out parents and everything else!"

Why do these people have the impression that the elderly and children suffer less from stress than they do? It's precisely because their definition of stress revolves around time pressure. Since older people are retired, they have all the time they could want and therefore time pressure cannot be causing them stress. In addition, we often stereotype the elderly: they walk slowly; they drive slowly; in short, they do everything slowly. They therefore cannot possibly suffer from time constraints and, by extension, cannot be more stressed than we are.

Similarly, our children also do not appear to suffer from time pressures. They do not have a domineering boss, or urgent bills to pay at the end of the month, or rushed shopping to do; they have only to spend time with their friends and pursue their favorite activities. So they too would not experience stress.

Here is the first myth in the public perception of stress: because we consider stress a consequence of time pressure, we conclude that the elderly and children are necessarily less stressed than adults are. This is wrong.

Scientific discoveries during the last two decades show that the opposite is in fact true. The elderly and children are actually much more vulnerable to stress than adults. Their brains are much more affected by stress than ours. In fact, this vulnerability increases among the elderly as a result of the impact stress has on a brain that is aging and slowly deteriorating—it has been shown that stress has the capacity to accelerate the aging of the brain in the elderly.

Children's brains are also very vulnerable to stress because their brains are still developing. It has also been shown that stress can delay the development of some parts or functions of the brain in children.

Along with the myth of time pressure as a cause of stress, there is a variant that has appeared in recent years, this time associated with children. According to this belief, parents are constantly pushing their children to rush to do all sorts of activities: go to school, do their homework, engage in one sport or extracurricular activity after another, both during the week and on the weekend. So, parents themselves are creating time pressures for their children. You see this repeated all the time in newspapers and magazines, which suggest the possibility that the many sports and cultural activities in which our youth are enrolled in the evenings and on weekends cause them to rush and therefore have become a source of stress. Since stress is time pressure, the link is obvious: children, like adults, are stressed.

The poor parents, in addition to having to manage their own stress, must now consider whether getting their children involved in sports activities—given the persistent message that exercise represents the key to preventing obesity in young people—could create stress for them. One day a totally distraught parent expressed his confusion on the subject: "It's crazy. Either we stress out our children, or we make them obese!"

But is it really time pressures that put stress on our children? Children are bundles of energy, and sports often replace the distance that children in another era would have walked to school. Not only do they no longer go to school on foot, but video games are now a major part of their activities. So, before concluding that sports activities create stress for children because they generate time pressure, it's best to ask whether stress is really due to time pressure. I state clearly that it is not!

Stress Is Not the Same As Time Pressure

To reassure you about registering your youngest in the next hockey camp, allow me to demolish the first myth about stress. Stress is not generated by time pressure. Let's examine the evidence to the contrary.

If stress is strictly the result of time pressure, then how is it that we can be stressed during a visit to the dentist on a day off? In such a case, you will agree that time is not a factor because you are off work. And the receptionist or dental hygienist will not rush you, stopwatch in hand, to the dentist's chair! Yet the average person is stressed by a visit to the dentist, and the stress is considerably eased on leaving the dentist's office, even with a hefty bill.

Consider some more examples. What about the enormous stress you experience when you learn that you or someone you love has a serious illness? Or when you are summoned to the boss's office during a major corporate restructuring? Or when your mother-in-law shows up on a Friday night and announces that she has come to spend the weekend, when you have been looking forward all week to having a restful few days? How do we explain stress in these situations in terms of time pressure?

I am sure that in all these situations, you will see a surge of stress at least as significant as if you were late to pick up the children at daycare. Yet in each case, there is no time pressure involved. Therefore, stress is not the result of time pressure.

But then, what is it that causes stress? The most thorough way to answer this question would involve stepping back in time to see how the concept of stress arose, how it has evolved over the decades and how scientists perceive it today.

I know, I know, you're in a hurry to get to the heart of the subject and read more in depth about what will induce a stress response. That is why I will not bore you with a long chapter on the history of the science of stress. However, if you are interested in better understanding how researchers have come to discover the information that I summarize in this book, you can go to Appendix 1, where this history is recounted.

In the meantime, I'll just list some very important facts that have marked the evolution of the science of stress during the last century. Researchers have understood that it is not our emotional sense of pressure that forms the basis of physical and mental disorders associated with stress. Actually, these disorders have their origin in the physical: they are related to stress hormones produced in response to situations that the brain has identified as posing a threat.

As we shall see in later chapters, our brain plays a critical role in helping us survive: it helps us detect threats in our environment. When the brain detects a threatening situation, it triggers a series of actions that result in the production of stress hormones. These hormones enable us to do the only two things one can do in the face of danger: fight or flee.

Both of these actions require energy. The two stress hormones give us the energy to fight the threat or flee if the risk is too great. It is this wonderful response that allowed us to hunt mammoths in prehistoric times or flee successfully when they were too big.

However, research has also shown that when secreted, these hormones have the capacity to return to the brain and affect our memory and our emotional control by acting on regions of the brain involved in these functions. Because of the effect of stress hormones on the body and the brain, ongoing and significant production of these hormones forms the basis of various physical and mental disorders associated with chronic stress.

And here is the most important information that has emerged from the scientific study of stress in the last century. Researchers have shown that a situation must contain at least one of four characteristics to induce a stress response that could have long-term deleterious effects. With any of these four characteristics, it does not matter who you are—whatever your gender, your age or your work, you will produce stress hormones, and you will do so every time.

The researchers also demonstrated that a situation need not necessarily contain all four characteristics to induce a stress response, but the production of stress hormones increases the more a situation has these elements. These four characteristics are discussed throughout this book, and I hope they prove an effective tool for lowering the extent of your reaction to stress.

Chapter 2
Stress Is Really NUTS

As I often enjoy pointing out, I really have a bizarre line of work. In the laboratory, my work consists of getting people stressed each day—and I get paid for this! Anyhow, when participants are subjected to stress creators, we always play on one or more of the four characteristics of such situations, and we measure the resulting stress hormones. In short, people are going to produce a biological stress response when exposed to a situation involving any of these characteristics:

NOVELTY: The situation is new to you.

UNPREDICTABILITY: You find the situation unexpected or unpredictable.

THREAT TO YOUR EGO: The situation is threatening to your ego.

SENSE OF LOW CONTROL: You have the impression that you lack control over the situation.

These characteristics form the acronym NUTS, which may be an easier way for you to remember them. I challenge you to find a situation that stresses you and that you can't explain through one or more of these characteristics. For nearly 20 years, I have attempted in my laboratory, and through experimental research, to find a fifth characteristic, but without success. For your part, try analyzing your stress reactions on the basis of these four parameters, and you'll find, to varying degrees and in various combinations, that they're the real source of your stress response.

A Note On Ego

Ego is what characterizes our personality compared to other people's personalities. If I asked you to describe yourself, you'd know what to say. You could, for instance, tell me you are someone who is generous, funny and athletic. Each time we interact with someone, there's always a risk that our ego could be threatened. Here's an example: you're at the coffee machine at work, and a colleague questions your ability to do your work properly—in front of two of your bosses. The sensation you experience when you get back to your office (tensing of the hands, a sensation of heat and a faster heartbeat) is a stress response. As I like to say, the coffee machine at work can sometimes be dangerous for the ego!

What About Time Pressures?

Let's come back to the time pressures many people see as *the* cause of their stress. When we examine this factor more deeply, we realize that time pressures are not what's causing our stress but rather *the impression of losing control over our time.*

You may have a sense that you're losing control of your time, just as you may have a sense that you're losing control of your job, your family or your health. This feeling of losing control, like any of the other three characteristics, is enough to set off a physiological stress response in your body. But you should note that I'm talking here about a "sense" of losing control and not actually losing control. You don't really need to lose control over your marriage to get a stress reaction. Just having the impression that you're losing control over your marriage (arguing more than usual, feeling that your spouse doesn't care and so on) will produce stress hormones in large quantities.

This distinction between the *impression* and the *reality* of whether you have control is essential. It lies in the fact that each of us has our own stress recipe because we perceive stressful events according to our own vision. Discovering this lets us get a better grip on the phenomenon, just as knowing the ingredients in a soup recipe helps us understand why the soup causes an allergic reaction and how to avoid it next time.

Your Stress Recipe

What surprises me the most in the course of my research is that when I ask all the stressed people I'm examining to tell me about the origin of their stress, more than three-quarters of them have absolutely no idea how to respond. Their stress is chronic and sometimes brutal, but they are unable to describe its cause. It's almost as if they were suffering from food poisoning but didn't know what the harmful ingredient was in the dish that caused it.

The only way to understand what forms a stress factor is to break it down. The NUTS method, with its four universal stress characteristics, helps us break down stress and identify the factors that lead our brain to detect a threat and then produce large quantities of stress hormones. By doing this, we can spell out exactly what our stress recipe is.

The following examples will show us that everyone is capable of discovering their own stress recipe. To illustrate this idea, let's take the examples of people in different age groups who are facing stressful situations, and together let's break down each situation based on the four NUTS characteristics. We'll then see that, depending on the age of the person who feels stressed, the stress response may lead to different physical manifestations.

Example 1. Stress in Children

We saw before that, contrary to popular belief, our children are even more vulnerable to the effects of stress than we are because their brains, which receive the stress hormones, are still growing. Even though stress in children may sometimes turn out to be quite intense, it is not always clearly expressed or visible. Very young children, for instance, tend to show their stress in the form of physical illness (stomachache, headache and so on). Parents, who sometimes think they're too young to be afflicted by any sort of stress, don't always understand what these illnesses mean.

Nonetheless, these symptoms often enable us to understand that real stress exists in children, and if it is chronic it can sometimes harm their development. This makes it absolutely vital for us to pay attention to our children from a very early age to help them break down their stress. Let's take a look together at how one situation can cause stress reactions to differing degrees among children, depending on their life experience.

The Situation

Let's take a potentially huge stress creator in children from ages 5 to 7: their parents' separation or divorce. We'll see that children can experience varying levels of stress, depending on how the divorce is initiated.

The Players and Their NUTS Factors
Jonathan, age 5½

After months of disagreements and disputes, Jonathan's parents suddenly decided to separate. Jonathan had become quite accustomed to his parents' conflict and was hardly expecting this decision. His mother, with whom he would be spending his weekdays, moved to Edmonton, and his father, who would be with him on weekends, stayed in Calgary. He gradually made friends at his new school in Edmonton, but he had a sense of missing things on weekends when he was with his father in Calgary. He was left without his Edmonton friends and had trouble making new friends in Calgary. After the divorce, Jonathan complained of severe abdominal pain several times a week, especially on Thursdays and Fridays.

Jonathan's NUTS factors: He was stressed because he had to face a radically new situation (no longer living with both parents, and changing schools and cities). This split was totally unpredictable for him since his parents had never said a word to him about it, and he was accustomed to their fights. In addition, at no time did he have any input into how events would unfold, giving him a sense that he had no control over the situation.

Added to this, he had the impression that his new friends would no longer be interested in him because of his weekend absences. The situation therefore became threatening to his ego. This family crisis thus combined all four NUTS characteristics for a single individual, making it perfectly normal for this young boy to undergo a strong stress reaction in the form of severe abdominal pain, especially on Thursdays and Fridays. Why on these days? Because this was when Jonathan began to anticipate his weekends in Calgary and the loss of his friends. This anticipation produced as strong a stress reaction as the actual loss of his friends on Saturdays and Sundays in Calgary. As a result, he experienced these physical symptoms starting on Thursday or Friday.

Sabrina, age 6

Sabrina's parents had not been getting along for the last few months, and they decided to separate. About three months before the planned separation date, they told Sabrina about their decision. The parents agreed that their respective new homes would be located less than three miles from Sabrina's school so that she could take the same school bus, regardless of whether she was at her father's or mother's home. In the first three months, Sabrina would be allowed to decide with which parent she would spend the week. Sabrina's parents were rather perplexed at their inability to detect any stress in Sabrina, which would have been normal in this type of situation.

Sabrina's NUTS factors: During this crisis, Sabrina's parents handled the situation very well. Although the situation was new for Sabrina, it was not wholly unpredictable because she had been told about it long before the separation actually occurred. The child had the sense that she had things under her control since she could choose which parent to spend the week with. The situation was not threatening to her ego, because she stayed in the same school and could keep all her friends and be close to familiar places. This made it entirely possible for the child to experience her parents' divorce without a strong stress reaction.

Example 2. Stress in Adolescents

Adolescents' brains go through extraordinary growth from age 8 right up to the end of their teenage years. As most parents know, adolescents are great sleepers. This is due largely to their substantial brain development and, accordingly, the need to recharge their batteries when night comes along—until noon the next day! When stress hormones reach these fast-growing brains, they affect areas that are still developing, such as the frontal lobe and the amygdaloid nucleus.[1] The frontal lobe plays a role in the ability to pay proper attention to surroundings and memorize them better, while the amygdaloid nucleus has an important role in regulating emotions. It's therefore not surprising to find that, when adolescents experience significant stress, it can take the form of sleep problems, lack of attention or anxiety.

Here again, the appearance of these symptoms in adolescents may be an important sign their parents can use to tell that their child is undergoing stress. However, there's no need to await these symptoms to establish this. Deconstructing a situation into its NUTS is often enough to tell that it has a strong chance of inducing stress in an adolescent.

The Situation

Let's take a situation that can cause a huge amount of stress in adolescents: a new school year involving the move from elementary school to junior high school. Who can forget the stress experienced at this crucial stage in life? When children leave elementary school, they are moving from a relatively small and familiar world to a big school with many more students. When children are in Grade 6, they have a sense of being in control of their situation because they know everyone around them and are the oldest pupils in the school, putting them at the top of the social hierarchy. But when they switch to junior high school, they find themselves in a school that's much bigger than their little neighborhood elementary school, with many more people they don't know, and now they're the youngest people in the school. These factors may produce a stress response, but here again, we'll see that the scope of the stress response depends to a large extent on what's going on between individual adolescents and their surroundings.

The Players and Their NUTS Factors
Emily, age 11

Emily doesn't live in the same neighborhood as her new junior high school, and as a result she doesn't know anyone there. She has no idea which bus to take to get to her new school, and she's wondering how she can find the classrooms without help. She asked her parents to accompany her on a visit to the school to get a better understanding of how it operates, but they're very busy with the care required by her younger sister, who suffers from a congenital deformity. Emily no longer feels truly at home and is worried that she won't make friends or that her older schoolmates could make fun of her. She really feels afraid of switching to junior high. Since the end of June, Emily has experienced sleep problems and has become very irritable with her brother and sister.

Emily's NUTS factors: The situation is new and unpredictable for Emily, because she doesn't know anything about her school or how it operates. Things are also outside her control, because she has no choice concerning the school. And her parents are too busy with her sickly younger sister to join her on a visit and meet the teachers before the start of classes. Finally, the situation is threatening to her ego, because she's going from a milieu where she was among the oldest to one where she'll be surrounded by older students and where she doesn't know anybody.

Combining all four NUTS characteristics, the new school year is turning out to be highly stressful for Emily. This may explain the sleep problems she has experienced since late June. Elementary school, a source of comfort, has ended, and Emily has started to think about back-to-school time in September.

Alex, age 10½

Alex has lived for a number of years in the neighborhood where his new junior high school is located, and he attended the elementary school near home. He thus has various pals who will be going to junior high with him, and his big brother Max has already been there for a year. Although he sometimes fights with Max, he is sure his brother will help him out when it comes to finding classrooms. In addition, Max plays hockey and has a very imposing physique. If the older guys in the junior high give Alex a rough time, he knows he can count on Max to defend him. But he still feels some apprehension at the thought of moving on to this new phase in his education, though he's not sure whether this feeling comes from the excitement of experiencing something new or whether it's stress.

Alex's NUTS factors: The slight apprehension felt by Alex may induce a minor stress response, because the situation is new for him. On the other hand, having several of his pals with him making the leap to the same school and having his brother Max to guide him gives him a sense of having control of the situation. Also, this provides some reassurance for his ego, because he feels less vulnerable at the thought of being among older students. The stress he feels is thus not nearly as strong as what Emily is feeling with all four NUTS characteristics combined.

Example 3. Stress in Adults

As I mentioned earlier, adults' brains are less vulnerable to the effects of stress hormones than the brains of young or elderly people. But this doesn't mean that adults don't feel stress or that they don't produce stress hormones that can affect their bodies and brains. Adults suffering from major chronic stress show the same array of symptoms as are found among children and adolescents, but there are broad individual differences in the occurrence of stress symptoms in adults.

Thus, one adult under stress may suffer severe attacks of acid reflux, while someone else may develop migraines or serious sleep problems. Irritability and anxiety are also among the signs found in adults who are in a state of chronic stress. As we'll see below, the characteristics leading to a stress response in children and adolescents are exactly the same as those leading to a stress response in adults.

The Situation

A new manager has just been appointed to head a corporate department, and he is planning a major restructuring, letting the "troops" know from the outset that, although he's not intending to lay anyone off, that could change depending on his group's performance at the next quarterly assessment. He indicates that, in moving toward the company's new development plan, employees will have to work extra hard to ensure the plan's success. His approach makes it clear that employees who agree to work overtime to ensure the plan's success are those who can expect rewards at the end of the restructuring.

The Players and Their NUTS Factors
Martin, age 32

Martin, a bachelor with no children, has just been hired by the company after completing his bachelor's degree in economics as a part-time student. He likes this new company he's working for but knows he won't spend his entire working life there. He sees the job merely as a step in his professional life. His career plan involves working a few years for this well-recognized firm, which will help him get a better-paid position in another company that really interests him. With no children to look after, he is willing to work more than 50 hours a week to keep his job and add it to his résumé. He sees this new restructuring as a challenge that he is ready to take on.

Martin's NUTS factors: For Martin, this is a new situation, because he had not foreseen this major restructuring in his career plan. He doesn't really have a sense of unpredictability in this situation, because he was ready from the start to put in extra hours to meet a new manager's requirements. Also, he has a sense of having control over the situation because, as a bachelor with nobody to look after, he can control his time as required. Finally, the situation is not threatening to his ego, because he sees it as a challenge that, if met, will be a positive addition to his résumé. Martin is therefore not experiencing much stress in connection with the restructuring.

Peter, age 41

Peter, a father of two children, has just been promoted within the department and is very proud of this. He worked for 10 years to get this promotion, often to the detriment of his family life. His wife misses few opportunities to chide him for this. In addition, the new position lets him silence his brother-in-law, Adam, at family gatherings, where he previously liked to tease Peter about his "low-level" job.

The announcement from the new boss makes him worry about losing his new job and being demoted to his former, less prestigious position. This would get his brother-in-law talking again. Moreover, he doesn't know how to tell his wife he'll have to work overtime, without facing a divorce. But if he doesn't work overtime, he fears losing his new position. He feels stressed and literally trapped. Yesterday, he lost patience with his young son while giving him a bath, and started shouting loudly at the toddler for no good reason. The child began crying and ran into the arms of his mother, who glared at Peter with a furious look in her eyes. He hates getting into these moods with a child he adores, but the moods seem to be getting more frequent as time goes on.

Peter's NUTS factors: For Peter, as for all other employees in the office, the situation is new, because nobody really expected a restructuring in the department. In addition, the situation is unpredictable, because he doesn't know whether he'll lose his new position as a result of the reorganization. He has a sense that he's not in control of the situation, because if he wants to regain control over his job he'll have to put in extra hours, to the potential detriment of his marriage and the children he loves.

Finally, the situation is highly threatening to his ego, because this new position was a source of social affirmation for Peter, and he knows that if he loses the position, he will again have to put up with mockery from family members. The situation is very stressful for Peter: it encompasses all four NUTS characteristics. His irritability with his son has made his stress spill over onto his children. This could result in his child also having a stress response, because his dad has now become a factor of unpredictability, producing a stress response in the child in reaction to his father's behavior.

Mona, age 45

Mona heads a single-parent family with three children. She is an un-skilled worker hired long ago through an elderly aunt who has since left the company. Each day, morning and night, it takes her an hour to get to and from work by bus. After some time, she managed to per-suade the former manager of her department to let her leave a little earlier, giving her time to pick up her children at school and daycare. She finishes her work at home in the evening after putting the children to bed, and the former manager never had any complaints about the quality of her work.

Mona is worried now that she may be unable to persuade the new manager to let her leave early to look after her children. In addition, it will simply be impossible for her to stay at the office and work the extra hours being requested. She fears that she could be fired and end up unemployed, with a family to look after. Since she found this good job through help from an acquaintance, she is well aware that, with her lack of basic training, she would probably never find as well-paid a job. What will she do to look after her children if she loses her job or winds up in a lower-paid job?

She feels stressed and has been finding it hard to fall asleep at night. She tosses and turns in her bed into the wee hours and wakes up very tired. This is now having an impact on her work and her ability to take care of her children. In addition, her hands have begun to tremble at odd times and her stomach is knotting. What's going to happen to her?

Mona's NUTS factors: Of course, the situation is new for Mona, for she, like the others, wasn't expecting this restructuring. In addi-tion, the situation is totally unpredictable, because she doesn't know whether the new manager will agree to let her have the same working conditions as his predecessor did and this decision will have a major impact on her ability to look after her children. She doesn't have the impression of being in control of the situation, because it is utterly impossible for her to work overtime, meaning she risks losing her job. Finally, the situation is threatening to her ego, because she knows very well that she lacks the vocational training for this job and that, if she loses it, she'll never again be able to find as well-paid and respected a position. She'll have to go back to working at minimum wage. Like Peter, Mona is going through a situation that combines all four NUTS characteristics. Mona is therefore experiencing just as much stress as Peter, but with different results. While Peter's stress is spilling over onto his family, Mona's stress causes her to worry about her situation night after night, leading to sleep and anxiety problems.

Example 4. Stress in the Elderly

Just like children, the elderly are much more vulnerable to stress than other adults are, because as their brains age they become more sensitive to the effects of stress hormones when they are secreted. Unlike children and adolescents, among whom stress can be reflected in gastrointestinal or sleep problems, stress among elderly people is very often associated with memory problems and confusion. This is due to the impact of stress hormones on an aging brain. Among the elderly as well, it is therefore essential to break down stressful or destabilizing events in their lives to help them deal more effectively with the stress-creating effects that they are almost certain to experience in their circumstances.

The Situation

After more than 30 years in their own homes, two elderly people have to move into retirement homes because their everyday tasks and care are becoming increasingly arduous for them.

The Players and Their NUTS Factors

Alice, age 79

Alice has to move at the end of the week. Her children have decided that she will go to a retirement home at the other end of town, near the home of her daughter Barbara, who will be looking after her. Barbara is convinced that bringing her mother to live in a retirement home nearby is a positive step, because then she can visit her mother more often. Alice doesn't know anybody at the retirement home, and this means she will have to leave her entire social network, consisting of people living in her neighborhood. For the last few weeks, Alice has been suffering from numerous memory lapses, so much so that Barbara is wondering now if her mother will be able to live in that particular retirement home, which houses people who are elderly but self-sufficient.

Alice's NUTS factors: This is a new situation for Alice. She will be moving somewhere absolutely unknown to her. With nothing familiar to latch onto, the situation is also unpredictable for her, and she can't help wondering: *What's going to happen to me?* Because she doesn't know anyone at her future residence, things are posing a threat to her ego: she's worried she'll be unable to make new friends. Finally, the situation lies outside her control, because the decision was taken unilaterally by her children, for her own good. Her case combines all four NUTS characteristics, and the stress experienced by Alice can easily explain the memory problems she has been showing in the last few weeks.

Gertrude, age 82

Gertrude also has to move to a retirement home. However, this will not be her first time there: she goes to the home every Saturday to play bridge with two of her friends, Pat and Ed, who are already living there. She knows most of the staff and likes the atmosphere of the home. That's why she has decided to go and live there.

Another reason that led Gertrude to choose this place in particular is that the director is allowing her to bring her cat, Colette, whom she cherishes and looks after every day. With her cat by her side, life can never be sad for Gertrude.

Her two children, Roger and Dennis, are coming to move her on Saturday. During the move, her daughters-in-law, Lucy and Paula, will take her out to lunch at her favorite restaurant, and they'll go to Gertrude's new dwelling when they're told that everything is ready. Gertrude sees the move as a sort of celebration that she is sharing with loved ones. She's in a rush to beat Pat and Ed at bridge!

Gertrude's NUTS factors: Since she has gone regularly to where she'll be living, Gertrude doesn't find the situation new or unpredictable. And since she's the one who has chosen this establishment and knows what to expect, she doesn't see the situation as being outside her control. Also, since she has several friends who are already living there, she feels no threat to her ego at the thought of having to make new friends. Finally, Gertrude benefits from excellent family support that makes this potentially stressful situation feel like fun. In contrast to the case of Alice, this situation creates almost no stress for Gertrude, and the chances are good that she can beat her two friends at bridge thanks to her super memory!

Now What?

This exercise has shown us that similar situations can cause a little stress, a lot of stress or no stress at all, depending on whether one or more of the NUTS characteristics are present. This applies regardless of age. As mentioned early in this chapter, the four NUTS factors are what cause your brain to react as if it faced a threat and to produce stress hormones. In the long term, the effects of these stress hormones can damage your physical and mental health.

If you told me you felt totally powerless in reading these examples, I would have to agree with you. What are you supposed to do in similar situations to help your loved ones? You can't haul a former spouse in front of a judge because he or she has moved across the country after a divorce and your child is affected. Nor can you stop a teenage daughter from enrolling in the city's top private high school on the grounds that she has to be protected from change-related stress. Nor can you stage a hunger strike in front of corporate offices because a new manager is making life difficult for employees. And you can't let an elderly mother live in her own house when she has become unable to look after herself and could get hurt.

Did I say you had to?

As you'll see in the following chapters, and as I've already written, we can *never* eliminate stress factors from our lives. Never. We can never stop others from making poor decisions, we can never protect our children from all change in life, we can never prevent people in positions of authority from abusing it and we can never slow the aging of our parents.

And this is all very well, because taking these actions is not the way to get rid of our stress. The reason for this is simple. Without stress responses, we would all be dead. Stress responses are what enabled our prehistoric ancestors to survive by hunting mammoths to eat. Without stress responses, our ancestors would never have been able to kill the mammoths and ensure the survival of the human race.

In the same way, without stress responses, our children, adolescents and parents—and ourselves as well—could never have the vigilance needed to get up in the morning, go to school to learn and develop, work all day long and look after our family's needs, or play bridge when the time comes. We could not cross the street without being hit by a car, we could not engage in sports without suffering serious injury and we would not have the ability to ensure our children's survival. Stress is a necessity of life.

As we shall soon see, stress, when acute, is a response that is extremely well adapted to the body, enabling us to live, survive and perform. It is only when stress becomes chronic that it begins to have harmful effects on our physical and mental health.

What I would like to do now is to explain, step by step, how we can end up stressed to the point of getting sick. I'm doing this because I feel that, if you know exactly what can lead you to *chronic* stress, you'll be better able to avoid it the next time you face a stress-creating situation.

Chapter 3
Acute Stress to Help Us Survive

In the early 1980s, evolutionary biologists[1] joined stress researchers in asking a basic question: *How is it possible for a stress response to exist and for it always to be harmful to the body?* We have known for a very long time that the body evolves, developing all the responses that enable us to survive over the ages (Darwin's theory). According to the law of natural selection, only factors enabling us to adapt to changes in our environment should be maintained over the course of evolution. Now, if stress is so negative for life, why has it been preserved throughout history? The reason is simple: because stress isn't negative, and it's necessary for life.

It's the same thing with other bodily functions. For example, glucose isn't bad in itself and is even necessary for life. However, if you're suffering from diabetes, glucose may become a serious problem for you. Should we conclude from this that glucose is bad for the body? No. The same reasoning applies to stress.

Stress in itself is not bad for the body or the mind. On the contrary, stress responses are necessary for survival. The brain's detection of a threat, along with the body's production of stress hormones and access of these stress hormones to the brain, is what makes us able to ensure our survival and, by extension, the survival of our children and hence of the species. Here's how the system works.

Acute Stress and Survival of the Species

First, the most important thing to know is that our brain is a "threat detector." As we'll see in greater detail in Chapter 6 on stress and memory, the brain was not created to memorize a list of words on the back of an envelope. The brain's primary function is to detect threats in the environment. If there's no immediate threat in the environment, your brain will let you memorize a list of words, fill out a census form or conduct any other day-to-day task. However, once the brain detects a threat, it will immediately stop paying attention to the task underway and turn to the surrounding threat. Its aim is to ensure your survival by mounting a stress response.

When your brain detects a threat, it sends a message to a small area inside it called the *hypothalamus*. When the hypothalamus receives information that a threat to survival is present in the environment, it produces an initial hormone called *corticotrophin-releasing hormone* (or CRH). This hormone then goes and activates another gland located at the base of the brain, the *pituitary* gland, which in turn produces another hormone called *adrenocorticotropic hormone* (or ACTH; yes, that's quite a mouthful!). This hormone then travels through the blood and activates two small glands on top of your kidneys, called the *adrenal* glands. When these glands are activated, they produce the two most important human stress hormones, *adrenaline* and *cortisol*.

When secreted, these two hormones enable you to do the only two things that you *can* do when faced with a threat: fight or flee.[2] In both cases, you need only one thing, energy. It is the concerted action of these two hormones that gave your ancestors the necessary energy to fight the prehistoric mammoth and eat it (thus ensuring survival of the species), or flee because the animal was too big (ensuring again the survival of the species because they would still be available for the next combat). This superb stress response allowed prehistoric humans to survive to fight the mammoths, procreate, and here you are, thousands of years later, reading this book!

The path that leads from the initial message sent by the brain to the production of hormones may seem long, but it isn't really. When a threat appears, adrenaline is secreted anywhere from a few seconds to a few minutes after the threat is detected, and cortisol a few minutes later.

When both of these stress hormones are produced, you're in an acute state of stress. This results in a powerful machine that will help you kill the mammoth, or flee if it's too big. Adrenaline and cortisol act on the body to help it mobilize the energy needed to react effectively and on the brain to let you focus your attention on the threat.

First, all your senses will become more acute, turning you into a superfighter. Your pupils will dilate so that you can see better, even in the dark. Blood will leave your extremities (fingers, toes, etc.) and head toward your heart, enabling it to pump more blood and thereby increasing your energy. If you look at your fingers during a time of intense stress, you may find that they appear whitish, because at this time when you need more energy the blood flowing in the extremities is directed toward your heart. A waxy color is one of the criteria that ambulance attendants use to detect a state of shock in trauma victims. But make no mistake about it: you don't need to suffer the impact of trauma to have a stress response that will affect your color. A nontraumatic stressor will cause the same physical reactions in you, though to a lesser degree.

When you're experiencing stress, if you look at the hairs on your arms and legs, you'll notice that they're completely straight. This phenomenon is especially easy to see on a dog that meets another dog it regards as a threat. The hair of the threatened animal will literally stand up on its back (it's the same with cats and most other hairy mammals). The role of this response is to make an individual more sensitive to the touch and to make this individual look bigger and more threatening. Of course, this is far more effective for cats and dogs than for you, with much less hair on your body. Remember, though, that prehistoric humans were almost as hairy as your mutt. This response, then, was undoubtedly quite effective in making a mammoth believe that a prehistoric human was big and threatening.

To help reduce blood loss in case of injury, the blood vessels in your skin tighten. You get hot. Your sweat glands are activated to facilitate perspiration and cool your organism. To lessen the pain from the attack by the mammoth, your brain produces *endorphins*, powerful painkilling substances. Filled with blood from the extremities, your heart becomes a superpump. This enables it to send more blood to your muscles, increasing your muscular strength and your chances of killing the mammoth or of fleeing at top speed if it's too big. To aid your heart, your arteries contract to raise your blood pressure. All the blood reaching your muscles is pumped very quickly. And your veins dilate so that the blood can get more easily to the lungs and help them reoxygenate. You can then run longer without losing your breath! You breathe more deeply, enabling you to howl and frighten the mammoth—and to give yourself the courage to fight it.

The glucose that you produce continuously and that you've stored for use when you need it is suddenly released and metabolized into another substance that helps create an instant source of energy (more effective than energy drinks). The fat stored in your fat cells is also metabolized to provide extra energy. The blood vessels in your kidneys and digestive system tighten to interrupt the operation of these organs. When you're facing a mammoth, it's no time to use energy for digesting food! You'll want to use this surplus energy to kill the beast.

Finally, the stress hormones you've produced to give you the energy to fight the mammoth will go right up to your brain. Once they get there, the cortisol will stick to its receptors, located in the areas that take care of vigilance, attention, memory and regulation of emotions. At that moment, your brain is at its top concentration level, and your degree of vigilance is at its peak.

You'll see the mammoth clearly in front of you, and time will seem to slow down as if to let you analyze your adversary's movements more effectively. On the other hand, it will be impossible for you to think about your morning breakfast. Your brain just won't let you. You've got to focus on the menacing mammoth and nothing else, or you're dead!

This moment you're experiencing will forever be lodged in your memory, again to ensure your survival. By "engraving" this stressful situation in your memory, your brain ensures that you'll remember it during your next confrontation, giving you a greater chance of success.

It's very easy to prove that an event producing acute stress will be lodged in your memory forever. For example, if I ask you what you were doing and whom you were with on February 23, 2004, you would surely give me a funny look and tell me that it's frankly impossible to remember events that are so distant in your memory. If, on the other hand, I ask you what you were doing and whom you were with when you learned about the events of September 11, 2001, you would say, "Aha, that's easy!" and answer my questions in great detail. You could even provide me with other details such as the time when you heard the news, the identities of the other people around you and probably even what you were wearing that day! Even though 2001 is further back in time than 2004, you have a clear memory of the events of September 11, 2001. Why? Survival of the species.

Do you remember your physical sensations when you learned about the events of September 11, 2001? You were hot, your hands trembled and you told yourself that this event would change the course of history. Your full attention was focused on a TV screen or on the radio. These reactions were nothing other than the result of a strong stress response that was activated at the moment you learned about the events of that day because your brain had detected a major threat. This set off the stress response, and the stress hormones that reached your brain after being produced by your adrenal glands lodged this event forever in your memory and in the memories of millions of people around you!

It's almost as if your brain had said to you, "Never forget this event, because it's important for survival." And here you are, years later, still with a clear memory of that day.

Through this example you can see that the brain, by lodging stressful events in your memory, ensures survival of the species. With this superb device in open mode, your chances of killing the mammoth and surviving are greatly enhanced. You can easily understand that the stress response is absolutely necessary to life and that, without this response, we would surely have succumbed to the threat of the mammoth a long time ago. However, you might tell me that nowadays, this response is no longer really necessary. We'll see about that.

Acute Stress and Survival: Present-Day Examples

Your child is playing in the yard with some friends. The ball the children are playing with gets loose and rolls gently toward the street. Trying to catch up to the ball, your child crosses a row of parked cars at the edge of the street. At this point, his brain detects movement to the right through peripheral vision, and without taking time to check the source, issues a stress response that causes him to lurch back toward the yard. The neighbor's dog is trotting in front, and your child realizes that this animal is the source of what was caught from the corner of his eye. Even though the response didn't serve any purpose in this situation, it would have been beneficial if what was seen peripherally had been the movement of a car. Survival of the species.

You are the mother of two children, and you're driving along a highway with your children in the back seat. It's winter, and you don't notice a sheet of black ice that's about to send your car out of control.

The vehicle spins several times and then comes to a stop at the edge of the road. You step out of the car and are struggling to regain your composure when you notice that the rear of the vehicle, with your two children inside, is still in the middle of a traffic lane, and you see a truck approaching in the distance, moving too quickly to avoid hitting your car. At this precise moment, the dose of stress hormones produced by your body gives you sufficient energy to make a superhuman effort, lifting the rear of the vehicle and moving it away, thereby saving your children from certain death. For many years afterward, you'll say to yourself, "I still wonder *how* I was able to do that!" Survival of the species.

You're at work, and the fire alarm goes off loudly. That dreadful alarm has the bad habit of going off for no reason, several times a month. You're not too worried, and you keep working quietly at your computer. Suddenly, the smell of smoke reaches your nostrils. You don't see any smoke, but you sense an unmistakable burning odor. You sniff to check, and the air you're breathing through your nose moves the hairs inside it. This motion causes these nasal hairs to activate sensors that, in turn, send a message to your brain that there is a certain odor in the air around you. (And you never thought that those annoying nasal hairs were of any real use!) When your brain receives this message and interprets it as threatening (if you had sensed the smell of apple pie, your brain would not have detected any threat), it will produce a stress response. This reaction means that, within a period of a few seconds to a few minutes, you'll be on the street in the company of your work colleagues, very much alive, able to look after your family when night comes along. Survival of the species.

These present-day examples will help you understand that the acute stress response is just as necessary today as it was in the time of the mammoths. However, how can this condition of acute stress in the face of a clear threat such as fire be linked to the stress that attacks us when we're up against NUTS—for example, when Jenny at work threatens our ego at the coffee machine on Tuesday morning? That woman is definitely not a threat to our survival, yet we have a stress reaction. This is precisely where it becomes important for the brain to distinguish between two type of stress, absolute and relative stress.

Absolute and Relative Stress

Absolute stress is a clear threat to an individual's survival. If you were quietly reading this book in your spouse's company and someone burst into your house shouting "Fire!," it's not very likely that you'd glance at your partner and say, "Yep, this is something new and unpredictable, and we don't really have the impression that we've got things under control. Darling, I think we should leave the house." Obviously, when this absolute threat is detected by your brain, it won't even leave you the time to analyze the situation, and you'll be out of the house in under 10 seconds, with your spouse right in front of you or right behind. Your brain and the stress response it generates have ensured your survival.

In contrast to absolute stress, relative stress requires an interpretation (conscious or unconscious) by the individual to generate a stress response. What I mean by relative stress is that our brain will produce a stress response when it analyzes a situation as new, unpredictable, threatening to our ego or suggesting lack of control (NUTS). Recent stress studies have shown clearly that, when the brain detects one or more characteristics of NUTS, it produces a stress response.

Unlike absolute stress, relative stress results from an exchange or transaction between an individual and his or her surroundings. Thinking of it as a transaction is entirely appropriate, with research showing increasingly that whether or not you produce a stress response will depend on how you interpret a situation. If this response becomes chronic, it may have harmful effects on your physical and mental health. A second distinction, between *eustress* and *distress*, helps explain a major point in stress science.

Eustress and Distress

Eustress refers to "good stress," a notion arising from a very important observation among human beings. If you have a positive interpretation of a situation, whatever it may be, you'll never produce enough hormones for them to harm you in the long term. Think of teenagers looking for powerful sensations—like those young people who go up in a helicopter and leap from it to land directly on a ski hill, without thinking of the avalanches this could set off.

Very early in stress science, researchers suggested that this situation should generate a major stress response in these young people, which could be harmful in the long term. When the researchers tested individuals looking for powerful sensations, they found that these sensation seekers produced enough stress hormones to give themselves a real "high" but not enough to hurt themselves in the long term.

Distress, the opposite of eustress, refers to "bad stress." If you take me and throw me from a helicopter onto a ski hill, I'll be in total distress (even with my skis on), because I interpret this situation in a completely negative way. I don't want to be there and don't want to engage in an activity I find too dangerous. Because I personally have a negative interpretation of the situation, I may produce enough stress hormones to cause me long-term harm.

The situation is identical in both cases (jumping from a helicopter onto a ski hill), but the individual who interprets it positively will not suffer the harmful effects of stress, while the individual who has a negative interpretation will suffer these effects.

This example suggests how dramatically the interpretation of a situation can affect the production of good stress (eustress) or bad stress (distress). As we see in the coming chapters, the fact that good or bad stress can result from our interpretation of an event is excellent news.

In the last few decades, we have dwelled at length on how stress is necessarily always negative and we can't do anything about it. This statement is false. By showing that a stress response results from whether or not a situation is interpreted as threatening (relative stress), research has enabled us to understand that we have immense power over our stress response. However, before we see how we can control stress more effectively, it is appropriate to look into how chronic stress takes root and how it can make us ill. Once you know about the long, winding road that can lead you to chronic stress, I hope you'll be able to avoid it the next time you encounter it.

Chapter 4

The Long and Winding Road to Chronic Stress

Now that all the items that constitute the wonderful world of stress are in front of you, let's see what makes you become chronically stressed, enough for you to be physically or mentally ill. The first thing to understand here is that chronic stress always begins with an acute stress response. Chronic stress may result from an individual's exposure to the same stressor, or to different ones, on a chronic basis.

Each time the brain detects acute stress, it doesn't suspect that it will become chronic. Accordingly, in facing initial instances of acute stress, your brain implements a complex system of actions, in effect a mechanism that enables you to recover from your initial stress and thereby survive. Over time, as it deals with stress that is turning chronic, this mechanism falls into disarray and produces a range of effects on your body and your brain. Let's start by describing the process that moves into gear to restore balance after an episode of acute stress.

Everyone's brain and body are there to help them survive. As noted in Chapter 3, when a person faces acute stress for the first time, the brain initiates a stress response resulting in the production of stress hormones that give the individual enough energy to deal with the threat through fight or flight. Either of these actions results in a heavy loss of energy. After this great a loss, the body must rebuild its energy reserves to survive—otherwise it risks death in the medium term.

Hence, after the stress hormones have been produced by the adrenal glands and have done their job of marshaling energy, they will re-access the brain to give it the message that the body has lost plenty of energy and needs to feed itself to rebuild its energy reserves and avoid the risk of death. The result is that, following exposure to acute stress, the individual experiences hunger and goes out to look for food to rebuild the lost energy.

This mechanism for returning the body to a state where it can again initiate the process it employed to produce a stress response is called *allostasis*. This differs from *homeostasis*, the property of a system that maintains stability. When there is a major change in the environment, allostasis enables the body to go outside the balance that homeostasis ensures.

For example, if a normal glucose level in homeostasis is four to six millimoles per liter, then going above this level means you have a problem of glucose regulation. However, it's quite possible that acute stress could cause your body to produce far more than this normal level of glucose to give you the energy you need to fight or flee a threat. When the threat is gone, the glucose level will return to normal. Allostasis refers to this ability to go beyond the normal state of homeostasis to fight the threat and return to it after the threat is gone. Without our body's allostatic ability to produce the substrates needed to deal with the threat and return to normal afterward, we would not be able to survive threats in our environment.

This loop of actions, facilitated by the stress hormones that marshal energy and then reach the brain to initiate the active search for food, is a superb mechanism for the survival of the species. However, when stress becomes chronic and the body and brain are exposed day after day to conditions that appear threatening, two vital things happen—a process I sometimes refer to as the "domino effect."

First, stress hormones, the frontline fighters that give us the energy to fight or flee the threat, start to become dysregulated. Next, the rear-guard fighters—all the hormones or their derivative substances that are linked in any way to the stress hormones—also start to become dysregulated to adapt to the changes indicated by the stress hormones, creating what is called an *allostatic load*. When this happens, the body experiences a collapse of its survival systems, which can lead to physical or mental disorders, or both, as an outcome of chronic stress.

Stage 1 of Chronic Stress: Derangement of Frontline Fighters

Faced with chronic stress, our brain will produce a stress response each time it encounters a threat. The problem is that our body cannot sustain these constant recurrences of hormone production in the long term without inducing a change in this production over time. We see this as a dysregulation, but our brain sees it as an adaptation. It's as if your brain were to say, "My goodness, there are lots of mammoths in your environment! Okay, I'll adapt to help you deal with this herd of mammoths." When exposed to chronic stress, we begin to develop physical and mental disorders because our bodies, in an effort to adapt to the situation, create a dysregulation in the various physiological systems associated with the stress response by trying to respond chronically.

Up to now, four forms of dysregulation of the stress hormone cortisol have been observed among humans affected by chronic stress. However, two of these forms are especially useful for a better understanding of how exposure to chronic stress can lead to stress hormone dysregulation and how these forms of dysregulation can be reflected differently in our physical and mental health.

- In the first case, the brain hypersecretes cortisol. It has decided to provide an extended reaction to all the threats it perceives by constantly producing a high level of cortisol, a phenomenon observed in cases of depression. A high proportion of depressed people show hyperproduction of stress hormones.
- In the other case, the opposite happens: the brain falls into a kind of breakdown of stress hormone production, called hyposecretion. Your brain stops delivering an adequate stress response, and you then produce less stress hormone than most people. This phenomenon can be seen in burnout syndrome.
- Studies are currently underway now in my laboratory to see if cortisol measurements obtained through saliva sampling can differentiate between the presence of depression (*hyperproduction* of cortisol) and the presence of burnout (*hypoproduction* of cortisol) among workers who say they are chronically stressed.[1] (You may be able to read about the results of this research in the second edition of this book!)

When the initial studies showing hyposecretion of cortisol in the context of burnout appeared, most scientists were quite skeptical about these results. Since the 1930s, it had been believed that stress hormones could be harmful only when produced in large quantities. But here we faced a mental disorder, burnout, in which the individual showed low cortisol production. Up to now, we still don't know the exact cause of this sharp drop in cortisol production among workers suffering from burnout. But recent studies show that three other conditions are also associated with abnormally low cortisol levels: post-traumatic stress disorder, fibromyalgia (a painful and chronic muscle condition) and chronic fatigue syndrome. Some of my scientific colleagues in Europe are trying to determine whether administering cortisone (synthetic cortisol) could help bring low cortisol levels up to normal, with beneficial effects. We are all eagerly awaiting conclusive results from these studies.

A Word about Burnout

The notion of burnout was introduced by Dr. Herbert Freudenberger in 1974 to describe a mental symptomatology (the science of symptoms grouped in an illness, their presentation and the diagnostic indications that can be derived from them). At the time, this condition was observed particularly among health care and education professionals. He described burnout as a sensation of having failed, a feeling of no longer having the energy needed to conduct day-to-day tasks and a sense of lacking the resources needed to face demands in one's surroundings. According to Dr. Freudenberger, someone suffering from burnout becomes rigid, stubborn, inflexible and cynical. Dr. Freudenberger noted that the people most likely to develop burnout are those who must constantly devote themselves to the well-being of others, such as doctors, nurses and schoolteachers.

In 1986, Drs. Christina Maslach and Susan E. Jackson described the three main dimensions of burnout, dimensions that are still used today in the scientific literature. They are emotional fatigue, depersonalization (a person's lack of concern for what's happening to them) and lack of personal motivation. In science, the term burnout is not synonymous with depression. Studies use different criteria for these two conditions and put people in separate groups according to which condition is involved. However, the great popularity of the term burnout *in the 1990s caused some ambiguity in its definition and clinical presentation. In addition, its similarity to some characteristics of depression led to doctors rejecting the notion of burnout. Today, doctors working in occupational health prefer to speak of "work adaptation problems" when referring to signs of burnout.*

Stage 2 of Chronic Stress: Derangement of Rearguard Fighters

This puts us at the end of Stage 1 of chronic stress, when the stress hormone cortisol starts to become dysregulated. A long chain of events is about to follow. The hormones in our body never function in isolation. On the contrary, they are linked to one another by highly complex physiological feedback systems. You can regard hormones as part of a very close-knit family. The hormones in our body are like brothers and sisters who are very closely connected to their cousins and aunts and uncles. If there's a problem they will do everything in their power to join forces and work together as a team.

You'll recall that the stress hormones that march earliest to the front have started to become dysregulated. Considering their tight links with the frontline fighters, the body's other hormones will seek to adapt and will also slowly start to become dysregulated, creating an *allostatic load* or a *domino effect.* This is how our chronic stress gradually has the effect of upsetting our other mechanisms and leading to physical and mental disorders. The forms of dysregulation that occur in the other systems linked to hormones will, depending on your genetic codes and lifestyle, increase your risk of developing one or more of the chronic stress-related disorders described below.

Comparing Apples and Pears

The first of the disorders linked to chronic stress consists of an increase in the body mass index, the result of weight gain in the abdominal area. As you've probably noticed, there are two types of obesity: *total obesity,* affecting all parts of the body, and *central obesity*, affecting only the part of the body around the abdomen. Scientific research over the past decade has shown that abdominal weight gain is often a symptom of an individual's exposure to chronic stress.

How can chronic stress cause abdominal obesity? Again, the answer lies in the fact that your body is really your best ally and will do anything to help you survive.

Your body doesn't know that in fashion magazines, beauty requires having a flat stomach. When your body gets the same signal from stress hormones day after day, demanding a major input of energy, it becomes hard for it to find the lipids and glucose needed to get the necessary energy to kill the mammoth in every part of your organism. However, your body quickly understands that if it stores the lipids and glucose around the abdomen, it can use them more quickly to produce energy![2]

Because you are an overuser of the stress response (you are in a chronic stress state), your body has found THE solution to help you survive. By placing lipids and sugar stores around your abdomen, the body makes sure it can use rapidly these energy stores when the demand arises. And since you're in a state of chronic stress and you constantly require energy to fight the threat, the body is careful to protect your survival by instantly providing what you need.

But take note: an absence of excess weight doesn't mean you're exempt from this phenomenon. Your weight may be relatively normal, but it's quite possible that fat is distributed only around the abdomen, creating a high waist/hip ratio. The waist/hip ratio is the ratio of the circumference of the waist to that of the hips, independent of the person's weight. The higher the ratio, the greater the abdominal obesity. I can recall seeing a young woman who weighed 110 pounds and was thus quite thin, but what little fat she had on her body was concentrated around her belly.

A study by Dr. Elissa Epel of Yale University in New Haven, Connecticut, set out to confirm that people showing abdominal obesity react more to stress than people without abdominal obesity. The researcher exposed two types of women to seven consecutive days of stress. They were put in groups based on their fat distribution: on one side were "apple-shaped" women (with a high waist/hip ratio); on the other side were "pear-shaped" women (with a low waist/hip ratio). In analyzing their stress hormone levels during the seven days they were exposed to psychological stress, the researchers observed that throughout the study the apple-shaped women produced far more stress hormones than their pear-shaped peers. Gentlemen, you're not immune from this effect. A colleague in Göteberg, Sweden, Dr. Per Björntorp, has shown on many occasions that abdominal obesity among males is also associated with high stress hormone levels.

But, ladies and gentlemen, there's no need to panic. Abdominal obesity also has other causes that need to be considered. Among men, one of the most common causes of abdominal obesity is—you guessed it—beer! Among women, the arrival of menopause is quite often associated with the appearance of some belly fat as a result of a drastic reduction in estrogenic hormones.

When the Heart Beats like Crazy

As you now know, when the body is in a state of stress, it produces adrenaline. This hormone plays a vital role in the cardiovascular system. The adrenaline secreted in response to a state of stress speeds up the heartbeat, with the heart contracting at a faster pace and blood pressure rising. These responses are healthy, of course, in a situation of acute stress. However, when we require our body to undergo these major variations in the cardiovascular system over an extended period, the pressure put on the system may be too great and can even lead to cardiovascular disorders.

In the 1980s, researchers began to establish a clear link between depression and increased risk of developing a cardiovascular disorder. Dr. François Lespérance of the Centre Hospitalier de l'Université de Montréal and Dr. Nancy Frasure-Smith of McGill University, also in Montreal, showed that people whose coronary disease has stabilized have a 26 percent greater risk of undergoing another cardiac event in the next two years if they suffer from anxiety or depression. This makes it very important to treat anxiety or depression disorders among people experiencing heart problems, with the aim of preventing subsequent attacks.

The Joys of Cholesterol

During periods of chronic stress, sharp increases in cholesterol levels may be observed among humans. As we know, cortisol is one of the first stress hormones to reach the frontline, helping us produce the energy needed to fight or flee a threat. To produce cortisol, *we need cholesterol*. Through a complex set of biochemical stages, cholesterol is altered to produce cortisol. If you're constantly asking your body to produce cortisol to fight threats, it is thus entirely normal for your cholesterol rates to rise to provide for the greater cortisol production needed to fight the stress that is occurring on a chronic basis.

An abnormal increase in cholesterol rates has been associated with the appearance of the *metabolic syndrome*. This syndrome is defined as the grouping of various metabolic disorders in the body. It is reflected in an abnormally high glucose level in the blood, higher cholesterol levels, lower levels of "good" cholesterol (high-density *lipoprotein* cholesterol) and higher blood pressure. Metabolic syndrome is generally diagnosed when three or more of these dysregulations are found in the same person.

A link between exposure to chronic stress and development of metabolic syndrome has been suggested by many scientists. Curious resemblances have been observed between signs of this syndrome and indications among patients suffering from Cushing's syndrome, which is due to a pituitary gland tumor that results in the adrenal glands producing abnormally high levels of cortisol stress hormone in response to the *adrenocorticotropic hormone* (ACTH) secreted by the pituitary gland.

Patients with Cushing's syndrome all present the disorders observed in metabolic syndrome, while also showing abdominal obesity. This similarity between manifestations of the metabolic syndrome and those of Cushing's syndrome, with abnormally high cortisol levels observed, suggests that exposure to chronic stress among humans, leading to high concentrations of cortisol, could lead to the development of the metabolic syndrome. Recent results from scientific studies show that people presenting metabolic syndrome also have abnormally high levels of cortisol stress hormone.

When Sugar Runs Wild

As we saw in the previous section, when we're exposed to acute stress the glucose stored in our body is altered to create another substance that helps us create an instant energy source. When we ask our body to metabolize this glucose on a chronic basis, glucose levels in the blood will rise so that it can be metabolized into an energy source. With this rise in glucose, insulin will work harder to recover the excess glucose in the blood and store it in the form of *glycogen* (an inactive form of glucose to be kept in reserve) in the liver and muscles. In the long run, this will lead to insulin resistance, which occurs when insulin becomes less effective in reducing glucose levels in the blood. When insulin loses its effectiveness, glucose levels rise, and this leads to development of Type 2 (non-insulin-dependent) diabetes.

Recent results from studies that follow participants over a long period show that exposure to chronic stress is associated with an increased risk of developing Type 2 diabetes. The diabetes observed among children is generally Type 1 (insulin-dependent), a type of diabetes characterized by the absence of insulin produced by the body, which in turn creates the need for these children to be injected with insulin on a daily basis.

However, over the past decade, a sharp rise in Type 2 (non-insulin-dependent) diabetes has been observed among children. The increase in cases of Type 2 diabetes has alarmed the scientific community, because Type 2 diabetes is associated with many of the characteristics of the metabolic syndrome, such as abdominal obesity, hypertension and abnormally high cholesterol levels, characteristics that all present risks for children's physical health. While various factors may explain this rise in the number of Type 2 diabetes cases among children, some researchers tend to believe this growth may be associated with exposure to chronic stress. However, there has still been only very limited research in this field, and there is not enough evidence to conclude that this association really exists among children.

Why Do We Always Get Sick on Weekends or Just before Leaving for a Holiday in Mexico?

It never fails: when the weekend comes, or when it's time to leave for a vacation, or at the start of a long holiday—this is the very moment when we get sick!

I can assure you that this strange phenomenon is not a matter of bad luck. There's a fully scientific explanation for it, an explanation found in the effects of chronic stress on the immune system. When someone is exposed to chronic stress, as we have seen, there is chronic increased production of cortisol stress hormone. Cortisol has a direct effect on the immune system's ability to protect against viruses and other outside agents. When cortisol is produced over long periods, its effect is to reduce our immune system's ability to defend against outside attacks.

That's a fine explanation, you may say. But it hardly explains why we always tend to get sick on weekends, or just before leaving on our dream vacation on a sun-drenched beach in Mexico.

Once again, we're often sick on weekends or holidays because our body is our best friend and will do anything to keep us going in the face of chronic stress. Scientific research on the effects of stress hormones on the immune system is one of the most complicated fields to describe, with dozens of hormones involved in the chain of events that occurs during chronic stress. However, my mentor and friend Dr. Bruce McEwen of Rockefeller University in New York once provided me with the best image for explaining the effects of chronic stress on the immune system in simple terms. I'll share Dr. McEwen's image with you.

Regard stress as a 10-pound barbell that you carry on your shoulders. Stress is often said to result from an imbalance. This isn't quite true. In fact, stress results from a system that is too well balanced and that does everything to maintain this balance and thus ensure your survival.

If I put a 10-pound barbell on your shoulders, what do you think will happen? Do you think you'll suddenly lean left or right? No. You'll remain standing up straight, with the barbell correctly placed on the middle of your back so that its weight is distributed evenly on both shoulders. You are coping with your acute stress.

Then, the following week, I add 10 more pounds to the barbell you already have on your shoulders. Your stress starts to feel like it will never end. You now have 20 pounds distributed on your shoulders. With this added weight, what do you think you'll do? Will you suddenly start leaning left or right? No. You'll still be upright, but your knees will start to bend a little under this additional weight.

A week later, I add 10 more pounds to the barbell. Again, you're still standing up straight, but your knees are bending a little more. This indicates the effort applied by your immune system in response to stress that is becoming chronic. The system lets you remain upright and well balanced, but the price you pay is a slight bending of the knees. Now let's fast-forward to the fifty-first week, the second-last week of the year, a few days before *the* week of vacation you've offered yourself at a five-star villa in Mexico. The weight now on your shoulders is enormous (510 pounds: you're very strong!). But you're still standing, though you're bent very low, close to the ground. Your immune system is still holding up. You haven't yet fallen ill because of chronic stress. Then comes your last working day before your vacation, just before your departure for a stress-free week.

I'm coming right up behind you (you're still bent down, close to the ground, with your 510 pounds of stress on your shoulders), and I remove this huge burden from your shoulders all at once (vacation time is starting). What do you think will happen? That's right. You'll lose your balance and fall flat on your back, because you were bent so close to the ground that the removal of the weight threw you off balance. That's exactly what happens to the immune system. During most of the period of chronic stress, the immune system will do everything in its power to enable you to function with the weight of the stress on your shoulders. However, when you end the stress and take the weight off your shoulders, you'll have gone too far to prevent the loss of balance and the onset of illness.

I once heard a young girl in an elevator tell her friend, "I'm so healthy that even when I'm stressed I don't get sick!" If the manners my father taught me to use with strangers had not stopped me, I would have snapped back, "Hold on! It's coming. Keep working, and you'll be okay. But go on vacation, and then see what happens!"

There's not much we can do about this situation, except to learn how to prevent the onset of chronic stress, as we'll see in the last part of this book. As I often enjoy saying in speeches, when faced with this state of affairs, you have two choices: either you never take another vacation and you avoid getting sick, or you take two weeks of holidays in a row. You use the first week to get sick, and the second week to go to Mexico!

Why Do We Sometimes Get the Flu When Getting a Flu Shot?

As you know, each year we are urged to get vaccinated against the flu virus. Some vaccines contain a tiny dose of the virus, which activates our immune system so that it can develop its own antibodies for recognizing and fighting the virus the next time it's found in the organism (live-attenuated vaccines). With the presence of a tiny dose of the virus, there's always a risk that some people receiving the vaccine will develop the disease it is intended to prevent. Many studies in the field of chronic stress and the immune system have shown that exposure to chronic stress increases the likelihood of a person catching a mild cold when injected with a very low dose of a rhinovirus. Similar results have been obtained for vaccinations against hepatitis B and rubella.

Dr. Sheldon Cohen of Carnegie Mellon University in Pittsburgh is a pioneer in the study of the effects of chronic stress on the development of illnesses following inoculation by a virus. In one of his studies, he asked 276 adults to fill out questionnaires on stressful situations in their lives. Later, all participants received a low dose of rhinovirus (a virus associated with colds), and they were followed for a month. The study's results showed that the presence of *acute stress* (stressors that appeared in the previous month) was not linked to contracting a cold following inoculation with a rhinovirus. However, the presence of *chronic stresses* (stressors present for a month or longer) was associated with a significant increase in the risk of developing a cold after receiving the rhinovirus. The chronic stressors affecting participants that were most likely to increase the risk of developing a cold after inoculation were unemployment and interpersonal difficulties with family and friends.

If you develop the flu after your next annual shot, ask yourself whether you were in a period of chronic stress before being vaccinated! Several years ago, I was in a very demanding and stressful period at work, and I had a chance to get a flu shot at my workplace. I refused it at that time, because I knew quite well that my chronic stress would significantly increase my risk of catching the flu, and this would have prevented me from completing the work that was causing me so much stress. I managed to complete it, waited a few days to see if I would get sick (with my allostatic load to thank!) and then got my flu shot. I made it through the winter without the flu.

Chapter 5

Measuring the Weight of Chronic Stress: The Allostatic Load Battery

In the last chapter, we saw that exposure to chronic stress can cause a variety of systems in your body to fall into disorder. In 1997, two renowned researchers, Dr. Teresa Seeman of the University of California at Los Angeles and Dr. Bruce McEwen of Rockefeller University in New York, worked together to develop a way of measuring allostatic load. Using various biological parameters, the researchers sought to determine the level of dysregulation associated with chronic stress in human beings. To this end, they used data from the MacArthur Study of Successful Aging. This was one of the broadest studies on this topic, with 1,313 elderly people as participants, and it measured the different biological variables that we looked at earlier. Dr. Seeman and Dr. McEwen aimed to find a means of measuring how a body may start to become dysregulated, even before an illness appears.

As we saw before, there's a normal range for each biological variable. Take the example of glucose level. Let's arbitrarily define the normal range for glucose as 4 and 6 millimoles per liter. It's only when you produce concentrations exceeding the normal range that your doctor will prescribe a drug to bring your glucose production back down to normal. For example, if your next annual checkup shows that you're producing it at a level of 9 millimoles per liter, your doctor may suspect you have diabetes and will prescribe either a drug or a special diet. If your glucose rate is within the normal range of 4 to 6, the doctor will conclude that things are okay.

Research on allostatic load has shown that the body's various biological systems start becoming unsettled very gradually. When the domino effect of dysregulation of these systems begins to pick up speed, the process becomes very hard to stop. Rather than waiting for a given biological variable to go outside its normal range before taking action, researchers have noted that it would be better to look at the array of biological variables associated with chronic stress (cholesterol, glucose, insulin, waist/hip ratio, cytokines, cortisol, etc.) when they are high without being abnormal. As more and more biological variables linked to chronic stress are found to be at the high end of the normal range, the person in question increasingly manifests a state of chronic stress that has begun to unsettle various biological systems.

A small example can give you a better understanding of allostatic load. Let's measure four biological variables associated with chronic stress, say glucose, cholesterol, cortisol and the waist/hip ratio. For the sake of this example, let's arbitrarily set the normal range as being between 1 and 10. We have two individuals for whom tests obtain the values in the table for these variables.

Biological data	First individual	Second individual
Glucose	4	9
Cholesterol	6	9
Cortisol	8	8
Waist/hip ratio	3	8

Normal range for each measurement: 1 to 10
Upper quartile: 7.75 or higher

We can see here that values for the first individual are at average levels, close to 5. But the second person shows values very near the upper limit of the normal range, close to 10. Since none of these values is outside the normal range (i.e. greater than 10), a doctor would see no reason to detect an illness and act accordingly.

However, researchers specializing in stress science understand that since these values are very close to the upper limits of normality, they show that the body has gradually begun to dysregulate its various systems in response to chronic stress. Therefore, in their quest to develop a biological measurement of chronic stress, researchers devised the allostatic load battery. Toward this end, they measured the various biological variables that are known to fall into disarray during periods of chronic stress, such as:

- the concentration of cortisol (a stress hormone and frontline fighter);
- the concentration of adrenaline (a stress hormone and frontline fighter);
- the concentration of norepinephrine (a stress hormone and frontline fighter);
- the concentration of total cholesterol (a rearguard fighter);
- the concentration of high-density lipoprotein (good cholesterol, a rearguard fighter);
- the concentration of glycated hemoglobin (an indirect measurement of glucose, a rearguard fighter);
- the concentration of interleukin-6 (immune system, a rearguard fighter);
- systolic and diastolic blood pressure (rearguard fighters);
- the waist/hip ratio (a rearguard fighter).

For each person tested, researchers calculated the number of biological variables in the upper quartile of the normal range. A quartile is similar to a quarter, but not exactly equivalent. For example, on a scale of 1 to 10, the upper quartile covers any figure over 7.75. A person who shows a level of 8 for one of the concentrations will be considered to be in the upper quartile of the normal range. This would not yet constitute so-called pathological derangement of this variable, which would require a level over 10, but it would be observed that dysregulation is gradually moving in and is getting dangerously close to the absolute threshold.

With this tool in hand, researchers calculated the allostatic loads of participants in the MacArthur study, determining the number of biological variables associated with chronic stress that were in the upper quartile of the normal range. A larger number of biological variables in the upper quartile means a higher allostatic load and thus a greater risk of developing one of the physical disorders associated with chronic stress.

Let's go back to the example above. In this table, the normal range is 1 to 10 for each variable. When we look at the data for the two individuals presented in the table, we see that the first individual shows only one variable, the cortisol level, in the upper quartile (above 7.75). This individual thus has an allostatic load of 1. The second individual shows upper-quartile data for four of the variables measured (all of them being over 7.75). This person thus has an allostatic load of 4. It can be seen that the second individual has four systems that have begun to go into dysregulation, even though this person does not yet show any variable over 10, which would mean a medical diagnosis.

Researchers have suggested that, if this early measurement of allostatic load is a valid way to detect states of chronic stress among individuals, a high allostatic load should be able to predict the development of various illnesses associated with chronic stress, years before any such illness appears.

Using the measurement of allostatic load among the elderly participants in the MacArthur study, researchers showed that elderly people with high allostatic loads generally died three years earlier than those with low allostatic loads. Other studies showed that a high allostatic load is also associated with memory disorders and a variety of other health problems.

Subsequent studies in the United States and Europe dealt with allostatic load among workers. An early study by Dr. Marja-Liisa Kinnunen and her colleagues at the University of Jyväskylä in Finland showed that, for people between the ages of 27 and 36, instability in relation to their career triples the risk of having a high allostatic load when they reach their forties. More recently, my student Robert Paul Juster and I showed that high allostatic load among workers is associated with symptoms of burnout.

Working with adolescents, Dr. Gary Evans of Cornell University in Ithaca, New York, showed that those who experienced difficult conditions (such as poverty or violence) had high allostatic loads. Dr. Evans said these results help explain how exposure to adverse conditions in childhood can lead to the development of cardiovascular disorders and depression in adulthood.

What if All the Tools for Detecting Chronic Stress Were Already in the Doctor's Bag?

You probably go for a medical checkup every year, and each time your attending physician probably orders a blood test. The results contain a list of biological variables the doctor wants measured to ensure that you're in good health.

For the most part, the biological variables that doctors request in these tests are just a list of the variables associated with allostatic load. However, relatively few doctors are familiar with the allostatic load battery, and so they rarely deliver an allostatic load analysis when they receive your blood test results. Some doctors will tell you that the allostatic load battery is just another way of talking about the metabolic syndrome, which we looked at in the previous chapter. This is incorrect. Metabolic syndrome is characterized by dysregulations in the metabolic variables only, such as hyperglycemia, higher cholesterol levels, lower levels of "good" cholesterol and higher blood pressure. In contrast to the metabolic syndrome, the allostatic load battery also includes stress hormones and some markers of immune system operation. In addition, the allostatic load battery focuses on variables with a level of dysregulation that has not yet reached the threshold of medical detection. This is a very significant difference.

I have been trying for a long time to get family physicians interested in new discoveries linked to the allostatic load battery. Who knows: maybe this book will succeed in reaching some of them, and they will then attempt to use the simple analytical method of upper quartiles to calculate a patient's allostatic load. To illustrate the effectiveness of this approach, here are results from an individual who took part in one of my studies of elderly people. The study followed a group of elderly people over a 10-year period. Each year, the participants came to the hospital for blood tests, cortisol hormone concentration measurements and various memory tests.

In this study, we measured four biological variables related to allostatic load: cortisol, cholesterol, triglycerides (a type of lipids) and glucose. We measured these four variables every two years from 1990 to 1998. The table below shows the results for one of the participants. For each variable, we used the clinically determined normal range, and I determined the upper quartile. Data with a black background are outside the normal range (these are cases that a doctor would treat), while data with a grey background are in the upper quartile of the normal range.

It can be seen that in 1990, this person had an allostatic load of 3. But none of the variables exceeded the threshold of normality, and therefore no illness was detected. Two years later, the allostatic load was up to 4, and the glucose level began to climb above the normal range. The glucose level remained above normal for the next seven years, and diabetes was detected in this person. Starting in 1994, a second system showed the effects of allostatic load, and we saw an abnormal level of cholesterol. This person then received antilipid treatment, which was combined with the treatment for diabetes. After nine years, three biological systems were medically unsettled and produced data outside the normal range (cholesterol, triglycerides and glucose). The system was in domino mode, and the doctor had to prescribe several types of medication to keep all these systems under control.

	Cortisol	Cholesterol	Triglycerides	Glucose	Allostatic load
Normal range	150 to 650	2.8 to 5.2	0.51 to 1.7	3.6 to 5.3	
Upper quartile	525 and higher	4.6 and higher	1.4 and higher	4.8 and higher	
Year					
1990	565	4.6	1.3	4.9	3
1992	602	4.8	1.4	5.8	4
1994	459	5.2	1.4	5.7	3
1996	349	5.6	1.5	6.4	3
1998	639	5.2	1.7	14.9	4

In this case study, we can see that in 1990 this person's system had already started going into dysregulation as a result of the allostatic load. However, because we were not paying attention to data that did not exceed clinical standards, the change in allostatic load could not be detected. If the allostatic load battery had been used back in 1990, this individual's stressors could have been analyzed, and various techniques for stress response control (see the last section of this book) could have been developed to help manage this person's stress and thereby prevent the allostatic load from resulting in physical illness.

I sincerely hope that this book will inform doctors of the allostatic load battery so that this method of calculating the level of chronic stress in humans can be part of the tools used by medical doctors to treat stress in their patients.

Chapter 6

When Stress Affects Our Memory

In the previous chapters, we saw how stress can help us survive by rallying the energy we need to fight or flee, and how chronic stress can gradually undermine our health and cause a variety of physical ailments. But anyone who has ever been in a highly stressful situation for a short or long period of time knows that stress can also greatly affect our memory and our emotions. As I've said, chronic stress can, in some cases, be associated with depression and burnout. Any manager also knows that stress can greatly affect employees' performance, and all parents have seen stress affect how their children do in school.

The effects of stress on memory are due mainly to the fact that the stress hormones produced when the brain detects a threat have the ability to reach the brain. When these hormones do reach the brain after being secreted to fell a—real or virtual—mammoth, they have very different effects on the memory, depending on whether you're facing acute stress or chronic stress.

The memorization process consists of a series of major steps. When we finally memorize something, the last step is to bring the piece of information gathered in our environment into our long-term memory system. Once the information makes its way there, it will never disappear. But there's a long, hard road between the first and last steps.

At each of these memorization steps, stress may have positive or negative effects, again depending on whether we're facing acute or chronic stress. Let's look in detail at each step.

Step 1: To Memorize a Piece of Information, You Have to Be Vigilant

The first step in getting a piece of information into your memory is vigilance. You have to be alert. Without this initial step, the memorization process cannot move forward. Have you ever woken up after having had a few drinks the night before, not being able to remember very much about the celebration? The reason for this is simple: alcohol reduces vigilance, and without this vigilance you're simply not able to encode anything. The morning after the night before, don't try remembering anything: this will be impossible, because the information simply wasn't stored in your long-term memory. By reducing your vigilance, the alcohol reduced your ability to take in information from the environment and encode it in your long-term memory. It's not that you forget key elements from the night before. It's simply that they weren't engraved in your long-term memory!

Acute Stress Increases Vigilance

As we saw in Chapter 3, acute stress has the effect of increasing vigilance. When your brain detects a threat, this leads to the production of stress hormones that will then go back to your brain to increase your vigilance. At that moment, your brain is at its peak of concentration, and your vigilance level is maximized. You see the threat in front of you clearly, and time seems to slow down to let you analyze the situation more effectively. It's because your vigilance level is at its peak when you're facing a threat that you can remember events in your life that have been highly stressful, such as the events of September 11, 2001, or a car accident you may have had last February. By increasing your vigilance when you face acute stress, your stress hormones increase your ability to analyze this threat effectively.

Step 2: You Have to Select the Information You Want to Memorize

When you're vigilant enough to encode a piece of information, you're just at the first successful step in memorization. To continue memorizing this piece of information, you'll have to be attentive now, which isn't the same as being vigilant. When you are vigilant, the senses are alert, whereas when you are attentive you become proactive by focusing on what it is you want to remember.

If you're not sure of this, imagine that you're at home, late at night, and there's a power failure. You get out your flashlight, looking for something important—such as the emergency number for the power company—that was written on a piece of paper with a paper clip on it. As you sweep the room with your luminous beam, you're being vigilant. However, when you see a paper clip at the corner of a brochure, your full attention is focused on that part of the beam, and you become attentive.

The attention you need to memorize a piece of information is called *selective attention*. Selective attention is defined as our ability to distinguish the information in our environment that's relevant from the information that's not relevant. Only the relevant information will be encoded and transferred to our long-term memory. This ability to distinguish the relevant from the irrelevant is essential. If you encoded all the information found around you, your brain would record far too much information. This could turn you into someone like the character Dustin Hoffman played in the film *Rain Man*, who memorized the entire telephone directory because he was incapable of distinguishing what was relevant in that huge set of listings from what wasn't!

Every day of your life, you detect information in your environment that's relevant (most of the time without even noticing)—this is what will be transferred into your long-term memory and thus memorized. All the information you regard as not relevant (for example, the contents of your breakfast 10 days ago) will not be transferred into your long-term memory and thus won't be memorized. The tricky part here is that you have to be sure that what you view as not relevant really fits that category! If it doesn't, problems can arise.

Each year in the university courses I give, there are invariably one or two students who come to see me after an exam is marked to say they absolutely cannot understand the poor grades they received. They tell me they worked very hard at it and that they truly don't deserve such a poor result. And I believe them.

I'm sure these students studied relentlessly all week. However, I tell them they spent the week studying information that really wasn't relevant! I explain that, when taking their course notes, they failed to distinguish between what was relevant in my remarks and what wasn't relevant, and they thus spent the week studying irrelevant information. When they were tested in the exam on the information that I considered relevant, they failed. That's why students love being told to underline some bit of information three times, because that tells them what's relevant, making their task much easier.

Similarly, we often tend to conclude that children with attention disorders also have memory problems, because their grades at school don't measure up. However, these children have an attention disorder, not a memory disorder. Again, the poor performance some of these children show on memory tests is just a simple matter of what is or is not relevant to encode in memory from their point of view. For the teacher, what's relevant will be what's written on the blackboard. For a child with an attention deficit, what's relevant may be a strand of hair on the floor. Unfortunately for this child, the probability of being questioned on the strand of hair is nil. And so, poor grades are often not the result of some memory problem but are caused by a difficulty this child faces, because of an attention deficit, in distinguishing what's relevant in the surroundings from what isn't.

At a Time of Acute Stress, the Only Relevant Information Is the Threatening Information

As we saw in the previous chapters, the brain's primary function is to detect threatening information in the environment with the aim of helping us survive. Accordingly, the brain differentiates at all times between threatening and nonthreatening information in the environment. If your brain doesn't detect any threatening information in the environment, it may work at encoding other information, such as your youngest child's next dentist appointment. However, if your brain detects a threat in the environment, it will prevent you from encoding this appointment, and it will make you devote 100 percent of your attention to information that's relevant to it, namely what's threatening. In so doing, it will ensure that you can rally enough energy to fight the threat, or flee if it's too scary.

In the presence of a threat, the relevant information for the brain, which has helped us survive since the time of the mammoths, is always threatening information. Conversely, irrelevant information is always nonthreatening information. Your brain will always select threatening information, because you'd be unable to survive surrounding dangers if it didn't.

This explains how we can remember minute details about our location, the people we were with and even what we were wearing when we learned about the events of September 11, 2001. The brain had just detected a threat, and when the stress hormones that were produced rose to the brain, they caused it to turn its full attention to this information. You may thus have forgotten that you were supposed to give file 414 to Sophie at the office on that day. The reason for this is simple: at that particular moment, this information became totally irrelevant to the brain, which focused your full attention on the threat of the collapsing World Trade Center towers. Since the information related to file 414 was no longer relevant to your brain, it simply wasn't processed.

The effects of stress on selective attention and the great pertinence to the brain of a threat at a time of acute stress have major implications for work, education and life in general. You've got an employee who woke up this morning and saw that his toddler had a high fever. This caused great stress to the father, because his child tends to have epileptic seizures when his fever isn't controlled. However, he absolutely couldn't stay home with the child because of an important administrative meeting with you. His precarious position at the company made it vital for him to attend the meeting. His wife was away on a business trip, and the only person who could look after the child was a neighbor the father hardly knew. Of course, with the need to hold onto his job, the father entrusted the child to the neighbor and showed up at the office for the meeting.

However, I can tell you that the father will encode only a tiny portion of the information you provide to him at this management committee meeting. Why? Because his brain detected a major threat (the child's high fever and the risk of epileptic seizure) that morning, and this is the information that will be most relevant to the father for the rest of the day. Everything else will become less relevant. The father doesn't consciously differentiate between the relevant information (his toddler's fever) and the irrelevant information (the management committee). But to ensure the survival of the species, his brain will cause him to deal only with his toddler's fever, and none of the other information, which has become irrelevant, will be fully encoded. The father will attend the meeting, but he will be present only physically since his mind will be at home, at the bedside of his fever-ridden child.

Here's another example for teachers. In your class you have a young girl living in a family where the parents are heading for divorce and are always fighting. This little girl doesn't know what will happen to her brothers and sisters, or to herself, nor does she know how things will turn out. She faces all four NUTS factors. For her brain, it's this information, and this information alone, that's most relevant, because a threat has been detected (a threat to her well-being). Don't be surprised if she seems inattentive during class hours—her lack of attention is real. For her brain, what's relevant is information related to the conflict between her parents and to her uncertain future. All the rest, including the information you're trying to have her memorize, becomes irrelevant. She won't be able to process this information optimally, as she would have done if her parents were perfectly in love.

The effects of stress on selective attention can have major repercussions on traders at the stock exchange or brokers at their desks, causing market turmoil. A recent study conducted by Dr. John Coates and Dr. Joe Herbert at Cambridge University in Britain measured concentrations of stress hormones in traders at the London Stock Exchange for eight consecutive workdays. The results showed that, when these people face an unstable and volatile market, their cortisol stress hormone levels can rise by up to 400 percent in comparison with their initial base level.

Researchers draw a link between this sharp rise in cortisol and the extent of selective attention in the work of traders. At any moment in the day, they must make decisions about buying or selling financial products. To do so, they must be able to differentiate between what's relevant (shares in X are down or up in an unstable market) and what's not relevant (shares in X are down or up in a stable market) before making a decision. Considering the well-known effects of the cortisol hormone on selective attention, Dr. Coates and his team suggest that this sharp rise in cortisol observed during volatile periods in the stock market could have a serious impact on traders' ability to make the right decisions at these times. And if traders make the wrong decisions because of too great an increase in stress hormones, your investments and mine will suffer!

You'll understand the paradoxical effects of stress on selective attention and ability to memorize a piece of information in the environment. By focusing all your attention on threatening information, the brain ensures your survival. However, in doing so, it reduces your ability to memorize any other information, thereby creating difficulties in the processing of events unrelated to the threat, regardless of their importance.

One day when I was giving a talk to a group of senior corporate executives, one of them asked me the best way to raise the performance of employees affected by stress. My response reflected what 20 years of research on the effects of stress on the human memory have taught me. There's no way to increase employee performance at a time of stress. You can offer them all sorts of courses in time management, performance management and management of whatever else you like, but this just won't work. Why? Because employees' brains won't allow it.

Are you creating a stressful work environment? The price to be paid is that employees will constantly detect threats, and this is the information that will become most relevant for their brains. This means it will be the only information their brains will allow them to process. Anything else will become irrelevant, including all the work you want them to get done. What's the only way to raise employee performance at a time of stress? By reducing stress! By lowering the number of stressors in the company, you can ensure that employees' brains will not spend most of their time detecting threats and dealing only with these threats. If there are no more threats in the environment, the brain will be prepared to process other information and give it the desired relevance. In this way, employee performance will improve substantially, and so will your profits.

Step 3: You Must Be Able to Do Two Things at Once

Think what our world would be like if the brain could encode just a single piece of information at a time for the purpose of memorizing it. You'd be unable to remember the conversation you had with your spouse while you were preparing the evening meal. Your children would have trouble remembering to take their baths because, when you asked them to do this, they were watching TV.

Our brain is a fabulous tool that, over thousands of years, has developed to let us encode more than one piece of information at a time. This ability is called divided attention and refers to the so-called *multitasking* we read so much about in newspapers and magazines. Divided attention enables us to pay attention to two things at once, with the purpose of memorizing both.

Ladies, I see a hint of a smile on your faces. You've surely thought to yourself, as newspapers often suggest, that multitasking is something unique to contemporary women. Various magazines and newspapers keep telling us that today's women have become experts in multitask-ing because they have to manage their work at the same time as their homes, their children, a dog to be walked, errands to be run, a dental appointment to be canceled and so on. These articles make it seem as if multitasking is a new ability of the brain that cropped up when large numbers of women joined the workforce during the Second World War.

I'm sorry to tell you, ladies, that you're mistaken! Divided atten-tion (contemporary multitasking) did not just develop among con-temporary women who combine careers with raising children. It has been around for centuries. I still remember the reaction of an elderly woman who took part in one of my studies. One day she arrived at the laboratory in a fury because she had just heard a report on the radio saying that multitasking was something unique to modern women. Seated in my office, she exclaimed, "But do today's women really think they're exceptional because they manage to combine childrearing with responsible jobs? Well, isn't that something. During my lifetime, I've had 23 children. Twenty-three! Think about it! I've had so many children that I've menstruated only once in my life![1] Don't you think I know as much as modern women do about multitasking?"

I could hardly help chuckling. Obviously, multitasking has existed for many generations, in different forms. It's all very well to blame it today for every evil! But think about it, if our brain has evolved so quickly over the centuries and now we have the Internet, video games, satellites and all the rest, it has plenty to do with the brain's incredible ability to pro-vide divided attention in dealing with an increasingly complex world.

There's a hitch, however. Our brain can focus on two things at once for the purpose of memorizing them, but its ability to do this depends greatly on the kinds of information we try to encode simultaneously. Some tests will help you understand clearly what kinds of information the brain is suited to encode at the same time.

Get a few sheets of paper and a pen, and make sure you're alone so that no information from your surroundings can divert your attention. Here is a list of six words. Read them slowly in a loud voice (without writing them) and then turn the page. Then try to transcribe these six words on a sheet of paper in any order. Return to the test page and count your correct answers. How many do you have? You should generally have very good results (at least five out of six!), proof that you're at the peak of your performance. This is quite logical: you were doing only one thing at a time.

List 1

HOUSE

APPLE

MAGAZINE

DESK

DOG

TELEPHONE

Now here's the second test. List 2 has six new words. Read the six words on this list the same way as before, aiming to memorize them. However, while you're trying to memorize the words, tap your thighs repeatedly with your hands. When you've finished reading the words on the list, stop tapping and transcribe the words from List 2 onto the sheet. Check your results against the list.

List 2

COMPUTER

ORANGE

NEWSPAPER

FENCE

COW

TELEVISION

How do they look? They're generally not as good as the first time (4.5 out of 6 on average). The explanation is simple: you were doing two things at once. By tapping your thighs while trying to memorize the words, you're dividing your attention between two tasks, and this division in attention results in a slight decline in your performance.

But would you get the same results if you did something other than tap your thighs? Let's try a third test.

Here's a third list (List 3), with six new words. Read the six words on the list, again with the aim of memorizing them. You don't have to tap your thighs. But, before transcribing these words on the sheet, slowly and loudly read the words on List 4, without your having to remember them. After that, check your list against the words on List 3.

List 3

BOOKLET

MUSTACHE

STOVE

SAUSAGE

STAIRWAY

PIGEON

List 4

OVEN

PINEAPPLE

STORY

TABLE

MONKEY

PHOTO

How are your results? They're generally not as good as in the first two tests (on average, four out of six). Here again, you were doing two things at once. This contributed to reducing your performance. However, how can we explain that reading List 4 hurt your performance more than tapping your thighs when you were trying to memorize the list? In both cases, you were doing two things at once. But here, one of the combinations of tasks (the two lists of words) hurt your performance more than the other one (reading words and tapping your thighs).

I call this result the *BlackBerry effect*, in reference to executives at important meetings who keep sending messages, typing frenetically on their devices, while thinking they can listen to and retain everything being said at the meeting. As we've seen here, it can be done, but your performance in executing both tasks will decline by 20 percent on average.[2] The reason is simple. Reading the second list had a greater impact on your performance because, in this case, you were encoding two types of information that tapped into the same resource, the verbal resource. You were encoding the words on List 3, and were then reading the words on List 4. In the case of the thigh tapping, you were doing two things at once, but you weren't using the same resources. You were encoding words (using verbal resources) while tapping your thighs (using motor resources).

The use of different resources in divided attention is a very important element in gaining a better understanding of how two tasks can sometimes be memorized very easily, while in other cases it's much harder. Think of your brain's resources as a space divided into three separate "tanks": the motor tank (moving, running, tapping your thighs), the verbal tank (talking, singing, listening to songs) and the visual-spatial tank (driving a car, skiing, sewing). When you take a verbal action, you're using the resources of the verbal tank. That leaves the resources in that tank partly depleted.

If you're reading a paragraph and tapping your knees at the same time, your brain is being fed from the verbal tank and the motor tank. No problem: there are enough resources for both actions. On the other hand, when you read a paragraph while trying to memorize another paragraph, you're using the same resources twice, from the same tank. It's therefore completely normal for you to lose a little of your performance, because you're using material from the same verbal tank, and there's less to help you perform well.

On the basis of these results, you'll agree with me that it's perhaps not a good idea to send an e-mail while listening to messages on your voice mail. If you try this, I strongly urge you to reread the written message twice before sending it. On the other hand, you can easily talk on the phone while bouncing a ball off the wall—and memorize both these actions. You can also drive your car while talking with your friend Julie; in the evening, as you tell your husband about the major accident you saw while you were in the car, and how heartbreaking you found it, you will remember that Julie is supposed to call you to go shopping.

I'm often asked whether it's a good idea for our children (or our employees at the office) to listen to music on their iPods while studying or working, or have the TV on while studying. I've never allowed my children to watch TV or listen to their iPod while studying, because I know perfectly well that, in doing this, they'll be dividing their attention between two verbal resources (homework and songs on the iPod or what's on TV) and that this will decrease their ability to memorize their homework. I don't allow them to do this because I can offer them a work environment that's free of a variety of verbal stimuli such as a phone conversation, a TV blaring, a chat with my friend and so on. Because I can offer them this work environment free of stimuli that could distract and divide their attention, I can allow myself to demand that they do only one thing at a time.

On the other hand, for a child growing up in a family setting with many and varied stimuli over which he has no control (no bedroom of his own where he can stay away from stimuli, TV always on, parents always fighting, etc.), I sincerely believe it's better to let him listen to music he likes while trying to do his homework. However, in this case, I would suggest that he listen to music he's already familiar with so that he doesn't have to pay attention to new lyrics. Of course, his attention will be divided, and his ability to do his homework well will be slightly reduced, but I believe it's preferable for him to split his attention with something he has chosen and likes rather than with stimuli that his brain could find threatening (and thus relevant), totally preventing him from paying any attention to his homework.

The same reasoning applies to the workplace. If your employee has her own office at work and can function without being subjected to other stimuli, it is greatly preferable for her to work without an iPod on her ears. However, if this employee is sharing a work environment with 23 other employees jammed into their cubicles close to one another, it may be hard for her to devote her full attention to her work if, at the same time, Sarah is talking—loud enough for everyone to hear—about her tumultuous night out with Reggie. Your employee would divide her attention between her job and Sarah's antics, and it would certainly have an effect on her ability to perform. In this case, an iPod with familiar music could be a better choice for raising her performance.

We've seen up to now that, when a second task shares the same verbal resources as the task under way, this sharing has a major impact on our performance. But do we absolutely have to be reading words to affect our performance when we're trying to encode another list of words? Here's a final test to reply to this question.

List 5 has six new words. Read the six words on the list with the aim of memorizing them. However, while trying to memorize the words, say the syllable "blah" loudly and repetitively (blah-blah-blah-blah, etc.), without stopping until you've finished reading the six words. When you've finished reading the words on the list, stop saying blah-blah-blah and write the words from List 5 that you remember. Check your results against the list.

List 5
COUNTER
WHEEL
CURTAIN
DOG
WEATHER VANE
BAMBOO

How do your results look? They're generally pretty bad (three out of six, on average)! Think about it. With this test, I've just lowered your performance by 50 percent. How did I achieve this? Here again, you were doing two things at once, and this helped lower your performance. But how can we explain that the blah-blah-blah hurt your performance more than reading the second list of words? In the case of the second list, as in the blah-blah-blah case, you were simultaneously using verbal resources. Why did the blah-blah-blah hurt your performance more than the second list of words?

We've reached the heart of the enigma of the effects of stress on divided attention.

At a Time of Stress, You Keep Talking to Yourself . . .

You're reading this book, and it seems you're well focused. I tell myself that you're devoting your full attention to your reading and that you'll be encoding my message properly. But why should I think that? While you're reading this book, you may be wondering if your wife plans to leave you and go live with the neighbor, or if your youngest child should go see the doctor about those red blotches that keep developing on his body. These thoughts that are going through your mind are verbal, and they use plenty of the verbal resources you need to read this book.

These thoughts in your mind come from a threat detected in the environment by your brain and by the fact that your brain is causing you to regard this information as being the most relevant and, therefore, the information to which you should be allocating the most attention. "Allocating attention" is another way of saying "using resources to process this information." Of course, you could always *visualize* your wife with the neighbor or your child suffering with fever (which would make you use visual resources), but most of the time, because we're trying to find solutions to our stressors, we *verbalize* this information mentally. In doing so, we use a huge quantity of verbal resources, seriously hindering our ability to encode any other information of a verbal nature. I've lowered your performance by 50 percent just by getting you to say blah-blah-blah. Imagine the impact on your performance when you brood on the stressors in your life day after day.

You may very well try to tell yourself that you're going to stop thinking about your stressors and that everything will be okay. I hate to tell you this, but your brain won't let you free your mind of all your stressors just because you're meditating or taking a yoga class. It can't let this happen, because otherwise your survival would be in danger. For your brain, the threat is what's most relevant, and this is what it will pay the most attention to. In so doing, it will make you think about it all the time with the aim of finding a solution. This will soak up enormous resources and keep you from being able to do two things at the same time.

Since you began reading this book, how many times has your mind wandered to think about things that are causing you stress?

As we'll see in the last section of this book, these recurring thoughts can be used to understand the origin of your stress and to act on it. But until then, it is important to look at the effects of chronic stress on the memory.

When Chronic Stress Unsettles Our Ability to Detect Relevant Information

As we've seen, acute stress has very paradoxical effects on memory. It increases memorization of the stressful information while reducing memorization of peripheral information, which the brain considers irrelevant because it's nonthreatening.

Over the last 20 years, I've been trying to gain a better understanding of how stress, by acting on our memory system, can lead us to a state of chronic stress that will cause us to develop disorders such as depression or burnout. You know better than I do the kind of stigma that's attached to these mental disorders in the workplace. You've perhaps never said it out loud to a colleague, but at the dinner table you may have told your husband a story along the lines of "Funny, it's twice now that Marie has taken a three-month leave from work because she's depressed. But Marie and I have the same job! Not only am I still at work, but I get stuck with all *her* work! Kind of lame, don't you think?"

I'm rather skeptical about an ad I've seen on TV showing a man with his hands covering his eyes while a voice in the background talks about depression in the workplace. Suddenly, the man lowers his hands to see all his colleagues with balloons, cake and streamers welcoming him back after he's been away from work because of depression.

Sorry, but that's not how things happen in real life. Most of the time, the return to work by people who have been on leave because of depression or burnout is very tough. These people get judged by their peers because falling into burnout or depression shows how weak they might have been. Are depression and burnout really due to a person's weakness? Or could it be that, for unknown reasons (genetics, life history, etc.), when stress hormones reach these people's brains, they have the effect of altering how they see the world with the result that, gradually, the glass becomes half empty rather than half full?

I can tell you that the latest decade of research on this topic suggests that the second interpretation is the correct one. It's recognized now that, just as the body can't handle heavy doses of stress hormones for too long without going into disarray, the brain seems to try to adapt to the chronic effects of stress by altering its perception of what's threatening and what isn't.

A common belief in today's science is that chronic stress has two effects on the brain's ability to differentiate between a threatening piece of information and a nonthreatening one. In the first case, when the brain is bombarded chronically by stress hormones, it starts to detect threats where none exist. Everything then becomes threatening, as if the brain didn't want to take any risks. The person starts to detect threats where other people don't see any. This closely resembles an anxiety disorder. In the second case, the brain stops detecting threats, as if they were no longer worth paying attention to. Then nothing is threatening—the person stops caring. This closely resembles signs of burnout.

Of course, someone may develop just one of these patterns, and we still don't know the exact mechanism causing individuals to develop either of these thought models. But here again, this derangement may be nothing other than an attempt by the brain to adapt to a person's chronic stress.

Data from studies conducted among abused children give us a better understanding of how the brain, in attempting to adapt, may alter how we see the world. One of my colleagues, Dr. Seth Pollak of the University of Wisconsin, has studied for many years how abused children (exposed to physical, verbal and/or sexual violence) process threatening and non-threatening information. The aim is to gain a better understanding of how their brains may develop a means of adapting to the adverse conditions in which they are living. In one study, this researcher presented smiling, neutral or angry faces to a group of abused children and to a group of nonabused children. He asked the children to press a button as soon as they could say whether the face was neutral, smiling or angry.

The results of the study showed that the abused children detected the angry faces significantly more quickly than the nonabused children. Nothing comparable was observed for the detection of neutral or smiling faces. It was as if the brains of abused children, detecting threats on a daily basis in their family environment, led them to become super threat detectors to help them survive. In fact, quick detection of the moments when an aggressor parent is in a state indicating a higher risk of aggression (an unsteady gait, a tight jaw, etc.) is beneficial to a child's survival. By learning to detect this threat quickly, a child can then flee and try to escape abuse. This increases the chances of surviving in such adverse conditions.

It's quite possible that this child could become an adult who is more anxious than average and who detects threats more consistently, even if he no longer lives in a violent setting. When he was a child, his system was admirably well adapted to detecting threats that could affect his survival. When he reaches adolescence or adulthood, his stress system will remain alert and vigilant, on its guard, even in situations no longer requiring this.

It's worth noting here that nearly 75 percent of adults suffering from depression report having grown up in an adverse family setting, with a profusion of stressors and threats. Researchers now believe that exposure to these adverse conditions during the development phase may have had sizable effects on how these people later perceive the world and how they react. By adapting to the adverse conditions of childhood, the brain ensured the person's survival. But as with the body, there is a price to be paid for this adaptation. By altering the brain's propensity to detect a threat, chronic stress will have the effect of instituting a thought system that is more sensitive than normal to surrounding threats.

Chapter 7

Why Are We So Stressed These Days?

In the last two chapters, we saw how chronic stress develops and how, when stress hormones become dysregulated, they can have a domino effect on various systems in the body and cause a range of disorders. We also saw how the chronic access of these stress hormones to the brain can lead to memory disorders and to changes in our capacity to detect threats.

As stress science researchers examine the effects of chronic stress on the body and brain, a key question has arisen: Why is there so much stress these days? Why are rates of obesity, diabetes and depression so high? The prevalence of stress is paradoxical, because nowadays we've come to grips with many situations that generate absolute stress. Mammoths vanished long ago, and we're not living in a war zone where threats to survival are part of daily life. Our present-day societies are rich, educated and safe, with far less absolute stress than there would have been at the time of the mammoths.

However, nearly 500,000 Canadians miss work during any given week because of stress-related health problems, and there has been a 316 percent increase since 1995 in stress as a reported reason for missing work. The World Health Organization predicts that, by 2020, depression will be the world's second most common cause of disability, behind only the current leader, cardiovascular disease. As we saw earlier, depression and cardiovascular disease are both disorders that may be linked to chronic stress. But if there are no more mammoths on the prowl and our lives are increasingly safe, where does the problem come from?

The answer is disarmingly simple. Our present-day world experiences chronic stress because our brains are not aware that we're living in the twenty-first century. In other words, our brains don't make the distinction between absolute stress (which threatens our survival) and relative stress (those NUTS again). For our brains, Jenny who takes a bite out of our ego at the coffee machine each Tuesday morning is no different from a prehistoric mammoth. By failing to distinguish between absolute and relative stress, our brains generate the same stress response in both cases.

In contrast to the era of the mammoths, our society nowadays is continuously changing. Novelty and unpredictability have become constant factors in life: new technologies to master, jobs that are increasingly precarious, unstable marriages and so on. Each day the media tell us about events that we have no control over and that could affect our survival: stock market crashes, violence, war, earthquakes and more. In today's more complex and competitive social relationships, the possibility of a new threat to our ego may often be just around the corner. In short, we live today surrounded by a whole array of relative stress creators.

Mammoths entered the lives of early humans in prehistoric times much less frequently than the NUTS of today's world enter ours. Because we generate just as great a stress response to relative stress as we do to absolute stress, and because relative stress is the more common kind of stress nowadays, it follows that these occurrences of relative stress accumulate and generate states of chronic stress that can be harmful to us.

Mammoths in the Morning Traffic

A small example will illustrate what I'm getting at. Imagine, first, that you're a prehistoric human and that, one fine morning, you look at the members of your tribe and realize they're hungry. You decide to go hunting for mammoths so that you can feed the tribe. You set off, spear in hand, accompanied by your fiercest warriors. At the edge of a valley, you come upon a six-ton mammoth. We can agree that this constitutes a case of absolute stress for you. Now, let's return to the twenty-first century. It's 8:30 a.m. and you're stuck in morning traffic on your way to the office. This is a case of relative stress: depending on whether you have a 9 a.m. meeting, you may or may not generate a stress response (unpredictability, lack of control). In your case today, you've got a 9 a.m. meeting with your boss. You therefore experience relative stress.

Let's take it for granted now that your brain doesn't differentiate between absolute stress (the mammoth) and relative stress (the traffic). In either case, your brain will detect a threat and will generate a strong stress response enabling you to rally a massive dose of energy to fight or flee the threat. As a hairy prehistoric man, you'll find your pupils dilating, your hairs standing on end, your muscles tensing, your breathing getting faster and your lungs swelling to let you emit a strident howl at the mammoth. Even now, as a semi-hairy man in the modern era, at the wheel of your car, you find your pupils dilating, your hairs standing on end, your muscles tensing, your breathing getting faster and your lungs swelling with air to shout—but you don't shout. For prehistoric humans as for modern humans, energy is mobilized to the utmost to be used in combat or in flight. But today, stuck in traffic, you won't do either of these things!

The prehistoric man effectively consumed all the energy that was rallied, because he either killed the mammoth or ran to escape it if it was too monstrous. You'll agree with me that it's not easy to run while inside a car. Our modern-day man has therefore mobilized a massive dose of energy that he hasn't expended. The feeling of the hands tensing on the wheel that you experience when you are stressed in traffic comes from this unspent energy.

Your brain, failing to distinguish between absolute and relative stress, takes it for granted that you got rid of the energy you mobilized by killing or fleeing the mammoth. The stress hormones produced will thus go back to the brain to induce a feeling of hunger so as to restore your energy reserves. You'll therefore aim to find food to build your energy reserves.

In prehistoric times, this was much more easily said than done: if a prehistoric man fled the mammoth, he would have to go hunting again to find food. Our modern man just goes to his office and heads straight to the vending machine to buy carbohydrates (candy, chips, etc.).

This is exactly what the body wants, because carbohydrates contain energy that can be used quickly. And since the brain takes it for granted that you've gotten rid of all the energy you rallied, it will send you the message that you have to replenish your energy reserves—and do it quickly!

In the case of the prehistoric man who has spent the energy that was mobilized to kill or flee the mammoth, the total energy reserve doesn't rise, because the energy mobilized has been spent. However, the modern man, who has retained the energy mobilized as a stress response (since it's impossible to run inside a car), has surplus energy that turns to fat—right around the abdomen, just where he doesn't want it.

Time Marches On

A fabulous system, don't you think? A perfect system for helping us survive. The only problem is that it hasn't yet adjusted to the modern era. And we suffer from these stress responses that haven't yet adjusted, because by generating frequent responses to occurrences of relative stress, we're straining a system that was originally devised to save our lives.

I sincerely believe that in the next century, humans will have learned to adjust their stress responses to the new era. All I have to do is look at how different the elderly people I examine in my laboratory are from the young adults I test. We recently discovered that simply getting to the laboratory for the first time, without previously knowing where it is, how to get there and whom they're going to meet, generates an enormous stress response in elderly people. This response is so substantial that it can induce temporary memory disorders, which, if we weren't so vigilant in my laboratory about the effects of stress on elderly people's memories, we might have attributed to their age.

In contrast, young people have no apprehensions about getting to the laboratory. Even if they lose their way, they still arrive at the lab relaxed, telling themselves that this isn't serious because we waited for them before we began the tests. Their stress hormone levels on arrival are minimal.

These elderly people and these young adults are living in the same century and the same year. But there's a large age gap, and the young adults have a big lead over the elderly people when it comes to their potential to adapt to the modern era. If my hypothesis is correct, this means that the brains of young people in future generations will have even greater mastery over their stress response, which, over the years, will have adjusted to the new realities of our time.

The Joys of Interpretation

That's all very well, you say, but what do we do until then? Nobody really wants to wait until the next century to gain better control over their stress response—and in any case, few of us alive today will survive beyond the current century.

There is a solution, however. Remember that relative stress depends on whether a situation is interpreted as being novel, or unpredictable, or threatening to our ego or outside our sense of control. A situation that is interpreted in one or more of these ways will generate a stress response. This suggests that, nowadays, a situation is stressful only if we interpret it as being novel, unpredictable, threatening to our ego or outside our sense of control. If you change your interpretation, you can prevent a stress response that could be harmful in the long term. I'll talk about this more in the last section of this book.

Of course, there are still cases of absolute stress in our present-day world, as we saw in the section on acute stress. For example, if your child suffers from leukemia, this condition is clearly a source of absolute stress for you. However, starting in 1963, Dr. W.A. Mason and his colleagues showed that stress hormone production among the parents of children suffering from leukemia (and therefore facing absolute stress) also depended on the parents' interpretation of their child's illness.

For eight months during 1963, Dr. Mason, in collaboration with Dr. Stanford B. Friedman, a pediatrician at the National Institutes of Health in the United States, followed a group of parents whose children suffered from leukemia, measuring their stress hormone levels. He also interviewed each of the parents (fathers and mothers) in great depth to gain a better understanding of how parents assimilated their child's illness.

In 1963, the chances of surviving childhood leukemia were very slim. In fact, every child in Dr. Mason's study died within eight months of the study. The researchers observed that the parents who refused to acknowledge that their child's illness could be fatal produced stress hormones in lower quantities than the parents who didn't deny the seriousness of their child's illness. However, Dr. Mason's results showed that denial was only a temporary solution. By following parents after a child's death, Dr. Mason observed that stress hormone levels subsequently rose dramatically among parents who had denied the seriousness of their child's illness but remained stable among parents who hadn't. These results showed that denial merely delayed a major stress response in those parents.

Dr. Mason also reported that parents who took the trouble to learn about their child's illness by asking the doctor questions and by reading books and magazine articles on the subject generally produced stress hormones in lower quantities than other parents. This facet is important, because it clearly shows the power of NUTS even where absolute stress is concerned. What was going on among parents when they were learning about their child's illness? In making this effort, these parents reduced the novelty and unpredictability of the illness (they knew what the illness was and how it would manifest itself), and they increased their sense (with the emphasis on *sense*) of having the situation under control.

In actual fact, these parents couldn't have their child's illness under control. But in learning about the illness their child suffered from, they had the *impression* of having greater control over the situation. This greater impression of control reduced the threat they perceived from their child's illness, and this in turn brought down the stress hormone levels in these parents. This effect continued after their child's death. This means it's the *sense* of having control over a situation that's the key factor in the notion of control in NUTS, rather than control itself.

However, actively seeking information to increase the impression of control is not a miracle solution for all parents of sick children. As we'll see in the next chapter, if you're an anxious type of person, doing research on your child's illness through today's Internet may increase your anxiety about your child's illness and cause you to produce a larger quantity of stress hormones.

At the time of Dr. Mason's 1963 study, only books and magazine articles were available. But now, the Internet generates a wide array of information as well as links to other sites that may result in research on an illness leading you to similar information on a different illness. This leaves you stuck with two illnesses rather than one!

My son suffered from gastric reflux when he was a baby. At age 2, it was obviously very hard for him to verbalize his disorder, which complicated my task of understanding his constant crying during the night. One day I decided to check the Internet for information on the symptoms associated with gastric reflux among 2-year-old children.

I discovered some important tips for detecting my young son's gastric reflux, but in following the links provided by some of the sites, I learned that gastric reflux among children can lead to Barrett's syndrome, a disorder that can produce cancer of the esophagus. This threw me into total panic. I made an urgent call to his doctor, convinced that my son showed all the symptoms of cancer of the esophagus. Of course, my son's doctor calmed my anxiety, explaining to me that this was not the case. However, I can guarantee you that, while waiting for the doctor to call back, I must have produced a massive dose of stress hormones!

That said, Dr. Mason's results are extremely important, because they show that our way of interpreting the stress around us (absolute or relative) may be a decisive factor in determining the size of the stress response the situation causes us to generate. If our interpretation of situations around us is always negative, it's clear that the stress response we produce on a chronic basis could cause us long-term damage.

But what makes us more, or less, inclined to interpret a situation as stressful? In other words, what makes us more or less inclined to react to novelty, unpredictability, a threat to the ego and a sense of loss of control? Over the last two decades, scientific studies have shown that various factors may result in someone being more inclined than someone else to interpret a situation as stressful, causing that person to produce stress hormones more frequently. Some of these factors are intrinsic to who we are as people and result mostly from our personality and our gender. Other factors have external origins and come from the environment we live in at any given moment in our lives.

Chapter 8

Stress to Match Each Personality

Scientific studies of stress have shown that three personality traits have the potential to generate stress responses in humans. These traits are hostility, anxiety and low self-esteem.

Honing In on Hostility

In 1892, the Canadian surgeon and researcher Sir William Osler wrote an article in which he reported that most of the patients he treated for heart disorders had similar personalities: he found them brusque and ambitious. This theme was taken up again in the 1950s by two doctors, Meyer Friedman and Ray Rosenman, who confirmed that the patients they treated for coronary disorders all shared a set of emotional reactions that they called Type A personality.

According to Drs. Friedman and Rosenman, people with a Type A personality are characterized by intense ambition, a strongly competitive spirit, hostility toward others, a constant preoccupation with deadlines and a sense of time-related urgency.[1] These researchers designated anyone not showing Type A personality traits as Type B. On the basis of these studies, the researchers concluded that people with a Type A personality were the most likely to suffer coronary disorders. This conclusion became highly favored among psychologists, who adopted the concepts of Type A and Type B personalities (later adding other types of personality), linking them to scores on psychological questionnaires such as those dealing with life events or day-to-day problems. On the whole, the results of these studies showed significant links between Type A and Type B personalities and the scores on stress questionnaires.

If you work for a medium-sized or large company, there's a good chance a consultant hired by your firm once administered a questionnaire to determine whether you had a Type A personality. What was the verdict? In my own case, as I've already noted publicly, I have a Type Double A personality. According to psychological studies from the 1970s, I should therefore show increased risk of developing coronary disorders.[2]

But in the early 1990s, some researchers began to express doubts as to whether all traits associated with Type A personality could predict coronary disorders in a similar way and with the same intensity. They suspected that some characteristics of Type A personality could predict coronary disorders on their own. They then decided to test the predictive value of each characteristic in Type A personality for the risk of coronary disorders. They found that the only characteristic of Type A personality that predicted these disorders was hostility.[3] This gradually led to the decline of biological research on Type A personality and the rise of new studies aiming to cast light on the role of hostility in responding to stress.

Up to now, studies have shown that there are two types of hostility that increase the risk of developing a coronary disorder. The first type is cynical hostility. This type of hostility is defined as an individual's tendency to interpret all events with a combination of hostility and cynicism. He or she is the sort of person who will say to a work colleague at lunch, "Wouldn't you know that John got a promotion! He always sticks close to the boss and holds his little weekend barbecues with the group to get them to love him. Always the same gang!" Do you recognize yourself? If you do, there's a good chance that you show the trait of cynical hostility. Studies of cynical hostility have shown that people with this personality trait are at greater risk of developing coronary disorders and of producing a high dose of stress hormones (cortisol and adrenaline) in a stress situation.

Cynical hostility doesn't show up only at work. Studies done in the 1990s tested the effects of cynical hostility among couples. Dr. Janice

Kiecolt-Glaser of Ohio State University is a pioneer in the study of how hostility affects stress hormone production in couples. In one of her studies, she measured stress hormones in 90 newlywed couples who were exposed to situations that could generate conflicts between them.

How did these researchers generate conflicts "on demand" among couples? Easy. They asked each member of a couple to talk for a few minutes about a subject on which they usually disagreed. One day I asked a colleague in Vancouver, Dr. Norm O'Rourke, a specialist in this area of research, to tell me what subject of discord was most often discussed by couples. He replied instantly: money!

With the aim of studying couples' reactions in conflict situations, the researchers separated couples into two groups, with couples in which one or both members showed cynical hostility during conflicts on one side and couples who didn't show cynical hostility during conflicts on the other. The results showed that even though the newlyweds said they were all very satisfied with their relationships, the spouses in couples in whom one spouse showed cynical hostility had a significant increase in the adrenaline stress hormone in conflict situations compared to the spouses in couples in whom there was no hostile member.

In another study, Dr. Edward Suarez and his colleagues at Duke University in North Carolina grouped men according to whether they showed a little or a lot of cynical hostility. Then they asked the participants to solve a difficult anagram. While that was going on, they subjected half the men in each of the two groups to harassment from a research assistant, whose role was to keep questioning their ability to solve the puzzle, with time running out. The men who showed cynical hostility and who were harassed by the research assistant presented significantly higher levels of the cortisol stress hormone than the less hostile men who were also harassed. There was also a sharp rise in blood pressure in the men who showed cynical hostility, a marker of their cardiovascular reactivity.

The second type of hostility that places a person at greater risk of being highly reactive to stress is repressed anger. This type of hostility is defined as an individual's tendency to repress his or her anger and not show it. This is the type of person who will say to a work colleague after a dispute, "Everything's okay! No need to talk about it, it's looked after! There's no problem! And anyway, even if we did talk about it, you wouldn't listen to me!" If you recognize yourself, there's a good chance you have the repressed anger trait.

A study conducted by Dr. John W. Burns and his colleagues at the Chicago Medical School asked participants to make up stories based on various drawings that were presented to them. While they told their stories, participants were subjected to harassment by a research assistant or, alternatively, placed in a control situation in which they weren't harassed. Using a questionnaire to measure the tendency toward repressed anger, the researchers classified the participants on the basis of whether they presented the repressed anger trait and measured the cardiovascular response of all participants, looking at those who were harassed in comparison with the control group. The results indicated that only the participants who showed the repressed anger trait had an increase in cardiovascular activity in response to the harassment.

Taken as a whole, these studies show that individuals showing cynical hostility or a tendency to repress their anger produced higher stress hormone levels and increased activity in the cardiovascular system when in a conflict situation.

Anxiety, or Fear of Being Afraid

The second personality trait that can cause a person to interpret most situations as stressful is anxiety. This trait (which should not be confused with anxiety as an illness) is characterized by someone often being worried about the future—about what will happen, what might happen or even what didn't happen. Anxiety can be either a state or a trait. A state of anxiety may be short-lived and fade away after the disappearance of a stressful event. In contrast, anxiety as a trait is part of an individual's personality. If you're not usually the anxious type (and thus don't display the trait of anxiety) but if you suddenly show a little anxiety—when your first child arrives, say—it will be said that you're in a state of anxiety. This state will be short-lived and will soon disappear.

On the other hand, if you tend to show an anxious trait, this aspect of your personality will follow you everywhere, and you'll show anxious behavior in facing an array of situations that would not generate as much anxiety in someone who didn't have this trait. An anxious trait and an anxious state must be differentiated from anxiety as an illness, which can constitute a serious pathology. It's now believed that people who show an anxious trait are more likely than other people to develop anxiety disorders such as generalized anxiety disorder, social phobia or obsessive compulsive disorder.

A study by Dr. Aafke van Santen and his colleagues at VU University in the Netherlands measured the production of cortisol stress hormone in 2,981 participants, classified according to whether or not they presented anxious traits. These researchers measured cortisol in the saliva of participants when they were at home. They asked participants to collect several samples each day to take account of the 24-hour circadian rhythm of cortisol. This stress hormone is at its peak in the morning and the levels decline in the course of the day, hitting bottom during the night. The study's results showed that people who show anxious traits present significantly higher cortisol levels in the morning than people who don't. This could mean that people who show these traits have a greater tendency to interpret day-to-day situations as threatening, leading to increased cortisol production at wake-up time.

Another interesting characteristic of people who show anxious traits is that they're likely to produce a stress response even when there's no stress! We often see this result in my laboratory. When we expose people to stress conditions, we always leave them a little time to anticipate the imminent condition so that we can measure the effects of anticipation of a stressor on the stress response. People who have anxious traits often produce as great a quantity of stress hormones while anticipating stress as they do when facing the stress itself.

When we compare the results observed in people who display hostility to those found in people who show anxious traits, an important fact emerges. In both of these personality types, the person often isn't facing any stressor. However, merely interpreting the potential situation as a source of aggression (hostile personality) or as something frightening (anxious personality) results in the person producing as great a quantity of stress hormones as if the stress factor were present.

The reason for this is simple. Hostility and anxiety lead to rumination. Stress doesn't have to be a big hairy beast that attacks you from outside. Stay home and ruminate long enough, and I can guarantee that you'll produce a large enough quantity of stress hormones to cause yourself long-term harm! Some of my colleagues are starting to think that, if depressed individuals show large increases in stress hormones, it's because they tend to ruminate all the time. If you always take a dark view of the world and find it constantly threatening, and if you turn this over continuously in your mind, it's clear that your brain will detect a threat from this (even if it isn't real) and will produce stress hormones.

Low Self-Esteem

The personality trait that's most highly predictive of strong responsiveness to stress is self-esteem. Self-esteem is the idea we have of our own value, the sense that we're unique and important. This character facet is formed very early in a child's life. A child with high self-esteem will move on easily to new experiences and won't be afraid of failure. A child with low self-esteem won't believe he or she can succeed and will avoid taking on new experiences. As people grow up, this personality trait will become more firmly anchored in them, leading children to become adults with either high or low self-esteem.

Someone with low self-esteem has the impression of never having control of a situation, one of the NUTS factors. Research by a colleague and friend, Dr. Jens C. Pruessner at McGill University in Montreal, has shown that when participants are exposed to laboratory stress, self-esteem is the trait that best determines whether or not someone will react to a stressful condition by producing stress hormones.

In one of his studies in collaboration with Dr. Clemens Kirschbaum of Dresden Technical University in Germany, Dr. Pruessner exposed participants to five consecutive days of stress. The results again showed that people with high self-esteem reacted less to stress during the five days of exposure than participants with low self-esteem.

In the 2000s, Jens and I discovered something quite fascinating. The hippocampus, you'll recall, is a small area in the brain shaped like a seahorse (which explains its name). It plays a very important role in memory and is one of the areas that stress hormones reach when they return to the brain after being produced in response to a stress incident. In one of our studies, we observed that people with low self-esteem have smaller hippocampi than people with high self-esteem. We made this observation among elderly people and among young adults. These curious results led us to wonder if stress experienced in childhood might just possibly have effects on a child's self-esteem, leading the child to respond to stress by producing high levels of cortisol that could damage the hippocampus. Unfortunately, I don't have the answer to this question, but studies are underway in both our laboratories to attempt to cast light on this intriguing discovery.

Chapter 9

Two Sexes, Two Types of Stress?

In your view, who produces more stress hormones when confronted with a stressful situation, men or women? Each time I ask this question in my public lectures, the majority of people in the room say *women*!

This is not the correct answer. Scientific studies over the last two decades show that, in fact, men produce a greater quantity of stress hormones when exposed to acute stress—at least when I'm the one causing the stress! That last part is a joke, but the finding is real. It has been demonstrated many times, both in my laboratory and at labs in the United States and Europe. Faced with acute stress when exposed to a novel, unpredictable and ego-threatening situation outside their control, men produce significantly higher concentrations of cortisol stress hormone than women do.

These curious results were first reported by a colleague, Dr. Clemens Kirschbaum of Dresden Technical University in Germany. Dr. Kirschbaum exposed men and women to psychological stress and observed that the men showed stress hormone production three times higher than the women. This was quite the result! Men, those prehistoric mammoth hunters, have kept this survival response well anchored inside them. Women, who in prehistoric times were busier looking after their offspring than hunting mammoths, appear not to have maintained the stress response!

Nonsense, you'll tell me, and you'll be right. Initially, researchers told themselves this result made sense, since men are generally more likely to suffer from cardiovascular disorders.[1] But this hasty conclusion was soon called into question by other researchers, who reminded us that women are twice as likely as men to develop depression. And since many researchers think depression may be linked to chronic exposure to stress, this notion of greater stress among men and its association to cardiovascular disease no longer makes sense. It would seem that women in the modern era also suffer from the weight of stress. But then, how is it that we can't observe this when we expose them to stress in the laboratory?

When Stress Was Male

One of the primary reasons cited to explain this troubling fact is that the scientific models that were developed failed to take account of the inherent differences between men and women in terms of stress response. The dominant model of stress response was the fight or flight response as defined by Dr. Walter Cannon almost a century ago.[2] As I've noted several times, this model asserts that, faced with a threat, humans rally all their energy to fight or flee.

The problem with this model is that it was developed using only males, in both animal models and human studies. Very early in stress science, researchers kept females out of scientific studies on stress because females, whether animal or human, have menstrual cycles characterized by sharp variations in their sex hormones such as estrogen and progesterone. Researchers suspected that female hormones might interact with stress hormones, making it harder to interpret results obtained from females. Consequently, to simplify matters, researchers used only males in scientific studies.

However, in 2000, the major organizations subsidizing scientific research made it clear that it was not ethical to keep women out of studies on the pretext that their hormonal cycle is different from that of men and that this could make it harder to interpret the scientific results. Men and women should be equal, given the need to make scientific discoveries that could be beneficial to both. Accordingly, granting organizations required scientific researchers to include equal numbers of women and men in their studies.

This was a very wise decision. From that moment on, some very interesting scientific discoveries were made and models were developed to explain how men and women may react differently to stress.

When Stress Became Female

The initial studies conducted among women showed, first, that women react to stress to a degree that differs according to the phases of their menstrual cycle. A woman's menstrual cycle is marked by a *follicular* phase and a *luteal* phase. The follicular phase is the start of the menstrual cycle, just after menstruation. At that time, a new *follicle* (egg) is being formed, potentially to be fertilized by a sperm. In contrast, the luteal phase is the end of the menstrual cycle, when the egg hasn't been fertilized. This is the phase just before a woman's menstrual period. It is this stage that has been associated with premenstrual syndrome (PMS) among women.

Studies conducted by Dr. Kirschbaum and his team showed that, when exposed to stress in the laboratory, women produce a significantly larger quantity of stress hormones prior to menstruation than when they are in their follicular phase (after menstruation). Subsequent research by Dr. Kirschbaum showed that women in the luteal phase show as great a responsiveness to stress as that observed among men, while women in the follicular phase show much less responsiveness to stress than men.

Contraceptive pills have the effect of leading to sex hormone concentrations similar to those observed just after menstruation, and Dr. Kirschbaum's results showed that women taking contraceptive pills have a lower responsiveness to stress than is observed among men.

The Dreaded PMS

Ladies, I see you smiling in the corner. These results seem to confirm the dreaded premenstrual syndrome and explain why we're sometimes so aggressive and stressed during those times. One day I held a public debate on premenstrual syndrome in one of my university courses. The students had to choose sides: on one side were those arguing that premenstrual syndrome is something real, linked to our biology; on the other were those asserting that PMS has no biological basis and occurs only in women's minds. All the women in the course were in the first group, and all the guys were in the second group, with a hundred pairs of female eyes shooting daggers at them!

I set out the scientific data to both sides. Yes, there really does seem to be a biological basis for premenstrual syndrome. However, studies also show that not all women in the world present this syndrome. For example, premenstrual stress is not always observed among South Asian women, with its existence depending on various factors such as whether a young woman lives in an urban or rural setting.

If premenstrual syndrome could be explained by female hormones (estrogen and progesterone) alone, South Asian women should show this syndrome as much as North American women do! Of course, you might argue that South Asian women are less likely to show premenstrual syndrome because their culture doesn't allow them to display this kind of behavior. Quite right. But it may also be that our own North American experience of PMS is also linked to our culture.

When I was young, women spoke of "being sick" when we had our periods. When a girl got her first period, her mother would make a face and tell her that the worst was yet to come, with cramps, headaches and so on. Some researchers suspect that the way mothers regard this part of the menstrual cycle may have an influence on how their daughters experience it—negatively or neutrally.

Up to now, there has been no conclusive study of the biological or cultural reality of PMS. Personally, however, I've decided not to take any risks. One day I told my daughter that when she got her first period, we would have a one-on-one mother-daughter supper to celebrate this major step in her life. Then we would go shopping to complete the celebration. I said to myself that by instilling in her a positive perception of this unique female condition, I could lessen the premenstrual symptoms she would have for the rest of her life.

Fight or Flight versus Tend and Befriend

As we've seen, the dominant model of stress response developed by researchers in the last century was the fight or flight model. But this model was developed only among males. Starting in the early 2000s, researchers called this model into question, at least in its applicability to women. By studying male and female animals in stress situations, researchers discovered that while males tend to become aggressive and look for fights when stressed, the response of females in stress situations is different. In these situations, females tend to adopt so-called affiliation behavior. They develop behavior that aims to protect their offspring and involves approaching the other females in the group.

On the basis of these observations among animals, Dr. Shelly Taylor, a researcher at the University of California at Los Angeles, came up with the protection and affiliation or "tend and befriend" model to describe women's responses in periods of stress. The model suggests that, in stress situations, women react by protecting themselves and their children (the protection part of the model) and by forming alliances with other females (the affiliation part). Dr. Taylor contrasts this response with what is observed among men, with their greater tendency to use a fight or flight response to deal with a source of stress. Results confirming this model, first tested on animals, have been obtained among humans.

In an initial study, Dr. Laura Stroud and her colleagues at Brown University in Rhode Island exposed men and women to two stress conditions. The first one involved success-related stress (people were asked to complete a difficult task in a very short period of time). The second one looked at social-rejection-related stress (people subjected to a condition involving social rejection). The results showed that men produced significantly greater quantities of stress hormones in the success-related stress situation, while the women had much higher stress hormone concentrations in the social-rejection-related stress situation.

These initial results showed that women produced more stress hormones in situations involving stress related to social affiliation, but not that women have a greater tendency than men to join with people of their own gender when facing stress. To answer this question, we need to look at a second set of experiments conducted among humans.

In an initial study, Dr. Kirschbaum asked men and women to come to his laboratory accompanied by their spouses. The spouses had the role of accompanying participants in their "stress experience," providing verbal support (encouragement) prior to exposure to the stressor. Then, Dr. Kirschbaum and his team exposed men and women to psychological stress.

You may recall that Dr. Kirschbaum's initial study showed that, in laboratory stress situations, men are three times more reactive to stress than women. He was surprised indeed to observe that, when men and women received support from their spouses before exposure to stress, the women were twice as reactive to stress as men! When a man was accompanied by his wife, this lowered his stress hormone production in the stress situation. In contrast, when a woman was accompanied by her husband, her stress hormone production increased. Wow!

But how can this result be explained? The researchers conjectured that the results may not have any link with the fact that the support was provided by a spouse but may have been connected to the fact that the support was received from someone of the other sex. To check whether this was indeed the case, the researchers subjected another group of men and women to a second experiment.

In this second situation, the researcher provided men and women with social support from an unknown person of the opposite sex. Each woman received social support from a man she didn't know, and each man got social support from a woman he didn't know. When these men and women were then exposed to stress, the researchers observed, again, that the men seemed to benefit from a woman's presence, with a lower stress response than when they lacked support.

In contrast, the women showed just as high a stress response when they received support from an unknown man as in the absence of support. With this second experiment, the researchers showed that men benefited greatly from the social support provided by a woman (whether their spouse or someone unknown to them, with greater benefit when the support came from their spouse), while the women got only minor benefit from the support provided by a man (whether their spouse or an unknown person).

In pondering these results, the researchers wondered whether women could benefit from the support provided by a woman and men could benefit from the support of a man. Dr. A.M. Smith at the University of Texas exposed men and women to stress after they had received social support from an unknown person of the same sex.

Women received support from an unknown woman, while men received support from an unknown man. The results of this study showed that, when men received support from another man, this led to an increase in their stress response. In contrast, when women received support from another woman, this reduced their stress response.

Let's go back over this. When men receive support from their spouse, their stress response is reduced. But when men receive support from another man, their stress response rises.

In contrast, when women receive support from their spouse, their stress response rises. When they receive support from another woman, their stress response falls. With these studies, scientific research has shown the viability of the "tend and befriend" model suggested by Dr. Taylor. Faced with a stressor, men may tend to use a fight or flight model (which may explain why they don't benefit from the support of another man at a time of stress), while women may be more likely to use the tend-and-befriend model (which may explain why they seem to benefit from support from other women at times of stress).

As I've often said at public lectures, these results suggest a course of action for women. Ladies, when you next find yourselves in a period of great stress, have a "girls' night out," and this will do you plenty of good. However, leave your cell phone turned on, because there's a good chance that your husband is calling if he's also suffering from stress!

Then What Are Husbands Good For?

If, as we've done throughout this book, we start with the principle that all stress behavior is aimed at survival of the species, a fundamental question arises from the set of studies reported on here. These studies have shown that men benefit from their wives' support at a time of stress, while women benefit from the support of other women. The $64,000 question that emerges from these results is: what are husbands good for?

Believe it or not, researchers have been asking the same question and have conducted an experiment to answer it! Dr. Beate Ditzen and her colleagues at the University of Zurich recruited women who had been part of a couple for at least 12 months and split them into three groups. The first group of women got support in verbal form (spoken encouragement) from their husbands before being exposed to a stressor. The second group of women received support in physical form (shoulder massage) from their husbands before being exposed to the stressor and the third group received no support.

The results showed that only women receiving support in physical form (shoulder massage) from their husbands showed a reduction in their stress response! Women who got support in verbal form (encouragement) from their husbands showed a stress response similar to that of the women who received no support.

These results—which I intend to frame and display prominently in my kitchen!—help us understand why the earlier studies on support from spouses at times of stress hadn't indicated a beneficial effect from spouses on women's stress response. All the previous studies looked at support in verbal form.

It appears that a woman benefits most from physical support provided by her spouse, while she benefits more from verbal support when it is provided by other women.[3] Meanwhile, a man under stress seems to benefit from verbal support provided by his wife. But no study up to now has attempted to find out whether a man may also benefit from physical support provided by his wife. All bets are on!

A Hormone for Affiliation?

Various researchers now believe that the "protect and affiliate" (or tend and befriend) behavior observed among women under stress may result from a hormone called oxytocin. This hormone, produced in stress situations, has the effect of reducing cortisol production. In animal studies, researchers have discovered that administering oxytocin has the effect of inducing protective behavior toward their offspring and affiliation with peers among females.

Both men and women produce oxytocin, but it's found in greater concentrations among women because it has a role in their reproductive systems. It is released in large quantities when women are giving birth, enabling uterine contractions.[4] In response to stimulation of the nipple by the newborn, this hormone also induces lactation, enabling a woman to breastfeed her child. It's interesting to note here that mothers are less reactive to stress during breastfeeding.

These data, often observed in animals, were reproduced recently by one of my students, Dr. Mai Thanh Tu. In contrast to female animals, human women have a choice between breastfeeding their children and giving them formula. On the basis of animal studies, only breastfeeding would provide for increased production of oxytocin, thereby leading to reduced stress response among women.

To test this hypothesis, Mai exposed two groups of women to psychological stress. The women in both groups had recently given birth. The first group breastfed their children exclusively, while the other group used only formula to feed their children.

The study's results showed that women who exclusively breastfed their children showed reduced stress response when compared to women who fed their children with formula. We interpreted these results in line with the production of oxytocin induced by breastfeeding and the effects of oxytocin on reduced stress response among mothers.

However, ladies, there's no need to blame yourself if your body didn't allow you to breastfeed your child or if you chose to feed your child with formula. We also observed in our study that the reduced stress response among breastfeeding women was present only when the mother was multiparous, meaning that she had already had other children. Among women having their first child (primiparous), breast-feeding or formula feeding had absolutely no influence on stress response: both groups of women showed a strong response when exposed to psychological stress. It was as if, at the time of the first child, the system wanted to take no risks and produced a stress response, irrespective of breastfeeding.

Of Fathers and Mothers

As soon as the tend-and-befriend model was put forth by Dr. Taylor to explain stress responsiveness among women, it was challenged by several researchers who didn't see how this stress response among women could be beneficial for survival of the species. You may recall that earlier studies showed that, from prehistory right up to the present, our stress response has developed to ensure survival of the species. It's easy to understand how the fight-or-flight response may be beneficial in enabling someone to fight and survive a threat. However, how could a protect-and-affiliate response be beneficial for survival of the species?

Once initial criticism of the model emerged, other researchers suggested that this tend-and-befriend response observed among women may also be beneficial for survival of the species, enabling women to avoid fleeing from a threat and leaving her offspring unprotected. In addition, the affiliation approach could enable them to link up with other women in the group with the aim of fighting any nearby threat as a group, without any men around.

Feminists harshly criticized the model, seeing it as keeping women confined to the predetermined role of the nurturing and protective mother. Psychosocial studies of gender differences show that young girls and boys will often adopt typical female or male behavior not because of a predetermined genetic code but simply because society favors this kind of behavior. Dolls are bought for little girls and trucks for boys, perpetuating socially determined gender roles.

Prehistoric women had the role of protective mother for many centuries, if not millennia. However, you'll agree that nowadays, with women entering the workforce in large numbers and the grow-ing involvement of fathers in family life, this model of the protective mother can no longer hold up, nor can the protect-and-affiliate response associated with it. Remember that our stress system doesn't seem to be aware that we're now in the twenty-first century, in an era of mothers who are presidents of companies and fathers who look after children at home. It may be that our system will continue to operate as it did in the prehistoric era, thinking it can ensure survival of the species in this way. Curious results obtained from young girls and boys lead us to think this may be the case.

An initial result comes from one of my studies conducted among children. The study aimed to find out whether poverty could be generating stress responses in children and adolescents. We measured stress hormones in 416 children and adolescents from ages 6 to 16 from varied socioeconomic backgrounds: low-income, middle-income and above-average-income. Results from the study showed that, from ages 6 to 10, children living in low-income families showed significantly higher cortisol stress hormone levels than children growing up in middle- or high-income families.

In this study, we also measured subjective stress levels and symptoms of depression among the mothers of these children. We first saw that mothers in low-income families reported greater stress and presented more symptoms of depression than the other mothers. In the final analysis, we showed that the more a mother reported stress and symptoms of depression, the more her own child produced high levels of cortisol stress hormone. This was the first evidence in scientific research of an effect we called the *spillover effect of parental stress on children*.

When I looked to see whether this effect was equally intense among boys and girls, I found that it was present only among girls. It seems that young girls are especially sensitive to their mothers' moods and that they react more strongly to the stress shown by their mothers.

Ladies, please, no guilt. I don't want you to read these lines and think it's always your fault. This is completely false, because results we obtain showing the mother's role in the stress experienced by children are often due to the fact that it's very hard to recruit fathers for our studies! Fathers generally tend to leave this kind of activity to their wives, which is why most of our results deal with mothers. However, results obtained among boys by a colleague, Dr. Mark V. Flinn, show that they react strongly to the behavior of their fathers.

These studies have shown that boys and girls seem to react differently to the stress of their fathers and mothers. But do the fight-or-flight or the protect-and-affiliate approaches come into play when they face a stressor? Here, intriguing results were obtained by Dr. Daryn H. David and his team at Yale University in Connecticut.

These researchers attempted to see whether the fight-or-flight response associated with men and the protect-and-affiliate response associated with women might also be found among young boys and girls. For this purpose, they studied the attachment to mothers among children exposed to stress. In this study, stress was generated by the mothers. They studied 65 mother-child pairs referred to social services because of behavior by the mothers that was sometimes problematic (neglect of the children, anger that frightened them, etc.). All the children were 18 months old at the time of the study, and the children's behavior was studied when they were interacting with their mothers.

The study's results showed that when a mother showed behavior that could frighten her child, young girls were significantly more likely to move closer to their mothers than the young boys were. In contrast, the boys tended more often to show aggressive behavior when their mothers' behavior frightened them. These results, although preliminary, seem to demonstrate a very different stress response among young boys and girls, responses that may appear very early in life.

However, boys and girls, men and women, mothers and fathers—all are always changing in an environment that may generate major stressors on its own. Studies in the last two decades have shown that factors unrelated to an individual may have a substantial influence on who will react more to stress and who will react less. Here, an individual's position in the social hierarchy is a very powerful indicator of the stress level that will be felt and whether high levels of stress hormones will be produced.

Chapter 10

Your Social Status, Your Stress

In a social hierarchy where there's a dominant individual and others who are subordinate, who produces a greater quantity of stress hormones? What do you think: is it the dominant individual or the subordinates? A colleague, Dr. Robert Sapolsky of Stanford University in California, asked this question, and to answer it he decided to study the production of the stress hormone cortisol in baboons in Kenya. Why baboons? Because it's very easy to determine a baboon's social status in a group: you just have to count the number of bites on the baboon. The more bites there are, the lower the baboon is in the social hierarchy!

Armed with this information, Dr. Sapolsky spent several months in Kenya measuring stress hormones in various baboon clans with the aim of determining who, based on social status, is most likely to produce stress hormones. Results from his initial studies showed that it was the subordinates who produced the largest quantity of stress hormones. In contrast, the dominant member of the group produced very low concentrations of stress hormones on a day-to-day basis. Of course, in the group, the dominant individuals will inflict stress on the subordinates, leading to high concentrations of stress hormones in them. Does this remind you of your work environment? But hold on! As usual in the wonderful world of stress, things aren't as simple as you might think.

This very clear result was, in fact, too simple for Dr. Sapolsky. He knew that, in his preliminary experiments, he had studied baboon clans that showed a very stable social hierarchy. A stable social hierarchy is one where the dominant individual is never confronted by subordinate members of the group. This is an autocratic society, in which power is focused at the top, and only death can dislodge the dominant individual from his position. In these very stable social hierarchies where Dr. Sapolsky's initial studies were done, the dominant individual was lord and master.

Dr. Sapolsky wondered whether he'd get similar results testing individuals in unstable social hierarchies. An unstable social hierarchy is one in which there's a dominant individual who may frequently be challenged by subordinate individuals in the group. Often in this kind of hierarchy, the dominant individual's behavior leads to his being provoked by some of the group's subordinates. In this situation, the dominant individual is not as aggressive as he needs to be to dominate the group completely.

In a second set of experiments, Dr. Sapolsky measured the stress hormones in baboon clans with unstable hierarchies. It was quite a surprise for him to discover that, in this kind of hierarchy, it was now the dominant individual who showed the highest stress hormone levels, with the subordinates showing low levels of cortisol stress hormone!

In a stable structure, the dominant individual is in sole command and makes his subordinates endure stress through his totally dominant behavior. In contrast, in an unstable social hierarchy, the dominant individual endures more stress, because he is constantly confronted by some subordinate individuals in the group who are trying to take power. While war goes on at the top levels of the hierarchy, the other subordinate individuals don't suffer attacks from the dominant individual and don't show increased stress hormone levels. This result reaffirms what I've said many times in this book: things are always relative when it comes to stress. Stress response depends not only on our sex and personality but also on our place in the social hierarchy and the stability of that hierarchy.

From Baboons to Humans

Dr. Sapolsky's results landed like a bomb in the scientific field, because they contained clear implications for human beings. Reading these studies immediately raises the possibility that the nature of the social hierarchy in a human group could have effects on the stress response of some individuals within the group.

Ask yourself whether the hierarchy in your work environment is stable or unstable. Does your boss completely dominate his employees, not hesitating to whip them into shape? If so, you're in a stable hierarchy, and employees should be the ones presenting the highest concentrations of stress hormones. What if your boss shows dominance but you know the vice-president of sales is hatching a plot to take your boss's place? Then you're in an unstable hierarchy, and it should be the boss who shows high concentrations of stress hormones. If the results found among groups of baboons could be confirmed among humans, researchers would have a formidable weapon in gaining a better understanding of why some workplaces induce higher levels of stress in employees than others.

However, when it came to transferring these animal data to humans, a major problem arose. Unlike animals, who often stay in the same social group until their dying day, humans change social groups several times in the course of the same day or week. They can be part of a broad network of social hierarchies, and depending on their surroundings may be in a different position from one moment to the next. Thus, an individual may be subordinate at work but play a dominant role at home. In contrast, another person may be dominant at work but completely subordinate in a family setting. The question for researchers is whether a person's position in a given social hierarchy may determine his or her stress response and whether this response may change on the basis of the social hierarchy in which he or she may be at any given time in life.

Socioeconomic Status: Jobs, Wages and Stress

The first type of social hierarchy that was studied is the one related to an individual's socioeconomic status. This status is determined by three main factors: income, job level (boss, executive, menial worker, etc.) and level of education.

The social hierarchy associated with socioeconomic status is generally constant. There are exceptional cases where someone moves from one socioeconomic status to another, such as a wealthy individual who loses his entire fortune after being defrauded by the likes of Bernard Madoff and also suddenly becomes unemployed. Another example would be a poor family that wins the lottery and suddenly moves from a low socioeconomic status to a very high one. But these cases are quite rare, and people at a given socioeconomic level generally tend to stay there for the rest of their lives, creating an enduring social hierarchy.

In the last three decades, scientific research has shown that an adult's socioeconomic status is related to physical and mental health. Rich people suffer fewer physical and mental illnesses than poor people, and middle-income people are in between these two groups. Studies have also shown that adults with low incomes show significantly higher stress hormone levels than adults with average or high incomes.

One of the most important studies in the world showing this result was Britain's Whitehall Study, which followed a group of British civil servants over many years starting in 1967. The aim of the study was to identify the most important social factors associated with the prevalence of physical illnesses among these individuals. The initial Whitehall Study results (the Whitehall I study) were derived from among British men. A second phase of the study was undertaken with the aim of including women (Whitehall II). Early results from Whitehall I showed a clear link between civil service job levels (bosses versus executives versus specialized workers, manual laborers, etc.) and mortality rates. Men with lower-level and lower-paid jobs (messengers, porters, etc.) had a mortality rate three times higher than men with higher-paid jobs (managers, executives, etc.).

As part of Whitehall II, Dr. Andrew Steptoe and his team measured stress hormone levels among the men and women taking part in this broad study. The results showed that men in lower-level jobs had high levels of cortisol stress hormone. Paradoxically, however, women in high-level jobs also showed high cortisol levels. Could it be that when men are in a position of dominance they function in a stable hierarchy, while when women are in a position of dominance they must function in an unstable hierarchy, with their leadership constantly challenged, causing them to produce more stress hormones?

The researchers asked themselves this question, and they very soon suspected that one of the factors explaining this result among women and men could be linked to stress experienced at work based on an individual's sex. The researchers then undertook a second study to check whether job-related requirements and the subjective level of control over their work could explain the differences between men and women observed in the relationship between type of job and production of stress hormones. Job-related requirements included factors such as time pressures in performing a piece of work, conflicting demands from superiors, the proportion and quantity of work having to be done under pressure, the level of concentration needed to perform a piece of work and work slowdowns that could be caused by colleagues' delays. The subjective level of control over work was represented by the latitude employees had and the degree of authority they could show in doing their work.

The results from this second set of experiments showed that heavy work-related demands were linked to high cortisol levels among women, while a sense of not having much control over their jobs was linked to high cortisol levels among men. Although the types of jobs held by men and women could predict the stress they experienced, it was a sense of having control over their jobs and job-related demands that differentiated the stress response among men and women.

Social Status: Power and Stress

Our socioeconomic status is not the only factor that can determine our place in a social hierarchy. As we saw earlier, someone may have different social statuses based on which group he or she is in at any given time. A top corporate executive may be at the peak of the social hierarchy within the company but low on the social hierarchy when sitting on the board of directors of another company or when in an athletic club. In contrast, a woman with a very low socioeconomic status may be at the bottom of the social hierarchy at work but at the top of the hierarchy when taking part in a discussion group or organizing a major event.

Someone's social status can thus change from one setting to another. The question for researchers was whether a person's social status (dominant versus subordinate) in small groups without a clear social hierarchy could also predict the stress hormone levels the person will produce.

Studies on social hierarchy linked to socioeconomic status are quite easy to do, because there are clear criteria (income, job and education) to determine a person's position in the social hierarchy associated with socioeconomic status. However, when it comes to determining the social status (dominant versus subordinate) of someone in a small group, a major problem arises. How do you measure the social status of a person in a small group? As we've seen, when studies are done among animals, it's easy to count the number of bites suffered by an animal and to determine, on the basis of this number, whether the animal is in a position of dominance or subordination. But humans don't usually bite one another,[1] so this form of measurement can't be used to determine the social status of a human.

However, researchers have managed to find a very creative method for determining the social status of someone in a small group. To do this, they create social groups and give the individuals in each group enough time to establish their own social hierarchy. They then establish a sociometric measurement of each person's social status. This method consists of asking each member of the group to write the names of the people in the group on separate cards. These people are then asked to put the names in order of the individuals' social status, with the dominant one on top and the others underneath in social order. The results are averaged, and the same name will often appear at the top of the different piles of cards. The group will have "acquiesced" in this person's dominance, and he or she will be called the dominant member. The other individuals in the group will be called the subordinates.

With this measurement of social status in hand, the researchers wondered whether the results obtained among baboons by Dr. Sapolsky's team would also be observed among humans. In an initial study, Dr. Dirk Hellhammer and his team at the University of Trier in Germany measured stress responses among 63 army recruits at the beginning and end of their intensive six-week basic training. As the boot camp got under way, the recruits were distributed randomly into nine groups. Sociometric measurements were conducted to establish the social status of each recruit within each group during the six weeks of training to determine which individuals would take the role of dominant member and which would take the role of subordinates. In both the first and last weeks of training, each individual was exposed to psychological stress. The results showed that the dominant member in each of the nine groups had the highest production of cortisol stress hormone when exposed to the stressor. In contrast, the subordinate individuals showed no rise in this hormone when exposed to the stressor either at the beginning or end of the training period.

You'll agree that these results are very similar to those obtained by my colleague, Dr. Sapolsky, on baboons! When individuals are in an unstable hierarchy, it's generally the dominant individuals who show the highest stress hormone levels. It is believed now that dominant individuals show higher stress hormone levels because their leadership (and ego) is constantly threatened by a potential loss of power. Remember that one of the NUTS characteristics is threatened ego. Each time someone feels that his or her ego (personality, character, skills and so on) is under threat, this triggers the production of stress hormones. In an unstable hierarchy, the dominant person sees his or her ego threatened while the subordinates have an easy time of it as the battle rages in the upper spheres of the hierarchy. Hence it's the dominant person who produces the highest stress hormone levels.

This initial study showed that the power attributed individually in a social hierarchy has a deep influence on stress response. However, anyone who has ever been part of a social hierarchy knows that the idea we have of our own power in the group may be very different from the idea that others have of our power. I can consider myself the dominant person in a group, even if the other team members don't think this is the case. It then becomes important to determine whether social status as established by one's peers is what determines the stress response or whether it's an individual's subjective social status (the idea I have of my own position in the social hierarchy) that's the best determinant of stress response.

To answer this question, Dr. Tara L. Gruenewald and her colleagues at the University of California at Los Angeles conducted a study among 81 students staying at university residences and thus living close to one another on a day-to-day basis. The researchers asked each of the 81 students to determine their subjective social status (their own impression of their position in the group's social hierarchy). On the basis of the results, they separated the students between those who saw themselves as the dominant members of the group and those who regarded themselves as subordinate members. They next subjected both groups to psychological stress and measured stress hormones in response to this stressor. The results showed that individuals who regarded themselves as dominant were those with the highest stress hormone production when exposed to the stressful situation. In contrast, the individuals who saw themselves as subordinate showed no responsiveness to stress.

These results are exactly the same as those obtained by Dr. Hellhammer when he established the social status of army recruits through peer evaluation. Thus, whether dominance is established by peers or whether it's felt subjectively by the individual makes no difference in terms of stress hormone production. A position of dominance in an unstable social hierarchy will always lead to higher stress hormone production, because the dominant individual will constantly be defending his or her position—and, by extension, ego—within the social hierarchy.

To sum up, dominant individuals who are able to establish a stable hierarchy in which their leadership is never called into question will show a very low stress level, to the detriment of the subordinates in the group, who will chronically show a high stress response. Dominant individuals whose personality traits hinder them from establishing a stable hierarchy may suffer chronic stress, seeing their ego threatened on a daily basis when their leadership is called into question. These differences in dominance and subordination will often appear only in very well-defined groups, such as workplaces, sports groups or various social groups, and may change in the course of an individual's interactions within these different groups.

The Cost of Dominance

If you're a corporate CEO sitting atop the social hierarchy, ask yourself what's preferable in terms of profits for your company: a single person at the top of the social hierarchy with a high stress level (unstable hierarchy), or 150 people at the base of the social hierarchy with high stress levels (stable hierarchy)?

Stable hierarchies are always autocratic, with a very high degree of dominance. In these hierarchies, the dominant person exerts total control over the troops, never hesitating to push them harder for increased performance. For the person who sits atop this type of hierarchy, all seems to be for the best in the best of all possible worlds. Enjoying low stress levels, the dominant person feels that these same levels ought to extend to the employees. However, recent studies show that the costs of absenteeism linked to the effects of chronic stress on employees' physical and mental health are enormous in this type of social hierarchy. This means that there is a very high cost to pay for complete dominance over a group, and this cost can be measured in hundreds of thousands of dollars annually. That is something to think about!

The very term "unstable" social hierarchy could lead some people to believe that this type of hierarchy has nothing positive about it. Why might constant challenges from subordinates be beneficial to employees' physical and mental health, and why should the boss put up with all the stress? First, because unlike employees, the boss has chosen to be in this position, and has the means to manage novelty and unpredictability and to control most situations. Besides, the notion of *challenge* is not necessarily negative. Studies have shown that when bosses give employees latitude to make certain decisions and encourage them to play an active role in the company's development, this has the effect of reducing stress experienced at work and enhancing employees' performance.

Of course, for a boss with a very dominant personality, it's not always easy to have to listen to employees' suggestions for increasing the quality of a particular department, or to have to explain the reasons for a decision that is going to have a substantial effect on the troops. However, by doing this, the boss increases the employees' sense of control and thereby reduces their stress level. This stress reduction is reflected in savings of hundreds of thousands of dollars in the costs of absenteeism linked to chronic stress at work, as well as in a pleasant and healthy work environment.

As I once said to a boss with a very dominant personality, if the need to dominate is too great, it's best to choose the social group in which the cost to be paid for this dominance is lowest. Learn to give your employees a little leeway, and apply your maximum dominance to a tennis match at the end of the day. Your profits will improve, and so will your health!

The Paradox of Adolescents

We saw earlier that young children and adults who have the benefit of high socioeconomic status produce stress hormones in lesser quantities than children and adults with low socioeconomic status. However, there is a curious paradox in the scientific literature. The influence of socioeconomic status on stress hormone production is not observed among adolescents. Up to now, studies show that a family's socioeconomic status (rich family versus poor family) is not an absolute predictor of the level of stress hormones produced by adolescents.

The first study showing this paradox came from my laboratory. I already talked in the previous chapter about measurements that I did of the stress hormones of children and adolescents aged 6 to 16. In this study, I showed that from age 6 to 10, children from poor backgrounds produce more stress hormones than children from well-off backgrounds. However, we observed that this effect disappears completely at the time of the transition from elementary school to high school, when children are around 12 years old (in Quebec high school begins in Grade 7). From age 12 to 16, adolescents from well-off and poor backgrounds alike produce high concentrations of cortisol. These results were subsequently replicated in other studies conducted among American adolescents.

The sharp rise in cortisol stress hormone levels when moving from elementary to high school is a hugely interesting result, because it's often during the transition from elementary to high school that adolescents begin to show certain disorders such as suicidal thoughts, symptoms of depression or conduct disorders. Most parents and teachers attribute these disorders to the onset of puberty. However, our experience in the stress field has led us to wonder whether a stress factor may not also explain these various disorders that often appear during the transition between school levels.

You may recall your days in Grade 6, when you were the "big" boys or girls, the oldest pupils in elementary school. You were in a small neighborhood school, and you knew everyone there. Your surroundings weren't new or unpredictable, and you had total control of the situation. Since you were the oldest in the school, you were atop the social hierarchy, and your ego was hardly threatened.

Now, think back to your first year of high school, if you live in Quebec, or junior high or middle school elsewhere. You went from a small neighborhood school to a school with hundreds of new pupils, and you were now among the youngest in the school. Everything was new, unpredictable and potentially threatening to your ego, and you in no way had the impression that you controlled the situation. You had gone from a dominant position to a subordinate position, and you faced all four NUTS factors. With these factors added to your life, one result, depending on your life history, personality and experience, may have been that you were producing very high levels of stress hormones during this first year in a new school.

For some children, who were already experiencing chronic stress at home, this rise in stress hormones during the transition from elementary school to junior high or high school may have had harmful effects, causing some adolescents to develop disorders related to chronic stress.

This interpretation makes plenty of sense, but it doesn't always explain why adolescents don't show the effect of socioeconomic status as observed among children and adults. What could be going on during adolescence to cause family income suddenly to cease being a predictor of who will produce the most stress hormones?

Adolescence: When Popularity Becomes More Important Than Wealth

To understand this effect, researchers turned to the adolescent experience. Adolescence is a very important period, in the course of which major changes take place. Of course, there are physical changes, such as the appearance of breasts and menstruation among girls and the arrival of facial hair and voice changes among boys. But beyond these physical changes, there are also major changes in what adolescents experience. During adolescence, we see an increased search for independence. Toward age 12, family influence over adolescents decreases sharply and the influence of friends increases substantially. This is when our child, who had always been enthusiastic about going on weekend camping trips with us, decides not to come any more because "camping is super uncool"—he prefers to stay home and spend time with his friends.[2]

A second major characteristic of the adolescent experience is the importance attributed to adolescent culture. During adolescence, belonging to a social group such as goths or nerds or a group of fans of hip-hop or sports largely defines a young person's identity. Researchers currently believe that socioeconomic status no longer influences the concentrations of stress hormones produced by adolescents because, at this time of life, status is defined more by belonging to a social group than by the family's socioeconomic background. Whether rich or poor, if an adolescent is *cool* or *in* because he or she is part of the most influential group at school, this new social status will have a greater effect on stress hormone production than family wealth.

With the aim of testing this hypothesis, Dr. Patrick West and his team at the University of Glasgow in Scotland measured the stress hormones of 2,824 adolescents aged 12 to 15 from families of both low and high socioeconomic status. In an initial part of the study, they confirmed our previous study by showing that an adolescent's family income had no influence on stress hormone production. In a second part of the study, the researchers asked adolescents to position themselves in terms of their social status (high or low) in three different social hierarchies. The first social hierarchy was related to school performance. Adolescents were shown a drawing of a multi-rung ladder, and they had to place themselves in terms of their school performance on the ladder (on the upper or lower rungs). The second social hierarchy studied was related to sports: were they very good or mediocre at sports? Finally, they had to define their popularity level (high or low), again using a multi-rung ladder.

The results of this study are fascinating. On the one hand, the researchers observed that, for the hierarchy related to school performance, the adolescents at the bottom of the social hierarchy were those who showed the highest stress levels. This effect was noted among both boys and girls, but the effect was significantly higher among girls. Similar results were obtained for the sports-related social hierarchy. This time it was boys' stress hormone levels that were significantly higher among those at the bottom of the hierarchy; this effect was also present among girls, but to a lesser extent. The results for the popularity-related social hierarchy are very surprising. They showed that it was the boys at the bottom of the popularity scale who showed the highest stress hormone levels, while among the girls it was those at the top of the popularity scale who showed the highest stress hormone levels.

Thus, in terms of popularity, it was the *least* popular boys who had the highest stress hormone levels, while it was the *most* popular girls who showed this same effect.

I find that this last result bears a curious resemblance to what has been observed among men and women on the basis of their job positions. You may recall that men with low job positions are those who show the highest stress hormone levels, while among women it's those holding the highest-level jobs who show the highest stress hormone levels. It seems, then, that the cost to be paid for popularity when you're a female adolescent or for a high-level job when you're a woman is increased stress hormone production. This result could be due to the sizable threats to the ego that come with this social status! In contrast, for male adolescents and for men, what seems to predominate isn't so much social status as determined by popularity but rather social status as determined by athletic ability.

The results of Dr. West's study showed unmistakably that, for adolescents, it's no longer family status that predominates as a potential stressor but rather their position in the various social hierarchies they are in at school and with their friends. Once they become adults, our adolescents will leave these social groups behind them to seek jobs and become part of a new social hierarchy, one now determined by socioeconomic status. This is when job-related social status will become important again in terms of stress, and also when the socioeconomic status of our adolescents who have become adults will again begin to emerge in scientific studies as a major factor in predicting increased stress response.

Popularity, Intimidation and Stress

Among animals, the dominant individuals in a group never hesitate to attack a subordinate who seeks to take power. The attack may often be very violent and sometimes it will be fatal. Of course, humans are not as aggressive as animals but, sadly, subordinate individuals in a group—and hence the least popular—do often face attacks from dominant members of the group. We're talking here about intimidation or bullying.

Bullying is characterized by a relationship of domination in which one or more aggressors inflict physical or psychological violence on a victim. Three key factors differentiate bullying from a simple dispute between two individuals: repetition, intentionality and imbalance of power. In a school setting, bullying is characterized by the repeated use of physical aggression, mockery and humiliation toward a child or adolescent. Reports from around the world on the prevalence of bullying among children and adolescents show that bullying occurs in every country on earth and affects one person in three during any given month. In fact, 11 percent of children and adolescents suffer severe bullying, including intimidation and physical violence, several times a month.

Of course, scientific researchers working in the area of stress science soon wondered whether bullying could be linked to high concentrations of stress hormones. Up to now, only three studies have been conducted on this question. The first one, conducted by Dr. Åse Marie Hansen and her colleagues at Denmark's National Institute of Occupational Health, dealt with Swedish workers who suffered intimidation at work. When researchers measured stress hormone levels among these individuals, they observed that people who were undergoing intimidation at work showed abnormally low concentrations of cortisol stress hormone. This result is very similar to the hypoproduction of cortisol observed in post-traumatic stress disorder (PTSD), and the researchers suggested that intimidation on a regular basis could lead to a form of PTSD, just as exposure to acute trauma does.

To see if these results might also be observed among adolescents undergoing intimidation, Dr. Wendy Kliewer of Virginia Commonwealth University in Richmond, Virginia, measured stress hormones among 101 11-year-old African Americans. The results showed that adolescents undergoing bullying presented significantly lower concentrations of cortisol stress hormone than adolescents who were not being bullied. These results are exactly the same as those observed among adults.

However, neither of these studies checked whether there were differences in stress hormone production based on the sex of the individual undergoing intimidation. Moreover, intimidation may take various forms: it can include physical intimidation (punching, kicking, slapping, etc.), verbal intimidation (verbal threats, nasty nicknames, bad jokes in front of others, etc.) and social intimidation (rejecting someone, talking behind someone's back, leading others to reject a person, etc.). The earlier studies hadn't taken account of the nature of the intimidation or its potential effects on adolescents' stress hormone production.

Dr. Tracy Vaillancourt and her team at McMaster University in Hamilton, Ontario, decided to look into this problem. They measured cortisol stress hormone among 154 12-year-old male and female adolescents, asking them to note the frequency and scope of the physical, verbal and social intimidation they faced at school. They then measured the adolescents' cortisol levels on a weekday, when they were at school, and also on a weekend, to see if the cortisol variations based on the type of intimidation were the same on school days and on days off.

The results showed that only verbal intimidation was linked to stress hormone concentrations among adolescents. These observed variations in stress hormone levels were found when measured both on a school day and on a day off. This shows that it's not just acute exposure to intimidation (on school days) that led to these cortisol variations—anticipation of this intimidation on weekends can be just as stressful for young people as the exposure itself on weekdays.

Now comes the most interesting result of this study. The researchers showed that, among girls, a high degree of verbal intimidation was associated with abnormally low concentrations of stress hormones, while among boys, a high degree of verbal intimidation was associated with high production of stress hormones.

Remember that, in males, stress response is reflected in most cases in rallying energy needed to fight or flee, while in females, stress response is most often reflected in an affiliation approach. It's quite possible that the increase in stress hormones observed among boys undergoing intimidation is linked to their natural propensity to fight or flee (very high doses of stress hormones are needed to do this), while the stress hormone reduction observed among girls undergoing verbal intimidation may be linked to their natural propensity to affiliate with the other girls in the group.

You'll agree that it's easier to pull our fists out and fight than to try to affiliate with people who are intimidating us. Boys may thus have a response anchored inside them enabling them to react to intimidation by rallying the energy needed to fight or flee. Of course, they'll produce very high doses of stress hormones to achieve this, and they may suffer from the stress hormone production in the long term.

In contrast, it may be that girls do not have this propensity to rally energy to fight or flee anchored inside them, and repeated but fruitless attempts to affiliate with members who are intimidating them could have a more harmful effect on their stress response on a chronic basis. On the basis of these speculations, some researchers go as far as to suggest that the very low concentrations of stress hormones observed in girls undergoing intimidation could represent a state of post-traumatic stress that may develop in response to the intimidators' chronic attacks and to the girls' inability to mount a response suited to this intimidation.

Clearly, studies on intimidation and stress among adolescents need to continue so that we can better understand the impact of bullying on our adolescents in the short and long term and the exact reasons for the intimidating behavior that some adolescents adopt toward their peers. Accordingly, I am collaborating with Dr. Mara Brengden and her team at Sainte-Justine Hospital in Montreal in a broad study aimed at gaining a better understanding of the short- and long-term effects of bullying on children's and adolescents' stress hormone production.

But until we have more scientific data, how can we help our young people negotiate intimidation-related stress? Of course, we can call in the teachers and the intimidators' parents to get this circus to stop, but these efforts do not always meet with success. Schools are developing new programs to fight intimidation and to try to do away with this problem, but developments are slow and aren't necessarily found in every school.

Unfortunately, I don't have an ideal solution to offer you. However, let me remind you of the often beneficial effects on an individual's stress level of moving from one social hierarchy to another. Parents may help their adolescents face the stress of intimidation by trying to do away with this intimidation. While they're working at that, they can also get their teenage children involved in various social groups (sports, social or school clubs and so on) with the aim of enabling them to change social status several times a week and thus move from the status of subordinates in front of their intimidators to that of positive leader in a hockey team, Scrabble club or hip-hop group!

Chapter 11

Recognizing When You're Stressed

As we've seen before, the body produces a very different physical response in a period of acute stress than in chronic stress. When you're facing acute stress, all your senses become activated and your vigilance is at its peak. Your hairs stand up on your arms, your heart is pounding and you're ready for a fight. However, when chronic stress sets in, the constant activation of this physical response results in some of your systems becoming dysregulated, leading to various conditions such as abdominal obesity and Type 2 diabetes.

You don't have to wait until you've developed Type 2 diabetes to recognize that you're in a state of chronic stress. You can use certain signs your body is sending you to get a clearer idea of how far this state of stress has set in.

The Acute Stress Stage

Let's start at the beginning. You're experiencing acute stress at work. At the time you detect this threat, your body rallies a massive dose of energy to help you fight the threat—or flee it if it's too great. Your fists are tight, your heart is beating like crazy and your digestion is slowing down so that the energy needed to digest is redirected instead to your muscles, enabling them to perform better in a fight. But the situation that was stressing you is ending. Your stress response returns to normal. All is for the best in the best of all possible worlds.

The Pepto-Bismol Stage

However, although your acute stress response has subsided, you haven't settled the situation that caused this response in the first place, and so the response recurs. You react a second time and then a third and a fourth time to the stressful situation, rallying a massive dose of energy each time. You are beginning to enter a state of chronic stress.

Your heart can keep beating like crazy without causing you too much harm. You're a fighter, prepared for the challenge. In the same way, your breathing can keep increasing without leading you to hyperventilate, because you're still dealing with the situation in front of you. After all, you're a fighter. However, you gradually begin to suffer gastric pain.

This is your sign. I call this initial stage of chronic stress setting in the Pepto-Bismol stage. When you begin having to take antacids on a regular basis to deal with digestive disorders and gastric pain, it's often a sign that you're developing a state of chronic stress. The reason for this is simple. Each time you generate a stress response to a recurring situation that's threatening to you, your body slows your digestion to enable the energy that would normally be used for digestive purposes to be redirected to your muscles and help you fight.

But now you've been slowing your digestion on a regular basis for a number of weeks. It's completely normal for digestive problems to appear after a certain time. We often attribute these disorders to poor diet. However, they may also be caused by fighting a stressor that's not going away. Next time you take an antacid pill, ask yourself whether you're dealing with a stressor that's simply setting in on a chronic basis. You may be surprised to realize that this is exactly what's happening.

The Rum and Coke Stage

Things continue. You haven't dealt with your stressor, and you're taking antacid pills, telling yourself that you really should be eating broccoli. The situation that's stressing you continues to weigh you down. You return home every night telling your husband just how much Jenny is stressing you at work. You decide to act. You find the perfect solution for managing this stress. You're going to the spa this weekend with Virginia.

At that point, you talk to Virginia about the best way of standing up to Jenny. She suggests that you attack Jenny's credibility in front of the boss as a way of getting back at her.

You return home Sunday evening, full of energy. You've got a plan, and you're going to implement it right away. You walk around the house telling whoever cares to listen that you're now going to manage this stress with a master's touch, no later than tomorrow! This surge of energy you're experiencing is often a sign you can use to recognize that you're in a state of stress. Faced with this stress, your body is producing a massive dose of energy, and you're feeling the effects. But you've got to make sure at this stage that your method of handling the stress attacking you is the right one, because if the method doesn't work, this massive dose of energy will start to put a heavy load on your shoulders.

You get to work Monday morning and head straight to the boss's office to discredit Jenny's work. But you've got a surprise in store: you discover not only that the boss disagrees with you but that you're the one who has just been discredited by repeating "gossip" (as the boss describes it) to company executives.

At that moment, the boundless energy you woke up to will begin to weigh on you, and a feeling of pressure will set in. You'll start to feel strained and run down. All the energy you rallied over the previous weeks to deal with this stress has had an impact on your muscles, which are becoming sore from repeated contraction. You tell yourself you'll go and get a massage at the end of the day. The perfect antistress solution, right?

Back at your workstation, you realize you're having trouble focusing. You have to read the same paragraph twice, because you're tending to forget what you read after your eyes get to the fifth line in the paragraph. The stress hormones that you've long been producing start to affect your selective attention. You then have trouble differentiating between what's relevant and what isn't in the document you're reading.

When you get back home at night, you open a good bottle of wine to share with your husband over the evening meal. You pour yourself a glass, then two, then three, then four. There's your sign. I call this stage of chronic stress the rum and Coke stage. When you start increasing your alcohol consumption beyond your usual level, this often means you're developing a state of chronic stress going beyond the Pepto-Bismol stage.

But look out. Not drinking alcohol doesn't make you exempt from this stage. If you smoke cigarettes, you may well find yourself smoking many more cigarettes each day at this stage of chronic stress. If you're an ice cream aficionado, you may find yourself sitting in front of the

TV and eating your second huge portion of this dairy delicacy straight from the container!

When you've been experiencing chronic stress for a long time, you'll often find yourself consuming more of certain products or devoting more time to certain activities (such as shopping or buying lottery tickets) that normally bring you comfort. It's as if the brain was tired of always having to do the work of helping us fight our stressors on its own and decided to offer itself something extra to reward itself for all this hard work.

The next time you pour yourself a fourth glass of rum and Coke while watching your husband dig his spoon deep into a second container of chocolate ice cream, ask yourself whether you aren't both undergoing chronic stress in relation to your family life!

The Final Stage: The Glass of Water Stage

Things continue. You haven't dealt with your stressor, and you're using rum and Coke to swallow your antacid pills. The situation that's stressing you keeps recurring, day after day.

Family conflicts are increasing at home. You no longer have any patience, and you keep flying into a rage at the children, who then start avoiding you as a way of surviving your continual fits of anger. You hide in the bathroom, where you can lock the door and weep in peace. This is your sign. I call this the glass of water stage because, when you reach this stage, you need a glass of water to swallow the antidepressants your doctor has prescribed.

Of course, nobody wants to reach this final stage, and this is just a caricature of a condition that can take years to set in. But this example shows that the signs our body sends us when chronic stress is setting in can inform us of its presence. On the other hand, you'll agree that it's not a good idea to wait until you're on your sixth glass of rum and Coke or your fourteenth container of ice cream before acting.

Ideally, you will detect stress as soon as it appears, with the aim of bringing it out and controlling it right away. In this way, you will prevent it from setting in permanently and making life hard for you. Bringing out stressors means taking them on one by one as they arise, for the rest of your life. You'll never be able to eliminate all the stressors from your life. On the other hand, you can learn to recognize them quickly so that you can manage them as they arise.

But how do you recognize your stressors?

Chapter 12

To Kill a Mammoth, You First Have to Know Where to Find It

As I've said before, what truly amazes me in my research is that, when I talk to people who say they feel stressed, and ask them to tell me the source of their stress, nobody can answer me! People are very good at saying they're stressed, but they generally have no idea what's stressing them. How can you kill a mammoth when you don't even know where to find it?

The first thing to do with a stressor is to find out where it comes from. That's easy for you to say, you'll tell me. How can we identify the exact situations that are stressing us in this crazy world? The answer is quite simple: by using the very stress response that's attacking us! Remember: when your brain detects a threat in the environment, it reacts by constantly making you aware of the stressors attacking you. In the chapter on stress and memory, we saw that this can create difficulty in memorizing any other information, because after the brain detects a threat it focuses its full attention on that threat.

Most of the time, you try to flee from the thoughts that are attacking you. This is the opposite of what you should be doing. When these thoughts weigh you down, it's because your brain regards them as potentially threatening. That's your stressor! You've just found your mammoth! Now you have to kill it. To manage this, you've got to find its weak point. This means you have to deconstruct the situation to get a better understanding of what NUTS factor or factors may be leading your brain to detect the threat. When you've found the origin of the stressor, you fight each factor by finding solutions to reduce its impact on your threat detection, and hence on your stress hormone production.

Jenny the Mammoth

Here's an example. Jenny is stressing you at work, and you hardly ever come home without mentioning this to your husband. At night, the very thought of Jenny prevents you from sleeping. That's your mammoth. Now, let's deconstruct this. Why does Jenny stress you so much? Is she novel? No. Is she unpredictable? No. Does she threaten your ego? Yes. Does she make you feel you've got no control over the situation? Yes. Well then, you've just deconstructed this stress.

Now you know that Jenny is stressing you because she threatens your ego and gives you the feeling that you've got no control over the situation. You've just discovered the origin of your stressor. Because she threatens your ego and gives you the impression that you've got no control over the situation, your brain detects Jenny as a threat, and you produce stress hormones each time you're in contact with her. This is all very well, but where do we go from here?

We Reconstruct

Relaxation is not the opposite of stress. Going to a spa for the weekend doesn't mean that Jenny won't be at the coffee machine on Monday morning, waiting to prey on your ego. The opposite of stress is resilience. Resilience, in this context, is the ability to have a Plan B, a Plan C, a Plan D and so on to deal with the situation that's stressing you.[2]

Jenny is stressing you because she threatens your ego and grabs away your impression of having control over the situation. Okay. Then what can you do to make her less threatening to your ego? Plan B: you fire her. Well, not a great idea, because you don't have anyone to replace her. Plan C: you meet with her to discuss your conflict and try to settle it. Fine. That may work, but it is far from certain. Plan D: you avoid her, and you also avoid going for coffee Tuesday morning. Plan E: you spend your time with other members of the group and no longer waste a minute with her. Plan F, Plan G, Plan H . . .

It's worth knowing that 85 percent of people will never actually implement their alternative plans. However, as a result of merely reminding yourself of these plans for dealing with the stressor, your brain detects less of a threat and produces a lower quantity of stress hormones. This sends the brain the message that you do have some control over the situation. And this sense of controlling the situation is precisely what your brain needs for it to detect a lower threat level in the environment and to produce smaller amounts of stress hormones.

Do you doubt this? Here's a study that should convince you. Dr. James Abelson of the University of Michigan administered a drug that had the effect of directly increasing cortisol stress hormone in the participants in the study. Dr. Abelson knew this drug could have certain negative side effects such as headaches, abdominal pain and so on. The protocol used to administer the drug included keeping a catheter in a vein, as a needle is left in the arm to administer the drug continuously over a given period of time.

In keeping with ethics committee requirements, Dr. Abelson had to explain to participants how the protocol would be applied and what the potential side effects were. He separated the participants into two groups. He gave the first group only basic instructions about how the protocol would operate and the potential side effects. But he told the participants in the other group that they could stop the administration of the drug, if they chose, by pressing a button placed in front of them.

By doing this, he increased their impression of control over the situation in the second group of participants. He also gave them detailed information on the drug's potential side effects to help them tell more clearly if the effects they felt were due to the drug or to normal nervous irritation on their part. In this way, he reduced the novelty and unpredictability of the situation.

Remember that the drug administered by Dr. Abelson had the effect of raising stress hormone levels chemically and not psychologically. The study's results showed that the group that was given a sense of control over the situation and that saw the situation as less novel and less unpredictable produced lower stress hormone levels in response to the drug than the other group.

Note that these participants did not press the button to stop the experiment! This is a phenomenal result, because we're not looking here at exposing participants to psychological stress. What this involved was using a drug that had the chemical effect of raising stress hormone levels. Merely increasing the sense of control over the situation and reducing its novelty and unpredictability resulted in participants producing lower stress hormone levels in response to the drug.

Think about it. If stress hormone production induced by a chemical drug can be lowered by controlling some aspects of NUTS, imagine the power you have to modulate your own stress hormone output caused by Jenny!

Deconstructing a stressful situation into its NUTS components and then reconstructing it and developing contingency plans may seem complicated, and you might question whether it has short-term benefits. So let me tell you the story of my daughter Jade, who one day found herself faced with a huge mammoth she couldn't fight—and of my contribution in helping her deconstruct her stress and then reconstruct it on her own so that she could fight it.

It was August. Our family had just moved into a new neighborhood, and my daughter was 5 years old. In September, at the beginning of the new school year, she would start kindergarten. Starting in early August, Jade had been complaining of stomach aches and trouble falling asleep at night.

I immediately recognized the physical signs of stress taking root in her. One day, I asked her to sit down quietly with me so that we could talk about going to school. It was impossible for me to ask whether she was stressed: a 5-year-old doesn't understand this concept enough to provide a suitable response. However, I set about helping her deconstruct her stress.

I asked her if the situation was new for her and if it made her a little nervous. She said it did. Novelty was emerging as a stress factor. Next, I asked her if the situation was unpredictable for her, in the sense that not knowing what would happen at school made her nervous. Again she said it did. Unpredictability emerged as a second stress factor. Then I asked her if it bothered her that she would have to make new friends among girls she didn't know. She said it didn't. That meant there was no threat to the ego. Finally, I asked her if she had the impression of having control over the situation, in the sense that she believed she would be able to do what would be asked of her at school. She answered no. Control emerged as the third stress factor.

With this deconstruction, I had just learned that my daughter had a stress response to going to school because the situation was novel and unpredictable, and because she lacked a sense of control over the situation. Now it was time to reconstruct. I knew this reconstruction would be more effective if the way it was done came from Jade and not from me.

I then asked her what she thought could be done to make the situation less novel and less unpredictable for her. After a few moments thinking about this, during which her pretty little face tensed up under the pressure of a very demanding intellectual task, she replied, "We could go lots of times to play in the school playground, and that way I'll be more used to it when I get to school!" This child was quite the strategist! She was making sure she would have quality time with her mom in the playground.

For four days, we went to the school playground every evening. It was very interesting to see the detection system my daughter brought to light. While we were having fun, she looked around and said to me, "Mommy, that's the door I'll be using to go in, right?" Yes, Jade. "Mommy, my classroom will be one of the rooms on the first floor, right?" Yes, Jade. She assimilated this new and potentially stressful environment in the course of four days. At the end, she announced proudly that she didn't need to go back to the playground because going to school no longer made her nervous. I thought I had succeeded in my task.

However, a few days later, her stomach aches and sleep disorder reappeared. The mammoth was still alive! Checking Jade's NUTS again, I understood that her sense of control over the situation had not been reconstructed. She still didn't have the impression of controlling this event, and this caused her to continue producing a stress response that brought on her stomach aches and sleep disorder. Hence, we had to continue reconstructing her sense of control.

But I knew it was impossible for me to give her absolute control over going to school. You can't just quit school at age 5! I thus had to find a way of giving her the *impression* of controlling certain aspects of going to school. With the impression of having control over one aspect of the situation, her brain could detect fewer threats and produce lower levels of stress hormones.

I tried the following experiment. I told her that for the first two weeks of school, I would give her whatever she wanted for lunch. She could decide to put whatever she wanted in her lunchbox, giving her total control over this aspect of the situation. A broad smile lit up her face, and she agreed to my suggestion. Her stomach aches and sleeping disorder disappeared right away, and the first thing she told her new friends in the schoolyard on her first day was that she decided herself what would go in her lunch box. This was a great victory over the mammoth!

Through this example, you can see that by deconstructing situations that may be stressful, you can help your brain reduce its perception of threats in the environment. You can also help your children, who don't have the ability to do this analysis of stressors in their surroundings. If my 5-year-old daughter could find some solutions to her problem and deal with half of them on her own, you can surely find solutions to your own problem and sleep better at night.

As I said in the introduction, I have no magical recipe to offer, and I can't tell you how to manage situations in your environment that are new, unpredictable, threatening to your ego and outside your control. These situations belong to you, and you have to deconstruct them one by one with your own Plans B, C, D and so on. But to do this you need to take some time. And as we know, nobody has enough time.

Having Time versus Taking Time

One day when I was giving a talk to a group of high-level managers, someone raised their hand and asked me the following question: "You're an expert on stress. You should know a universal method for managing it. What is that method?"

I replied, as usual, with what 20 years of stress research had taught me. There is no universal method for managing stress. Since stress is highly individual and depends on our life history and our interpretation of situations as threatening or nonthreatening, there is no method that can, in any overall sense, manage stress effectively in the same way for everyone.

I know, I know. You've surely been told that methods such as yoga or meditation are universal approaches to this end. But is this really true? Scientific studies have shown that if you take a hyperactive person (such as myself) and ask that person to practice yoga, it will have the effect of *raising* stress hormone levels! It's no joke: yoga would kill me.

As for meditation, plenty of studies show that not everyone has the ability to reach a tranquil state in a few minutes with the aim of "going into themselves." Again, studies show that for people who need a higher level of activity, meditation really isn't a panacea. And it's one thing to go into yourself and not think about anything, but that doesn't stop your stressors from continuing to attack you when you open your eyes!

I've waged a determined campaign against schools that have decided, with no scientific basis, to institute yoga classes for pupils as young as age 6. This is done under the pretext that it's a universal method that will relax our children and help them manage their stress better. Really? What happens, then, to a young child who is full of energy and wants nothing more than to play outdoors and expend the energy she's rallied to face the stress in her life? What happens to a hyperactive child who finds his stress hormones on the rise when he has to do this activity that's not really made for him? Where does this notion that there has to be a universal method of stress management come from? It's a notion that betrays a poor knowledge of stress.

Let's go back to my managers and their question about a universal method for managing stress. I sensed right away that my negative response just didn't suit them. The executive who had put the question to me retorted, "I see what you're saying about yoga, but do you really have nothing to suggest?" Noting his inquisitive look, I answered, "I may have a method that would work, but I don't think you'll like it." With a hundred pairs of eyes riveted on me awaiting the answer, I told them that a good way to manage stress would be to take an hour each day, all alone, with no stimulation at all. You should have seen their faces! "But it's impossible to find an hour a day with my busy schedule! And anyway, what would I do during that hour?"

I then asked them, "Why do you think stress keeps you from sleeping at night?" The reason is simple. Because bedtime is often the only time of day when our brain isn't stimulated by all sorts of things like ringing telephones, hungry children, e-mail messages to be sent, spouses talking about how their day went and so on. And let's be clear about one thing. The brain hates not being stimulated. The proof is that when you sleep, you dream. Even when you're sleeping, the brain generates information that sometimes seems to come straight out of a fantasy movie.

More evidence that the brain hates lack of stimulation comes from scientific studies on sensory deprivation that were conducted in the early 1960s. Researchers wondered what would happen if the brain received no stimulation. They put people into soundproof rooms (absence of sound) without light (absence of visual stimulation). The people were completely naked (absence of stimulation from clothes on the skin). The researchers found that after a few hours, many of the participants suffered from visual, auditory or motor hallucinations. It was as if the brain, in the absence of stimulation, decided to produce its own movie!

When you stimulate your brain every minute in the course of a day with various activities, you prevent it from having to deal with the absence of stimulation. Bedtime is often the only time of day when this constant stimulation ceases. And it's often when your brain, with no stimulation, will bring the day's stressors into your consciousness. Suddenly Jenny will appear in your mind, you'll start to ruminate on the stress she causes you and you'll be unable to fall asleep.

On the other hand, if you spend an hour a day alone, with no stimulation (no music in your ears, no company to disturb you and so on), then this lack of stimulation will cause your brain to bring your consciousness back to the events of the day that led to your stress. This is exactly what you want, because that's when you can start deconstructing the situation that's stressing you and try to understand which NUTS factors it contains. Next, you can start reconstructing the situation to seek out Plans B, C, D and more to act on the NUTS factors that are stressing you.

There's no need to say to your husband each evening, "Honey, I'm heading off to manage my stress. See you in an hour." Absolutely no need! You don't even have to tell yourself you're going to manage your stress. Spend some time alone, without stimulation, and I guarantee that within minutes the situations stressing you will start to emerge in your mind.

You didn't manage to find every Plan B for controlling the situation by the time the 60 minutes were up? This doesn't matter: they'll reappear in your mind tomorrow, during your next period alone. They'll come back because they're important to the brain, which detects a threat. As long as the situation is not under your control, it will reappear in your consciousness.

After 10 years at this, I can produce an organization chart of the stressors in my life. The biggest ones are those that appear most often in my consciousness, and those are the ones that I don't succeed in fully managing. I keep trying to find a solution for each of them, and I never give up, because I know that if I neglect it, the chronic effects of each stressor will affect my physical and mental health.

In performing this exercise day after day, you'll discover two important things. The first is that two situations are stressing you for very different reasons. Jenny is stressing you because she threatens your ego and gives you the impression of lacking control, while the morning traffic stresses you because it's novel (you've just moved) and unpredictable. Don't use the same methods to control these two stressors: it won't work! With Jenny, you'll have to deal with the threat to your ego and your sense of control, while with the traffic, you'll have to deal with its novelty and unpredictability.

The traffic is killing you little by little. With the stress of having to spend two hours in it at the end of the day, it makes you lose patience with your children in the evening and swear loudly at everyone. Is this hurting your family life? Act now. You've deconstructed the situation: might the only solution be to move to help you control this stress? Then move. Is your work killing you? Are you suffering from abdominal obesity, diabetes and depression? Change jobs. When a mammoth is too huge, you have to hunt a different one to survive.[3]

The second thing you'll discover by performing this exercise of deconstructing and reconstructing your stressful situations is that you're most sensitive to one of the four NUTS factors. In deconstructing your stressors, you'll realize that most of the situations stressing you always contain the same NUTS factor. This is the particular factor to which you're most sensitive. You can thus organize your life appropriately.

In the course of deconstructing my stressors, I realized I was most sensitive to unpredictability. Facing something unforeseen or unpredictable, I can become stressed in two seconds. I thus organize my life accordingly. For example, I'll tell my students that it's no use asking me for a letter of recommendation the day before I have to submit a grant application: they have to request it two weeks in advance. Is September 15 my deadline for submitting an application for a major research grant? I'm going to make sure I've completed the application by September 1 so that I don't get stressed if the photocopier breaks down!

Of course, we'll never find a solution to every instance of novelty, unpredictability, threats to our ego or low sense of control over our lives. But remember: the idea is to control most of these situations when we can, with the aim of not allowing our brain to detect threats on a regular basis. This protects our physical and mental health.

My way of taking an hour a day is to walk my dog. Anyone who knows me knows about this dog. Each time I face a stressful situation at the office, say a management committee meeting, I tell myself that before doing anything or making any decisions, I'll go walk my dog. Since the dog can't talk to me, he can't stimulate my brain. There are a hundred ways of getting time alone to deconstruct your stressors.

Here are some examples. I remember a man I met at one of my lectures who told me he now understood why, even though he was a top-level cyclist, he always refused to go biking in a group with his friends. He told me that while pedaling he could really be alone with himself and think about important things that were bothering him. Without knowing it, this man was deconstructing his stress in the best way, while keeping himself in tip-top shape.

A husband who carves wood on his own after the children are in bed, or a wife who sews or knits alone, thinking back to the day behind her—these are situations that let us escape life's constant stimulation of our brain, enabling us to become conscious again of the situations the brain detects as threatening so that we can act on them.

At the end of that talk I gave to the managers, one of them approached me to ask a personal question. When we were alone, he opened his laptop, showed me his calendar and said, "Madame, do you see a free hour a day in this calendar? No. But I've thought of something. Would 20 times three minutes a day, when I go to the bathroom, count as the hour you're suggesting?"

I looked at the smirk on his face and replied, "Sir, you've understood that this is what it's all about. There's a big difference between 'having time' and 'taking time.' Don't wait until you have the time: you'll never have it. But if you take the time from other activities, I can assure you that the benefit you'll get from this will easily make up for the hole you'll have to leave in your calendar. What's more, with less stress in your body and your mind, your work performance will improve greatly. You'll get two for the price of one!"

Chapter 13

Addressing NUTS for Adolescents

I had been doing research for 20 years to discover the exact mechanism by which acute and chronic stress can affect our physical and mental health. At that point, I told myself that all this research would make sense only if it enabled me to help people of all ages better control their stress response, which can often overwhelm them. This led me to take three concrete actions.

First, in 2004 I founded the Centre for Studies on Human Stress, whose mission is to educate the public about the scientific basis of the stress response. On the center's bilingual website, www.humanstress .ca, you will find a wealth of information on the science of stress, its application in your everyday life and its development over the course of my research.

You can also download the official magazine of the Centre for Studies on Human Stress, *Mammoth Magazine* (what else!), from the site. At the time of writing, my students and I have published 11 issues of *Mammoth Magazine*. These issues deal with the nature of the stress response (No. 1), stress among seniors (No. 2), the stress of children in childcare (No. 3), stress at work (No. 4), the stress of back to school

(No. 5), differences between men and women in the stress response (No. 6), the stress of adolescents (No. 7), stress and wealth (No. 8), genetics and stress (No. 9), the stress of caregivers (No. 10) and stress and men's mental health (No. 11). *Mammoth Magazine* is available in French and English, and it is the product of volunteer work by students and scholars of stress. Access is of course free.

Second, I decided to write this book for the public so as to inform as many people as possible about the science of stress. It came out in French in 2010. Finally, I decided to do something even more practical. With my group of students at the Centre for Studies on Human Stress, we set up various educational programs about stress among adolescents and workers to enable all these people to better understand their stress response and keep it under control.

In this chapter, I describe some exercises that we use in the program for teens to help them better manage their stress response. These exercises may be helpful in learning how to deconstruct and reconstruct the circumstances that cause stress in your life or your teenager's life. In doing so, you can diminish the number of threats detected by your brain and, by extension, the level of stress hormones that you produce in those situations.

DeStress for Success Program for Teens

You will recall that in 2000, I demonstrated that at the point of transition from elementary school to high school, young people exhibit a significant increase in stress hormones that could be explained by the novelty, the unpredictability, the threat to the ego and the low sense of control that young people experience when they reach their first year of high school.

I often thought about these results while walking my dog, as they suggest that our teenagers could be suffering on a long-term basis from a poorly controlled stress response. Then I decided to go further. For two years my team and I met with school counselors, principals, teachers, teenagers and parents to better understand their educational needs related to the effects of stress on physical and mental health. At the end of this period, we created the DeStress for Success program, which aims to teach teenagers in high school how to better control certain factors in their environment that can induce a significant stress response.

The main goal of DeStress for Success is that when they have completed the program, students will have an extremely detailed knowledge of how to deconstruct and reconstruct their own NUTS. To accomplish this, the program uses various fun activities, such as role plays in which adolescents must present a skit about a potentially stressful situation and members of the class must try to detect which of the characteristics of NUTS are present in the scenario.

In the next section, I summarize a few of the exercises that young people do to better understand their stress. Teachers and parents, you can help your students and children better understand their stress by using these exercises from the DeStress for Success program. You can even do the exercises yourself. If it's good for the kids, it's good for the adults too!

How NUTS Became SPIN

When we held a meeting with the teens to talk about NUTS, we immediately saw that this acronym did not resonate with them at all. We had to find a cooler acronym to attract adolescents. After a 60-minute walk with my beloved dog, I came up with the acronym SPIN (**S**ense of having little control, **P**ersonality under threat, **I**nability to predict what's going to happen and **N**ovelty of the situation), a formula that our teenagers accepted enthusiastically. So now we teach adolescents to "SPIN" their stress by deconstructing it.

To do this, we ask each student to write down two situations that they have found stressful over the past week. Next, we record those situations on the board, and we deconstruct one after another to demonstrate that each of these situations can be understood through the presence of one or more of the SPIN characteristics. Teens are fascinated by this discovery.

Subsequently, we give them a homework assignment to do for the week that aims to contextualize their stress response. In other words, it helps them understand that different situations may induce a stress response by playing on different characteristics of SPIN, and that the same reaction in two different people can be explained by different SPIN characteristics. Here's the exercise we give them to do.

The first part of the exercise is to write down, over a three-day period, all situations that the adolescents considered stressful. Beside each situation, we place the four SPIN characteristics. In each case, the teenager has to say whether the situation experienced as stressful involved a low sense of control, whether their personality felt threatened and whether it was unpredictable and/or new.

Stressful situation	S	P	I	N
Argument with my brother	X	X		
Sarah made fun of me		X	X	
Shopping with my mother	X		X	
Tennis game with Jim		X		
TOTAL	2	3	2	0

S – sense of having little control
P – personality under threat
I – inability to predict what's going to happen
N – novelty of the situation

On our second visit, we make them aware of two things. First, we ask them to count the number of occurrences of each of the SPIN characteristics over the previous three days. They notice that one of the SPIN characteristics arises more often than the others. The teen then knows that he or she is most sensitive to this particular feature.

Teenagers have a lot of fun comparing their level of sensitivity to one or the other characteristic and trying to give examples of situations from their own lives that include a particular feature. With this initial exercise, teens have learned that different people experience a stress response for a variety of reasons that can be related back to SPIN.

You might think that this is normal, because kids report very different stressors from one another. That's not really the case, though, and we proved it during the second exercise. We ask the teens, if they wish, to name a few of the stressors they have experienced over the last three days.

The goal here is to find stressors that are common to many adolescents. The common stressor that occurs most often among adolescents is a dispute with a brother or sister. We then use some of the common stressors that we have found in adolescents and ask each young person who has experienced this stressor to tell us which of the SPIN characteristics are associated with it for them. Another discovery awaits them. Here is an example of the results from this exercise.

Common stressor: Dispute with a brother or sister	S	P	I	N
Joshua	X	X		
Julie			X	X
Marcy	X		X	
Timothy		X		

Looking at this table, teens realize that the same situation (fight with a brother or sister) led to stress for all of these adolescents, but for completely different reasons in terms of the SPIN characteristics. Thus, for Joshua, the tiff was experienced as stressful because he did not seem to have control over the situation and this threatened his ego. By contrast, for Julie, the dispute was experienced as stressful because it was new and unexpected, as she usually does not quarrel with that sibling. For Marcy, this took away her impression of control, and it was unexpected. Finally, for Timothy, the incident simply threatened his ego.

With this exercise, adolescents understand that while the same situation might be stressful for two different people, the stress could stem from different SPIN characteristics. In this way, they learned to put their own stressors and those of others in context.

Now the teens must learn to rebuild stressful situations around them using the SPIN features. To accomplish this, we first show them the SPIN reconstruction method I described in the last chapter. Then they leave with another assignment for the week. This time, they must again describe the different situations that cause them stress and deconstruct them using SPIN. Then, for each of the SPIN characteristics that induced a stress response, they must describe the strategy they have decided to use to influence that characteristic.

The next step is to write whether or not the strategy worked for each characteristic. If not, they are then asked to find a Plan B for each of these characteristics. The table on the next page shows an example of results for this deconstruction and reconstruction exercise, based on the four stressful situations described above, using the SPIN method.

As you can see in this example, the teens are not always able to reconstruct on the spot each of the SPIN characteristics that induces a stress response. However, through this method, they can understand that even if we succeed in controlling only one of these characteristics, we have already improved our sense of having control over the situation, while continuing to work on other aspects of the situation that we find stressful. This sense of regaining control of the situation through the SPIN deconstruction and reconstruction method thus enables them to better control their stress response to this particular situation.

This method also allows them to understand that sometimes the stress response experienced in a situation can be beneficial, as in the case of the tennis game with Jim. The game induced a stress response because this young person's personality felt threatened. However, his attempt to stress his friend Jim before the game (so that Jim wouldn't play as well!) brought him no benefit in terms of stress, because he still felt pressure to perform at this event.

Stressful situation	S	P	I	N	Strategy used	Did it work?	What is Plan B?
Argument with my brother	X	X			S: Avoid him.	No	S: Talk to him.
					P: Tell my mother.	Yes	P: Long live Mom!
Sarah made fun of me		X	X		P: Change groups.	No	P: I know what I'm worth.
					I: Ask my friends what Sarah said about me.	Yes, but even more stressful	I: Talk to Sarah one-on-one.
Shopping with my mother	X		X		S: Explain to her that I hate this.	Not really	S: Show her that I will make good purchases.
					I: Ask for pocket money for clothes.	Yes	I: I have to set aside money to buy those shoes!
Tennis game with Jim		X			P: Get him stressed before the game!	Yes, but it's not cool to win under those conditions	P: I think that feeling threatened by Jim in tennis helped me win. I'll keep trying.

This is excellent because it is precisely this stress response before the next game that will enable him to win! Remember that stress allows a person to mobilize energy. Now if this youth mobilizes a massive dose of energy before the game because his ego feels threatened at the thought of losing to Jim, he can use that energy to win. Recognizing this, he decided not to alter the stress response, but to maximize it to his advantage.

In 2008, we tested the effectiveness of the DeStress for Success program among 504 adolescents in the Montreal area. My students and I measured stress hormones in these adolescents before and after their participation in the program, and we measured various aspects of their memory and their well-being. We are currently analyzing the results of this extensive study, but preliminary results show that the program has had positive effects, reducing stress hormones especially among teenagers who showed high levels of these hormones early in the program.

These adolescents seem to benefit greatly from the information and tips they received to better control their stress response. We also conducted a survey among the young people who benefited from the DeStress for Success program. The result: 80 percent of the students told us that the concepts taught in the workshops were useful, and 90 percent said they had a better understanding of stress following their participation in the program.

My team and I are currently working on an idea for making DeStress for Success available in the form of computer software to allow more teenagers to enjoy the benefits of this program.

Chapter 14

Addressing NUTS for Adult Workers

One day, I received a call from the father of a teenager who had participated in our DeStress for Success program. He was a very active man, who worked as a CFO in a very large company. He told me that during a family dinner, he was telling his wife about his very stressful day when suddenly his son interrupted him and said, "No problem Dad, I'll SPIN your stress for you in two seconds. This situation is stressful for you because it's new, it's unpredictable and you have absolutely no sense of having control over it. In addition, considering the way you've described it, I think this is also very threatening to your ego. So you have all four stress factors in this one situation, and that's why it stresses you so much!" The man told me he was stunned. He realized that his son was right, and he asked for additional information. His son showed him how to deconstruct and reconstruct the SPIN of his stress, and the father learned a lot thanks to his son's teaching!

He then asked me if I intended to adapt the DeStress for Success program to the workplace. Employees and managers would surely benefit from the program, he said, and this could have positive effects on the working environment in his company.

This man had a good point, for work-related stress has become a real scourge in contemporary society. In addition to potentially adverse effects on physical and mental health, stress has also become an economic problem for many individuals and organizations, and for society in general. Stress can be very expensive: the estimated annual cost of stress on businesses in the United States is between $150 and $300 billion; in Canada, it's between $8 and $10 billion in absenteeism and $36 billion in presenteeism (when the individual goes to work, but his or her productivity and effectiveness are reduced as a result of stress).

One in two employees who is absent from work because of a mental disorder will be out for at least 13 days or will never return to work. In 1991, 15 percent of insurance claims were related to various mental health disorders. By 2001, that figure had jumped to 40 percent, and today it amounts to an estimated 56 percent (generating costs that also add up to billions of dollars per year).

This problem is now taken very seriously—by the World Health Organization, which published a self-help book in 2004 offering systematic approaches for employers to deal with stress at work; by the International Labour Organization (ILO), which organized a conference on mental health at work in October 2000; and by the member states of these organizations. France, for example, adopted a national interoccupational agreement on stress at work on July 2, 2008 (extended by administrative order on April 23, 2009). The objectives of this agreement are to increase awareness and understanding of stress at work; to draw attention to signs that could indicate problems of work stress as early as possible; and to provide employers and workers with a framework that allows them to detect, prevent, avoid and cope with stress problems at work.

With some of the students in my laboratory, I had already started working on an education program on stress in the workplace. This man's appeal was very convincing, and so I decided to continue the development of the program, which we called Stress Inc. The program uses basically the same approach as DeStress for Success (deconstruction and reconstruction of NUTS), but without any role playing. We are developing it with the help of a Web program that will enable a significant number of workers to access it at any time.

Until the program is developed and scientifically validated just as in the DeStress for Success program, I would like to offer you some tips and methods, based on the science of NUTS, which can help you better understand and control your stress response—and better control that of your employees, if you are in a management position.

To Which NUTS Factor Are You Most Sensitive?

First, to contextualize the situations that cause you stress, you can easily use the tables described in the summary of the DeStress for Success program in the last chapter. In addition, my students and I recently developed a questionnaire (called the NUTS questionnaire) that will help you identify the NUTS factors to which you are most sensitive. We developed this questionnaire by creating nearly 100 situations that we see as being primarily characterized by one or another of the NUTS elements.

Let me give you a few questions from the questionnaire. Read each of the situations described, then simply assign a rating from 1 to 7 to indicate the level of stress that the situation would elicit in you (with 1 being a little bit stressful and 7 being extremely stressful).

1. You save all year for a great vacation in the south (all inclusive). Once you arrive, it rains all week.

1	2	3	4	5	6	7
Not very stressful					Very stressful	

2. You get a promotion at work resulting in significant changes to your position.

1	2	3	4	5	6	7
Not very stressful					Very stressful	

3. Your 18-year-old daughter has always been fascinated by Africa. She tells you that she is leaving for three months in Togo to volunteer at a clinic that specializes in treating AIDS.

1	2	3	4	5	6	7
Not very stressful					Very stressful	

4. Imagine that you have no talent in the kitchen and that you are known as a disaster area in that department. However, it is your turn to host the whole family for Christmas dinner.

1	2	3	4	5	6	7

Not very stressful   Very stressful

5. You have planned your summer vacation. You are leaving by car, and the day before your departure, the price of gasoline increases dramatically.

1	2	3	4	5	6	7

Not very stressful   Very stressful

6. Your colleague, who has less experience than you, is chosen to lead the team.

1	2	3	4	5	6	7

Not very stressful   Very stressful

7. It is Friday, the end of the week is here and instead of cleaning your apartment, which it sorely needs, you go for a long walk. At the moment you arrive back home, your brother-in-law arrives with his wife, his children and their dog.

1	2	3	4	5	6	7

Not very stressful   Very stressful

8. You have just learned that your father suffers from Alzheimer's disease and that you will have to take care of him.

1	2	3	4	5	6	7

Not very stressful   Very stressful

To analyze your results, add up the scores you gave for the following answers:

> Total score given to questions 3 and 5: _____
> Total score given to questions 1 and 7: _____
> Total score given to questions 2 and 8: _____
> Total score given to questions 4 and 6: _____

Now circle the highest score. This figure represents the NUTS factor to which you are most sensitive:

- The total for questions 2 and 8 represents your sensitivity to novelty (N)
- The total for questions 1 and 7 represents your sensitivity to unpredictability (U)
- The total for questions 4 and 6 represents your sensitivity to a threat to your ego (T)
- The total for questions 3 and 5 represents your sensitivity to a low sense of control (S)

Subsequently, we asked 150 workers to consider these 100 situations and determine the percentage weight of each of the NUTS factors in each situation (for example, 30 percent lack of control and 70 percent unpredictability). We then selected the questions that had the highest rates of agreement (70 percent or more) and constructed the questionnaire accordingly. The final product includes 60 questions, but this small sample gives you a good idea of your level of sensitivity to one or more of the four NUTS factors.

Most of the situations described in the NUTS questionnaire have nothing to do with work. Yet when I give lectures to workers and give them a short NUTS questionnaire, I am always surprised that most of the workers in the same company score high on the same factor of NUTS!

Thus, the majority of workers in telecommunications are most sensitive to unpredictability. In contrast, teachers mostly show a greater sensitivity to novelty. You could say that this is natural because all these people are working in the same work environment and are therefore all subject to the same stressful conditions. However, I remind you that the situations in the NUTS questionnaire are not related to work. Rather, they are related to everyday situations that have nothing to do with the telecommunications or school environment. Thus, the fact that the majority of workers in the same type of workplace have a high sensitivity to the same feature cannot be interpreted as being related to their work. Instead, we need to ask whether it's not precisely the common trait of their personality that led to these individuals being hired in that particular business or academic environment.

Stress, Performance and Presenteeism at Work

Let's return to the effects of stress on the job. As we've seen, they are many: absenteeism, increased accidents, reduced performance and productivity, poor company image, etc. The most surprising effect, however, is *presenteeism*—when the individual goes to work, but his or her productivity and effectiveness are reduced as a result of stress.

Presenteeism is assessed by asking a simple question: over the last 30 days, how many days were you forced to reduce your activities or not do as much as usual? At a conference on stress at work, I asked 250 employees of large companies to answer this question. The survey results showed that people who reported fewer than 10 days of reduced effectiveness were mostly women, while those who reported between 20 and 30 days of reduced effectiveness were mostly men. For those who reported between 10 and 20 days, there was no gender difference.

As we've seen, the initial effects of stress involve selective attention, that is, the ability to distinguish what is relevant from what is irrelevant. This difficulty in discriminating between relevant and irrelevant information in times of stress may be the source of the high cost of presenteeism in the workplace. Causing stress to someone will never increase that person's performance; it will only increase his or her memory of the stressful event, at the expense of other information. The only way to increase performance at work is, on the contrary, to reduce the number of stressors in the workplace. And in doing this, executives and managers can play a very important role.

Management, Managers and Stress

To prevent costs associated with diabetes among employees, it makes sense for a company to hold a week-long seminar on nutrition, so that at least some of its employees who might otherwise have developed diabetes do not. It's the same with stress. You may well offer a chair massage to your employees, but in so doing you are simply addressing a consequence of stress (back pain), not its cause. It makes more sense to manage novelty, unpredictability, a low sense of control and potential threats to employees' ego so that they don't suffer from stress at work and don't develop the physical and mental illnesses with which it's associated.

But before handling the NUTS factors in the workplace, managers must first determine whether their behavior toward employees could be an important source of NUTS for them. Each year at the university, I'm evaluated on my ability to properly deliver my teaching to the 150 students who've taken my course. Naturally, reading student evaluations can be hard on my ego, but there hasn't been a single year when this assessment didn't allow me to improve my teaching, which has become very popular with the students.

Similarly, you would think it would be beneficial to allow employees to evaluate their managers based on the four factors of NUTS. This confidential assessment would enable the manager to see whether his or her method of working with employees could induce some of the NUTS factors, which could explain much of the stress experienced by employees. I propose five simple questions that could be asked to employees in each work team, with the responses to these five questions sent to the team manager.

1.   Does your work cause you stress?

0   100
_____
Not at all   Yes, a lot

2.   Do you have the impression of having control over your work?

0   100
_____
Not at all   Yes, a lot

3.   In your work, do you often feel that your ego is being threatened, in the sense that you have the impression that certain aspects of your personality or your ability to do your job well are constantly being questioned?

0   100
_____
Not at all   Yes, a lot

4.   In your work, do you have to manage many new things on a regular basis?

0   100
_____
Not at all   Yes, a lot

5. Does your work involve a lot of unpredictability?

0	100
Not at all	Yes, a lot

The average of responses of employees in each team to these five simple questions will help managers better understand how the work that they ask of the employees can lead to stress responses, on the basis of the four NUTS factors. If managers receive the questionnaire results and see that the majority of employees report experiencing a high level of unpredictability, they will understand the need to act on this particular feature of NUTS to reduce stress for employees and thus increase their performance.

Only imagination and knowledge of the workplace will enable managers to really control the NUTS elements that are problematic in their group. For example, if the manager sees that it is novelty that causes the most stress to the employees, he or she may decide to avoid announcing important deadlines on short notice. Such a manager might smooth the introduction of changes well in advance by alerting employees that an important issue is coming up, and could even ask employees what they need to manage this innovation.

Managers who see that unpredictability is the problem can increase the frequency of team meetings to inform members of the nature and progress of various projects or develop a team journal in which this information will be transmitted on a regular basis. If a low sense of control is the problem, managers may establish new systems in which employees will be consulted on some important decisions or allow some teams to propose new ways of working. Finally, if threat to the ego is the problem, the manager may decide to select appropriate individuals for the work team. What would be better yet—if possible, of course—would be to leave this choice to the employees themselves.

A Company's Stress Flowchart

A company could even push this method to the point of creating an actual organization chart showing the origin of stressors in the company. For example, in responding to the questionnaires completed by each department, a manager may find that the stress in different departments is caused by different NUTS factors. He or she may find that stress is intense in, say, the human resources department, and that it is caused by unpredictable situations that employees must manage. On the other hand, high stress in the shipping department could be explained by a feeling of lack of control among most of the employees in that department. Finally, in administration, the stress level might be high as a result of the novelty of the work required of employees.

A flowchart showing the origin of stressors within a company would allow the manager to better target the actions management needs to take in these departments so as to control these aspects of NUTS that create high stress among employees. In doing so, it could certainly increase the performance (and fun!) at work for the employees.

NUTS at the Point of Hire

Typically, when you are interviewed for a job, you will be asked how you handle stress. What will you respond? Of course you will tell the interviewer that you manage stress very well and love being challenged. Any other answer would not be well received! Such a question actually tells the interviewer nothing. By contrast, if instead of being asked how you manage your stress, you were asked to describe how you negotiate novelty, unpredictability, threats to the ego and a low sense of control, the response could inform the employer much more about your ability to negotiate potentially stressful situations that arise in the company.

This would also allow companies to better manage the recruitment process. Indeed, a recruiter who knows that the department for which he or she is seeking a new employee is subject to a great deal of unpredictability can then focus the interview on this particular aspect to establish whether the candidate would be a good fit. Burnout and absenteeism are most often due to people not being in positions that really suit them.

In a survey conducted by the Robert Half Group, 1,470 human and financial resources professionals in eight European countries reported that 45 percent of their employees expect to change jobs within the next six months. In the face of this alarming figure, it is important to ensure that all employees find jobs that will enable them to better manage the factors of NUTS they may encounter in the company.

Know the Employees Personally

As I noted in the chapter on personality and stress, different personality traits may lead to an individual being more or less reactive to stress.

A manager cannot assume that every employee in a group will react to the same potentially stressful situations with the same intensity. Depending on their personality, some may have difficulty negotiating certain aspects of their work, while others may handle the same aspects of the same work much more easily.

Scientific studies of the relationship between personality and stress have shown that three major personality traits predict an increased response to stress—hostility, anxiety and low self-esteem. Clearly, people who have one or more of these personality traits are likely to be sensitive to different factors of NUTS. The table shows the NUTS factors to which these personality types are most sensitive and provides examples of situations at work that may have these factors and hence induce a strong stress response in these employees.

Personality	Will react to:	Stressors
Hostile	Low sense of control; Threats to the ego	Performance evaluation by manager; having little latitude within the job
Anxious	Novelty; Unpredictability	Deadlines; changes within the company
Low self-esteem	Novelty; Unpredictability; Too much control	Deadlines; overly high expectations from the manager

A Note on Hostile Personalities and an Apology to Jenny

We see from the table that an individual with a hostile personality is usually very sensitive to not having an impression of control over the situation and to threats to the ego. There are a host of situations in a work environment in which these two factors may be involved. Quarterly assessment by the manager may be seen as generating a strong threat to the ego and lead to a stress response. In addition, having little latitude in one's work can be perceived as lack of control.

I often say in my lectures that one of the hardest things for managers to deal with is having a hostile personality in their group. These people spend a lot of time making cynical remarks about their peers, and when confronted by some of their colleagues they channel their suppressed anger into avoiding the situation. Hostile personalities are very difficult to manage in the workplace, as they often tend to work their way into groups they can control through their hostile behavior.

At this point, I want to apologize publicly to all the people named Jenny who may read this book. Throughout the book, as you've seen, I've had fun talking about Jenny who wears down our ego in the morning at the coffee machine. I even compared Jenny to a prehistoric mammoth to help you understand some aspects of stress. Of course, "Jenny" is a fictitious name, but I really did know someone named Jenny with the personality I describe, someone who was very hostile and constantly seeking to undermine her colleagues.

In an earlier job, I often used to have lunch alone in the cafeteria, where I would deliberately sit near a particular group of employees. This group caught my attention because even though it was made up of about 10 people, it was always the same person who spoke. The other members of the group were abnormally quiet. By choosing a table nearby, I could hear the monologue and try to understand the dynamics within this group. I rapidly detected in this "Jenny" a very hostile personality, always shooting at the same target!

Every time I listened to one of her monologues, I heard Jenny talking about her target with breathtaking cynicism. For example, she could say, "Did you see so-and-so this morning? Didn't he look great with his little orange ladies' jacket?" or "It's common knowledge that so-and-so is being given the lead on yet another file. It's pretty easy to understand why, since he's constantly in the boss's office, sucking up to him!" What fascinated me the most was the silence of her colleagues. No one spoke and no one contradicted her. Of course, there's a strategic reason for this. Anyone who did speak up would be in danger of becoming the next scapegoat and being subjected to her hostility.

Having this type of personality in a work group often leads to bickering among its members. Hostile personalities also hate to be assessed by their superiors. They don't consider their superiors competent to perform this assessment, and therefore sense a threat to their ego. These individuals like to have full control over a situation. Thus, they often don't understand why senior management positions aren't offered to them, or why they're not chosen to lead an important project. They therefore become extremely cynical and keep on having one-sided conversations with their colleagues.

So I decided to use Jenny as an example of stress at work in all my lectures and in this book.

If I were running a company, I would use a retired employee to try to defuse the hostility of someone like Jenny. As we saw, Jenny's colleagues don't dare call her on her rant or tell her that her hostility is difficult to manage because they don't want to become the next scape-goat. This is quite normal, and it's a highly effective survival response to her hostility. However, a former employee with a strong personal-ity could easily be placed in the group with the goal of standing up to Jenny. By constantly questioning Jenny's arguments—in attacking her target or in any other situation—the retiree will of course incur her wrath, but will not suffer because he or she is no longer part of the work group. However, direct confrontation with Jenny could reduce her power over the other group members and create an unstable so-cial hierarchy in which the dominant individual, Jenny, is now con-stantly challenged by another person.[1] It would now be Jenny who would experience significant stress, and her brain would issue the order to deal with this situation as soon as possible to ensure her sur-vival. And while Jenny was busy doing that, the other group members could relax a little!

Anxious Personality and Low Self-Esteem

In the table, we see that for anxious personalities and personalities with low self-esteem, it's more the novelty and unpredictability of a situation that can be stressful. These people are very sensitive to the sudden an-nouncement of crucial deadlines, sudden and unexpected changes in the company and so on. However, unlike anxious people, those with low self-esteem will also be very sensitive to sense of control. But in their case, they will be sensitive to having too *much* control over a situation.

A manager might think that encouragement—saying "I know you're capable!" or "I know you can do it!"—should be beneficial for all employees. The manager may believe that showing confidence in the employee will lead that person to have greater confidence in his or her abilities and thus perform better. While that is certainly the case for most employees, it's important to understand that for a person with low self-esteem, an expression of too much confidence and overly high expectations can have the opposite effect. A person with a low sense of self does not believe that his or her work will be marked by success.

On the contrary, they believe that their success is due only to chance. These are the kinds of people who, when faced with a success-ful outcome to which they have contributed, say "Ah, that was luck!" rather than "Yes! I'm really proud of the work I did with my team!" So if you show too many expectations and too much confidence in the ability of a person with low self-esteem, this could result in the opposite of the effect you were seeking.

Swans and Eagles

Looking at the table, you could say that businesses should avoid recruiting these three types of personalities. This is easier said than done for hostile personalities, and may not be the correct conclusion for anxious personalities or individuals with low self-esteem.

Hostile personalities are quite difficult to detect in the hiring process because, in general, their true personality does not really become apparent until they're part of a group they can dominate. As we saw in the chapter on social status and stress, it takes time for a social hierarchy to establish itself within a group. When first starting a job, hostile personalities will play the game, behave very coolly and make every effort over time to establish themselves in a position of dominance within the group. It's after they've succeeded in doing this that their true colors will emerge.

Anxious personalities and people with low self-esteem are more easily detected during the hiring process, and many leaders tend to avoid such personalities when hiring. Many companies prefer to hire people who love stress—sensation seekers and those who love challenges. However, managers should know two things before making such a decision. First, sensation seekers look for novelty and unpredictability, which can be a positive for the company. However, they are also looking for loss of control—they like the feeling of not having total control over a situation. Now, if your employee is looking to lose control over most of the files at work, you, as a manager, will reap the consequences of this attitude. It's something to think about before you end up with 10 sensation seekers in your group!

This leads me to conclude this chapter by talking about swans and eagles. Dr. S. Mechiel Korte and his colleagues at Wageningen University in the Netherlands, all experts in evolutionary biology, asked themselves an interesting question one day. According to Darwinian theory on the evolution of species, any species that cannot adapt to the environment is gradually eliminated by the law of natural selection. If that is true, then why do we still have anxious personalities and people with low self-esteem?

If these personality traits were so negative for the survival of the human race, then people who exhibit them would not have survived over the centuries. They should have been eliminated by the law of natural selection, according to which the strong should mate with the strong and perpetuate the species, while the weak should mate with the weak and their genetic code should gradually be eliminated over time.

To answer this question, researchers studied the behavior of animals within a species and subjected them to what they called the game of eagles and swans. Within each species, there are eagle-like personalities that show aggression and uncommon courage, and there are swan-like figures that show cooperation and low aggression. To determine who in a given group is an eagle and who is a swan, the researchers set up interactions among the different members of the group. On the basis of the individual members' behavior, they labeled members who showed aggressive behavior "eagles" and those displaying cooperative behavior "swans." Then they studied the survival probabilities of swans and eagles in adverse conditions.

The researchers found that in a competitive situation, the eagle still showed aggressive behavior, continuously fighting either until it was injured or until its opponent submitted. The eagle almost always grabbed all the available resources within the group (power, females, etc.), but at the cost of losing a great deal of energy in combat. In contrast, when a swan was facing an eagle about to attack, it promptly withdrew from combat. Interestingly, the swan was able to quickly detect the eagle by its aggressive behavior, which allowed the swan to survive and not waste energy in a losing battle. When two swans met, they always shared the available resource without a fight and thus without expending energy.

By analyzing the different behaviors of swans and eagles, the researchers found that, in terms of survival, both strategies, the eagle and the swan, are successful. The eagle can afford to fight because it is almost always assured of winning, but in doing so it uses up a lot of energy. In contrast, by submitting to the eagle, the swan is sure to survive with a minimum of energy loss.

When winter arrives and food is scarce, eagles are more likely to die because all the fighting took its toll, leaving them little energy to survive the intense cold. Swans, on the other hand, don't perish because, having conserved their energy by avoiding no-win battles, they ensured that they retained enough energy to meet the rigors of winter. Thus, the swans were as well suited as the eagles to the environment around them—if not better. This explains why they have survived through the ages, even in a position of weakness.

I think there are eagles and swans in the workplace too. You can easily recognize the eagles by their competitive behavior and their sensation seeking. You will, of course, want to hire a maximum number of these frontline fighters. However, don't neglect the swans, who can often be recognized in anxious personalities and people with low self-esteem. Although less flamboyant than eagles, swan-type personalities generally show a high degree of cooperation and can always be counted on in difficult conditions.

Sarah at reception is a swan. She may have low self-esteem, but she always knows where the clasps are to tie up the last set of records that need to be sent urgently. We can always rely on her to find what no one else can find. Peter in human resources is a swan. Although he always seems a bit anxious, he does such a great job organizing the Christmas party and never forgets to wish everyone a happy New Year. It's when things start to go wrong in a company that we see the swans break away from the pack. They become highly effective and important to the company's productivity and the well-being of its employees.

In short, you like the eagles, but make sure to keep the swans around too. They are very useful for a company's survival. And between you and me, try to imagine a work environment where almost everyone is an eagle!

Chapter 15

Fleeing the Mammoth Can Help Us Control Our Stress

As we saw earlier, when the brain detects a threat in the environment, it mobilizes a massive dose of stress hormones, which allow us to fight the threat, or flee it if it's too large. In previous chapters, we described some methods for understanding the origin of our stressors to help us tackle them more effectively. However, it's important to remember that avoidance—or escape—is another valid strategy that individuals can use to ensure that they will survive a threat. Prehistoric humans sometimes had to run away from a mammoth that was simply too threatening. Fleeing allowed them to stay alive and begin the hunt again, this time chasing a mammoth of more manageable size. It was through flight that they were able to survive.

In scientific studies, we often use *escape* as a term for activities people engage in to avoid situations that cause them stress. We refer to escape through alcohol, gambling or any other activity that allows us avoid coping with our stress. In this chapter, I'm not talking about this type of escape. I'm talking about actual flight—avoiding the situation that stresses us out by simply leaving the scene!

I often see people in my lab who tell me they don't flee in the face of a threat. They always fight back in response to every threat, viewing this as the only possible solution. Flight is for the weak, and running away doesn't solve any problems. I always answer in the following way: "Are you sure that flight is really never a good strategy for any of the stressors that assail you? And are we talking about a good strategy for you or for the people around you?"

In fact, I'm not at all sure that flight should always be avoided as a stress-management strategy. And I'll use two very convincing examples to explain why.

Sir, let's say you arrive home tonight and discover that your wife has had a very stressful day at work. For some reason that is completely unknown to you, she seems to be trying to pick a fight with you on any one of a number of topics, all of them trivial. In plain English, she's after you.

You have two choices in this situation. You can choose to fight the stressor and get into the dispute. However, you then run the risk of ending up at midnight still arguing with your wife, perhaps not even remembering the initial cause of the conflict. The other choice you have is—to go walk the dog! Or to do anything else that will delay contact with your wife, giving her the time she needs to calm down. You will have avoided a senseless conflict and you will have helped preserve your relationship.

Here's another example that has more serious repercussions. Madam, you return home one evening after a particularly stressful day at work. You feel the pressure attacking you: your fists are clenched, your breathing is shallow, your muscles are tense and you feel the hairs standing up on your arms. Your stress response is at its maximum. Around eight o'clock, you're preparing to bathe your two young children. After the bath is prepared, you ask the older child to undress for the bath, and you get ready to help the younger one do the same. Your oldest just keeps fooling around and takes forever to take off his socks. You feel the pressure rising again. Your fists clench, your jaw tightens, your muscles tense up, your pulse is racing. You gently tell the children to hurry, because "Mom is tired tonight."

The children are finally naked as jaybirds, laughing and jumping in the bath. Water splashes over you. Suddenly, you just can't take it anymore, and you explode. Within a few seconds, you find yourself shouting at the top of your lungs at your two children standing in the bath, who are now watching you with fear. You sit the younger one down too firmly in the bath, and you yell at the older one to sit, and fast! In your mind you realize that this is not at all what you want to be happening, but you still hear shouting coming out of your mouth. The little one begins to cry in the face of your explosion, and the older one is trying to get out of the bath to avoid having to be subjected to it any further.

Don't feel guilty if this situation is familiar to you. The story comes from my own home and the mother was me, before I learned that sometimes avoidance is the best way for us to negotiate acute stress.

Why does this sudden fit of rage happen? For one simple reason. When we are in a state of very acute stress, we are angry. Think about it. You've mobilized enough energy to kill a mammoth, and to do so you've turned yourself into a fighter hyperventilating before the mammoth to give yourself strength and scare the beast. You could not fight a mammoth saying "Gently, Mammoth. Take it easy now"! No, you attack, screaming in a paroxysm of rage. As I said in previous chapters, this response hasn't adapted to changing circumstances over the years and is still there today in all of us.

In the moment of acute stress, your energy has been mobilized and is at its maximum, and this energy must be released one way or another. The slightest irritation will make you lose your cool, and that's why you can find yourself screaming at two children whom you in fact adore. When you do this, it's you who become a mammoth threatening your children, and they will produce a stress response to your aggressive, unpredictable and uncontrolled behavior.

No parent wants to behave like this, and yet it happens frequently, often as a result of good intentions toward our children: bathing them, helping them with homework, reading to them in bed. But despite our good intentions, if the child must pay the price of going through a stress response to take a bath, we need to ask ourselves whether avoidance of this situation (escape) might sometimes not be a better strategy.

Thus, walking the dog or going for a walk alone can enable you to quickly deconstruct the course of events in your day that put you in such a state. I sincerely believe that there would be great benefit for the little ones, your spouse and yourself. Your family would not have to suffer your acute stress and its potential consequences, and you would return home after this walk in a calmer state that is more conducive to healthy interaction with loved ones.

Chronic Stress and Tantrums

A fit of rage due to acute stress can also indicate the onset of chronic stress in an individual. Indeed, animal studies have shown that when an animal is subjected to chronic stress (the same stressor occurring several times a day for many consecutive days), this creates an effect of habituation to the stress response. Thus, we observe that the animal's production of stress hormones will decrease with the number of exposures to this stressor. However, Dr. Mary Dallman of the University of California at San Francisco showed that when the stress system gets used to a stressor that occurs chronically, the system becomes much more sensitive to any new stressor.

Thus, the price of becoming accustomed to a chronic stressor is increased responsiveness to any new stressor. And since, in humans, an acute stress response can sometimes lead to outbursts of anger, when someone has a sudden outburst of anger in response to a situation that appears innocuous to you but is potentially stressful for that person, it may well reflect the presence of chronic stress in that person that has settled in, or is beginning to do so.

Avoidance: Use Sparingly

It is thus sometimes useful to adopt an avoidance strategy to negotiate a highly stressful situation in which our stress can spill over onto loved ones. However, it's clear from the examples cited above that avoidance—escape, or flight—is only a temporary solution and should not be used regularly to control our stress response. Indeed, you will need to talk things out with your wife someday to save your marriage, if the problem at the root of the conflict isn't resolved. And you'll certainly need to give your children a bath some time.

What's important to remember here is that avoidance is a strategy to adopt in very specific conditions, and for a relatively short period of time. If you adopt a strategy of avoidance for all stressful situations in your life, you will undoubtedly find yourself in a state of chronic stress when you're faced with a situation that you haven't been able to manage.

Chapter 16
The Power of Others

Of course, we cannot always flee from an imminent threat. At some point, we will need to deconstruct and reconstruct the stressor. If we know the origin of the stressor, we can respond to the particular factors that led to it.

At the same time, other factors have also been shown to reduce stress hormones in difficult times. Depending on our social status in the groups we belong to, our social interactions with people in those groups can induce a stress response. But social interactions between people in general are not always stressful—in fact, they can have a hugely beneficial effect during periods of chronic stress.

But don't run immediately to your worst enemy, thinking that this will help you manage your stress! In general, those who generate stress make poor allies in helping us manage our stress. However, scientific studies over the last two decades have identified three factors related to the power of others that can be used to effectively manage a stress response.

Social Support May Protect against Stress
Humans are social by nature from birth. The newborn absolutely needs its mother to survive and to develop a secure attachment to its parents.

Similarly, young children need to interact with peers to develop emotional behavior that will be appropriate at different stages of life. Teens take advantage of their various social networks to develop their own worldview. Their parents use their social relationships to enjoy the good times in life and help each other during difficult times. Deprived of such networks, the elderly become isolated, which is a major factor in reducing their physical and mental capacity.

Social support refers to a person's social network, which can provide three types of resources: instrumental, informational and emotional. Instrumental support involves material or financial help that others can bring. Informational support refers to assistance we can receive from others through information that can help us deal with difficult situations (e.g., information on how the municipal court works or how to challenge a ticket). Emotional support is help in the form of care, listening, reassurance and emotional expression. People who provide emotional support are those we call when we feel the need to vent, people who will listen to us and give us advice.

All sorts of people can provide us with these three types of social support. Thus, for a young adult, instrumental support may come from parents while the informational component may come from Internet acquaintances and emotional support from a few close friends. Social support leads to social inclusion. An individual who enjoys good social supports in one or all of these three areas is generally well integrated into society and does not suffer from isolation. Conversely, people who do not have good social-support systems in place are less integrated in society and tend to suffer from loneliness.

Research on the link between social supports and physical and mental health shows unequivocally that people who enjoy a good social support network are healthier and live longer than people who don't. This has been observed equally in young adults, university students, working adults and the elderly. Subsequent studies have shown that people who receive good social support have better cardiovascular health than people who don't and who suffer from loneliness as a result.

Dr. John T. Cacioppo of the University of Chicago is one of the foremost experts on the study of the relationship between social support, social isolation and physical and mental health. Dr. Cacioppo has studied adults of all ages, and the results of his studies are similar regardless of age. Thus, people who enjoy a strong social network and who receive sufficient instrumental, informational and/or emotional social support produce fewer stress hormones than those who are socially isolated.

Social support has a major impact when it comes to the elderly, a group that has a tendency to be isolated. Studies by Dr. Teresa Seeman of the University of California at Los Angeles showed that middle-aged and older people who have few social supports have a higher allostatic load[1] than older people with a strong social-support network.

In another series of studies, Dr. Seeman and her colleagues showed that older people who enjoy good social support produce fewer stress hormones and manifest better performance on memory tests than elderly individuals who are lonely. These results demonstrate that some memory problems observed in the elderly may be caused not by a pathological aging process of the brain but rather by a level of social isolation that leads to increased production of stress hormones, which in turn may adversely affect our aging loved ones' memories.

It is often said that our societies have become very individualistic. I don't really believe this. I think that our societies are now marked by isolation, which is very different. I know many people who live alone and have little social contact, and I'm not sure that that's what they want. It's important to understand that our way of life has changed dramatically since World War II, when our society was characterized by very close family ties and people tended to live close to their families. Grandpa and Grandma would typically be living with one of their grown children, with Aunt Gertrude in the house next door and Aunt Betty down the street. Any problems experienced by an individual were experienced by the whole family and solved by the family as a group.

Today families tend to be scattered, with their members often many miles from one another. In most cases, social support is no longer provided by the family but by peers—this is true at all ages, and the trend is widespread. No research to date has studied the effects of the changes in the way we receive social support in contemporary society. However, the emergence of new social networks via the Internet fascinates me. As a research scientist, I wonder if computer-based social networks can have as positive an impact as more traditional face-to-face social networks on the production of stress hormones in people of all ages. I often tell myself that my next study will be devoted to this question!

But in the meantime, I bring you the following anecdote. The McGill Centre for Studies in Aging in Montreal tried an experiment with the elderly. Over a period of several weeks, they offered a course on how to use the Internet and e-mail to people aged 65 and older. A little reticent at first, the students ended up embracing the new technology and ultimately showed a strong interest in it. Through the program, they learned how to surf the Web and use e-mail.

After the course was over, the organizers asked the participants to tell them what of all the things they had learned they considered most important, and why. The majority answered without hesitation that it was the use of e-mail, and provided a very simple explanation. With this new tool, they could now communicate on a regular basis with their children and grandchildren. A grandmother reported that she had gotten to know her teenage grandchildren better through communicating with them on the Internet, and said that this was the best gift she had received from the initiative.

Of course, nothing will ever replace visiting our aging parents, which they desperately need. Any really functional society takes as much care of its aging parents as it does of its children. In addition to frequent visits to our parents, however, it would be worthwhile to consider buying a computer for the seniors in our families (and teaching them how to use it if necessary). A small "Hi, Mom" sent to your mother, a big "Hello, dear Granny!" from your children, and "Yo! Grandpa!" from your teens can only brighten your parents' lives and help them take advantage of the family support they greatly need.

Using Altruism to Combat Stress

To break the isolation, volunteering can work wonders in individuals who lack the support of a social network. Indeed, people of all ages who volunteer say they feel useful and feel a strong sense of well-being as a result of their experience. In addition, this act allows people affected by loneliness to come into contact with others who share their tastes and their desire to give, thus creating another social network.

The beneficial effect on health experienced by people who volunteer may have nothing to do with working with others on a daily basis, but may be associated instead with performing an act of kindness. Witnessing or engaging in altruistic behavior appears to have beneficial effects on our health.

One of the first studies ever done on this subject was undertaken by Dr. David C. McClelland of Harvard University in Cambridge, Massachusetts. The purpose of the study was to verify whether merely perceiving goodness in someone would have a beneficial effect on the production of the immune system marker S-IgA (salivary immunoglobulin antigen), as measured in the participants' saliva. The hormone in question has a protective effect on the immune system in times of stress.

To perform this study, Dr. McClelland separated university students into two groups. He showed a film about Adolf Hitler and World War II to the first group and a film on the life of Mother Teresa in India to the second group. He measured S-IgA levels in both groups before and after exposure to the films. The results showed that people who saw the movie on Mother Teresa produced significantly more salivary immunoglobulin antigen than those who saw the film on Hitler. Dr. McClelland called this "the Mother Teresa effect." With this study, he demonstrated that the mere perception of kindness leads to better immune system activity in humans.

Some researchers have interpreted Dr. McClelland's results as showing that the act of helping others often prevents us from ruminating on our own problems, and therefore diminishes our feeling of stress. Other researchers have speculated that the high induced by voluntary altruistic behavior will arise because the act of kindness itself creates a feeling of well-being and improved self-esteem, two consequences that have specific positive effects on the stress response. If this is the case, acts of kindness, generosity or any other form of altruism should reduce the potentially damaging effects of stress on physical and mental health.

To date, there are very few studies on the relationship between altruism and stress response in humans, perhaps because we do not yet have very good methods for measuring this human characteristic. However, Dr. Dennis Charney of the U.S. National Institute of Mental Health studied the factors that allow people to develop resistance to highly traumatic events. To do this, he analyzed 750 men who had fought in the Vietnam War. All had been taken prisoner during the war and had been kept in captivity for periods of six to eight years. All had been tortured, kept in isolation or both for very long periods of time. Surprisingly, none of them had developed depression or post-traumatic stress disorder in response to this highly traumatic experience. Dr. Charney interviewed the men in an attempt to better understand the factors that had enabled them to withstand this extreme stress.

At the end of the study, Dr. Charney was able to identify 10 critical elements that had led these men to develop this capability. Altruism was one of these factors. Indeed, Dr. Charney noted that the men often said that the fact of helping others cope allowed them to negotiate their own stress. This result confirms that altruism may be beneficial when an individual is facing acute or chronic stress.

Other factors identified by Dr. Charney as being associated with developing resilience were optimism, moral values, spirituality, humor, a role model, social support, the ability to cope with one's fear, the fact of having a mission and the training undergone to carry out this mission. You will notice that many of these factors have come up in this book as ones that have demonstrated their capacity to reduce the production of stress hormones in times of acute or chronic stress.

Even Those Who Don't Talk Can Help

We've seen that the fact of entering into social interaction with other people can be beneficial in countering the effects of stress on physical and mental health. Animals may help as well.

We've known the beneficial effects of pet therapy on human health for a long time. Several studies have shown that animals can be a great help for people with visual, physical or intellectual disabilities or psychiatric conditions. We've all seen a dog help a blind person get around or help someone in a wheelchair reach objects that would otherwise be out of range.

Recent studies show that animals can also have a significant impact on stress response in humans. One possible explanation for pets' positive impact is that their presence increases social interaction among individuals. Anyone who has ever walked a dog knows that this activity can lead others to approach you to initiate a conversation about your pet—its looks, its breed or anything else about it. The enhanced social interaction generated by the presence of a dog could explain its beneficial effects on an individual's stress response. However, this reasoning may not apply to pets such as cats, turtles or snakes that rarely leave the house with their owners.

Given this, scientists have wondered whether a physiological mechanism directly linked to the interaction between animals and humans could be the source of the beneficial effects of animals on people's physical and mental health. Such an effect has actually been observed. In 1929, a scientific study showed that when a person strokes a dog, that dog's blood pressure decreases. Some 60 years later, a second scientific study showed that people who interact with an animal also show a decrease in blood pressure!

In a more recent study, Dr. J. S. Odendaal of the Life Sciences Research Institute in Pretoria, South Africa, recruited participants between the ages of 19 and 55 and had them interact with dogs that were known to be placid. The researchers measured the cortisol stress hormone in all the participants before and after they interacted with a dog, and before and after a control situation in which they quietly read a magazine. The interaction with the dog consisted of admiring it, scratching its ears, and talking and playing gently with it. The results showed that participants exhibited a significant decrease in cortisol after interacting with the dog, while no difference in cortisol production was observed before and after the control situation.

Dr. Robert Viau was a blind researcher who was supported by a guide dog.[2] One day, he questioned whether the dog could have beneficial effects for children with pervasive developmental disorders. These young people suffer from various behavioral problems associated with autism, and most of them have difficulty communicating verbally with the people around them. Dr. Viau asked me if I could collaborate with him on a study in which companion dogs from the MIRA Foundation in Quebec would be provided to children with pervasive developmental disorders. The idea was to see whether a difference in production of the cortisol stress hormone would be detected after the dog was introduced into the child's family.

I agreed without hesitation to be part of this fabulous project. Dr. Viau's team measured cortisol in 42 children with pervasive developmental disorders at three defining moments. First, they measured the cortisol level before the dog arrived in the family, providing a base level of stress hormone production in these children. They then measured the cortisol level during the four weeks that the dog was with the family. Finally, they measured the cortisol level when the dog left the family.

The results showed a significant decrease in cortisol when the dog arrived. This lower cortisol level remained stable over the four weeks of the dog's involvement with the family. Then, when the dog was removed from the home, cortisol production increased significantly until it reached the levels observed before the dog's introduction. In addition, the children's parents noted a decrease in the children's problematic behavior during the time the dog was in the home. Following the study, which clearly demonstrated the positive impact of the companion dog on the child's behavior and production of stress hormones, the MIRA

Foundation offered to donate the dogs used in the study to any of the families that wished to keep them.

All the research to date has confirmed the positive and significant impact of pets on the stress response in humans (and in the animals in many cases!). Of course, running to your local pet shop to buy an animal is not a panacea to help you manage chronic stress. Indeed, other studies have shown that for a pet to have a beneficial effect on a person's health, the person must love the animal and want to interact with it. So if you hate dogs, it may not be a good idea to use this method to help you manage the stress in your life.

But for a lonely child who has difficulty interacting with his or her peers, a teenager suffering from bullying at school and feeling very isolated or a senior living alone, a pet could prove to be an effective tool for managing life's stress. Any adult reading this book may have already seen the benefit of a cat, a dog or even a turtle on a child's or a parent's behavior. Scientific research in recent decades has led us to believe that there is a physiological mechanism at the root of this positive effect, and that humans can produce fewer stress hormones if they interact with an animal than if they don't.

During the summer when I was writing this book, feeling stressed at the thought of not being able to finish before the start of the school year, I decided to combine two methods to help me control my stress response. Two for the price of one, you might say! Along with my children, I volunteered with the Society for the Prevention of Cruelty to Animals (SPCA) in my neighborhood. In doing so, I combined the positive impact of altruism on my stress response with that provided by interaction with animals.

Observing the delighted smile of the staff on seeing us arrive to help clean the animals' cages and walk the dogs before they opened the doors to the public, I felt a sense of well-being, and my children held their heads up high before this new challenge that enhanced their self-esteem. We had a lot of fun petting the cats in our care and watching the dogs we were walking do their tricks, and we continued to talk about it all the way home. The experience was so pleasant that we decided to continue volunteering through the school year!

Chapter 17

Your Body Is Your Most Effective Ally

We've already seen that to manage the stressors in our lives we need to deconstruct and reconstruct the situations that affect us, with the goal of discovering and controlling the NUTS characteristic causing our stress response. We've seen that flight can sometimes be useful in preventing acute stress from spilling over onto our loved ones. We've also seen that interaction with another being, human or animal, can have a beneficial effect on our stress response. There remains one last ally that we have not yet analyzed that can have an important effect in helping us quickly decrease an acute stress response: our body.

As we have seen, the body is a remarkable tool that allows us to produce a stress response when threatened, enabling us to mobilize enough energy to fight the threat or flee if the threat is too great. However, to enable us to survive continuous threats, the body has also had to create systems that allow it to suppress this stress response and prevent us from constantly producing excessive levels of stress hormones.

Thus the body is a wonderful ally in reducing stress hormones produced in response to acute stress. By using the mechanisms that the body itself has set up to reestablish equilibrium, you can act quickly and directly on the stress hormones you produce. Using these mechanisms as often as possible when faced with acute stress is a great strategy!

Breathe, Breathe, Breathe

We probably can't even count how many times we've been told to "take a deep breath" when faced with extreme stress. When we think about breathing while experiencing stress, we tend to picture someone sitting in the lotus position, going to great lengths to control how deeply and how frequently they take a breath. However, this image does not at all reflect how breathing can help us reduce our stress response.

The best way to use your breathing to diminish your stress response is to do what I call "belly breathing." The goal is very simple. Allow air to enter your body through your mouth or nose with the idea of filling your belly up with as much air as possible—making it stick out. That's it! That's the whole thing. There's no need to strike a fancy yoga pose. You can do this exercise while driving, during a meeting with the management committee or your boss, at the coffee machine with Jenny or while giving your kids a bath!

Practicing belly breathing will ensure that you reduce the concentration of stress hormones that you produce at times of stress. But how is it that such a simple act can have such a huge effect on our stress response system?

Let me begin my explanation by reminding you of the initial process that takes place during the stress response. When your brain detects a threat, it mobilizes a massive amount of energy to allow you to combat the threat, or to flee it if the threat is too great. What do we mean by *mobilize energy*? It's something like what you would do if I showed you a 100-pound weight and asked you to lift it. You would get close to the weight, take a deep breath, bend over, grab hold of the weight and lift it, all the while holding your breath. You would have used all your energy to lift the weight. Once you had lifted it up all the way, you'd continue to hold your breath, because otherwise you might lose your strength and have to drop the weight.

It's relatively easy to recognize when someone is in a state of acute stress. You only have to notice the unevenness of their breathing and the choppiness of their speech. This tells you that the person is in the midst of mobilizing all their energy and that to do so they need to hold their breath. If you had to give an oral presentation while holding up a 100-pound dumbbell, your words would be choppy, because you would necessarily have to keep on holding your breath to be able to continue mobilizing the energy you need to keep holding the weight above your head. This is exactly what happens during a stress response.

I'd like to explain another aspect of this with yet another illustration. When you get in your car to go to work in the morning, you step on the accelerator to make the car go forward. However, to stop the car, you have two choices. You can take your foot off the accelerator and hope to stop in time for the red light, or you can use the brakes.

When you mobilize your energy (and your breath) in response to a stressor and then do nothing afterward, it's similar to taking your foot off the accelerator and hoping to stop in time at the red light—it won't necessarily work! Thus, you may have undergone something stressful at 9 o'clock, and at 11 o'clock you still find yourself mobilizing your energy and holding your breath a little in response to that stressor. Your speech is choppy, and you're gasping. You don't know how to stop your stress response.

However, if you take one or two good belly breaths, you'll stop producing stress hormones, and by extension you'll stop mobilizing energy. Your speech will go back to normal and you won't have to continue the stress response after the threat is gone.

Why can belly breathing so effectively put an end to our stress response? Simple. Under your rib cage sits a muscle called the diaphragm. When you take in a lot of air, making your belly swell up, this expands the diaphragm. Once it has been expanded to a certain degree, the diaphragm activates the *parasympathetic response*, which terminates the stress response. The exact physiological mechanism of this reaction is very complex, but for our purposes here it's sufficient to understand that the more the diaphragm expands because of air in the belly, the more likely it is that you will activate the parasympathetic system, which will stop the production of stress hormones.

There you go! It's incredibly easy, and furthermore, it's free! You can do this exercise yourself and show it to your children, who can also benefit hugely from it when they are stressed. Belly breathing is easy to do and children enjoy it. One day when my son was particularly stressed (and stressful!), his sister looked him right in the eye and said, "Belly, Mattis, belly!"

Belly breathing is, however, decidedly unpopular with adolescents. When my team and I talked to teenagers in the DeStress for Success program about the importance of belly breathing to reduce their stress response, they made it clear that it was not cool at all, and that they had no intention of doing it in front of family and friends.

Of course I understood why they were reluctant, and so I studied the scientific literature to see if there were other methods of inducing diaphragmatic breathing in humans. I discovered that there are three activities that, even without our being aware of it, induce belly breathing, with all its stress-busting advantages. We now discuss them in the DeStress for Success program, and you can benefit from them too!

The Belly and Singing

The best way to do belly breathing without realizing it is to sing. When we sing, a significant amount of air enters our body and causes the diaphragm to expand. This expansion then activates the parasympathetic system that influences the stress response. Anyone who sings regularly knows that it involves diaphragm breathing.

My colleague and friend Dr. Tores Theorell of the National Institute for Psychosocial Factors and Health in Sweden has conducted several studies with individuals who sing in choirs. Dr. Theorell measured the cortisol stress hormone in singers before and after they sang in a choir and found a significant reduction in the concentration of stress hormones, especially among women singers. This result can be explained by the effect that singing has on breathing. Because it requires diaphragm breathing, choral singing activates the parasympathetic system, which reduces the production of stress hormones. Singing, it turns out, is a great way to reduce your stress.

I remember meeting a woman at a lecture I gave who told me an interesting story. She said that she had recently received a call from her sister, who asked her to come as quickly as possible to her home town, about 200 miles from Montreal, because their mother had cancer and was expected to die within the next 24 hours. This woman sang regularly in a choir. For some reason she could not understand, during the entire 200-mile ride, she had felt a strong need to sing. She gave in to this urge and sang the whole way in her car, all the while feeling guilty about singing while her mother was dying. When she heard what I was saying about singing, breathing and the stress response, she understood that her body, her best ally, had allowed her to better deal with this stressful situation by "pushing" her to sing.

The Belly and Prayer

Another way of doing belly breathing without realizing it is to pray. I'm not talking about a little 10-second prayer asking our favorite gods for a new car. I'm talking about a liturgical prayer that goes on for a good length of time. Why? Because when we pray for a long time, our breathing tends to slow down (*Holy Maaaaaarrrrrrrrry, prrrrrrrrrraaaaaaay for us*), thus causing diaphragm breathing the same way that singing does. Diaphragmatic breathing is also one of the basic elements of yoga. The question that researchers are therefore trying to answer is whether the effects of liturgical prayer on breathing and the stress response could explain some of the beneficial effects reported by people who practice yoga. Indeed, in Hinduism and Buddhism, the mantra is a form of prayer made up of a series of sounds repeated over and over again, following a certain rhythm.

Dr. Luciano Bernardi and his team at the University of Pavia in Italy tried to see if mantras or the lengthy rhythmic patterns induced by Christian prayer could have an impact on cardiac rhythm, and by extension on the stress system. They tested 23 adults, asking them to recite a Catholic rosary or a yogic mantra. The results showed that reciting a rosary or a mantra increased synchronization of cardiac rhythm. This positive effect of the mantra on diaphragmatic breathing could explain the positive health effects of yoga experienced by those who practice it.

Through its impact on respiration, can yoga help reduce production of stress hormones? Dr. Jeremy West and his team at Reed College in Oregon measured the cortisol stress hormone in 69 students who participated in one of three types of classes: an African dance class, a yoga class and a biology class. The African dance class was linked to an increase in breathing in response to the dance movements, while the yoga class induced diaphragm breathing and the biology class had no effect on breathing. The researchers measured the students' stress hormones before and after they participated in each of these classes. The results showed that cortisol levels went up in response to the African dance class and went down during the yoga class. There was no change in cortisol levels following the biology class.

These results suggest that the diaphragm breathing that takes place during yoga is the root cause of the beneficial effects reported by yoga practitioners. However, as we saw in previous chapters, for people who prefer to be active and don't enjoy sitting in a lotus position, yoga can actually increase the production of stress hormones.

Once again we see that there is no universal method of combating stress, and that's just fine. This way, when we're undergoing acute stress, we can choose to sing rather than pray—or even just listen to music!

The Belly and Music

We already know that a person's breathing rhythm tends to become synchronized with melodies sung or litanies intoned by the individual. Another interesting fact about breathing is that it has a tendency to keep time with a rhythm that a person hears, but doesn't produce. So when someone listens to music, his or her breathing tends to adjust to keep time with the music. The music's rhythm—the length of musical notes in relation to other musical notes—is more important than its style, such as techno or disco, in synchronizing breathing.

The fact that breathing becomes synchronized to a musical beat might help explain why some adolescents who go to raves end up in hospital, confused or unconscious. Of course, the confusion could have been caused by the teens taking ecstasy or other drugs, but there's another potential cause. The tempo of techno music played at raves is wild, at more than 100 beats per minute. Teens dance to the hellish pace of this rapid beat for two to 14 hours at a stretch. The dancers' breathing tends to speed up to match the tempo, which can cause some to hyperventilate or lose consciousness.

On the other hand, if you listen to music with a slower beat, such as classical, jazz or blues, your breathing will tend to synchronize to that rhythm and hence induce diaphragmatic breathing because you are allowing a lot of air into your body. Anyone who likes to sit for a long time in a comfortable armchair listening to classical music knows the feeling of well-being that eventually takes over after listening to a few pieces. This is due not just to the beauty of the music but also to the slowing down of our breathing to match the music's slow tempo.

Because one's breathing adjusts to match musical tempo, very fast music should increase stress hormones, while slower music should have the opposite effect. This is in fact what has been observed. A study by Dr. Gilberto Gerra of the Centre for Studies on Drug Addiction in Parma, Italy, concluded that there was a significant increase in blood pressure, respiration rate and concentration of the cortisol stress hormone in 18-year-olds who listened to techno music. In another study that I conducted with Dr. Isabelle Peretz of the Université de Montréal, we exposed university students to a stressful situation. After this, we asked a first group of participants to rest in silence for 30 minutes, while we exposed the second group of participants to relaxing music. The results showed that the level of stress hormones went down much more quickly in the group that listened to relaxing music after being exposed to stress than in the other group.

In another study that I conducted with Dr. Sylvie Hébert and her team at the Université de Montréal, we evaluated whether the very fast-paced music that is usually used in video games could have an effect on the production of stress hormones through the synchronization of breathing. We thus measured stress hormones before and after young men played a video game. Half the participants played with fast background music as part of the game, and the other half with no music. The results showed an increase in stress hormones among participants who played the game with music, while the level of stress hormones did not rise among the participants who played without music.

These results show that music has a very powerful effect on the synchronization of our breathing, and by extension on our production of stress hormones. Of course this doesn't mean we should force our adolescents to listen to classical music or stop playing video games. We would stress them too much by doing that! However, if you're stressed but you need to give your children a bath, it would be a good idea to listen to your favorite music before doing it. As for teens, it's always possible for them to de-stress by dancing to the music they love!

Get Rid of the Energy You've Mobilized!

In the previous section, we saw that breathing is a very effective tool for allowing our body to reduce its production of stress hormones. Another good way of reducing these hormones during a stressful time is to move: run, play an active sport, dance—in short, exercise. Again, the reason is very simple.

When your brain detects a threat in your environment, as you now know, it will produce a large amount of stress hormones in order to fight the mammoth or flee if it is too big, allowing you to survive. In the chapter explaining why we are so stressed nowadays, we saw that in prehistoric times people got rid of all the energy that they had mobilized by slaying the mammoth or by running away if the animal was too powerful. Nowadays, though, we don't usually dissipate the energy that we mobilize. Since the brain doesn't know the difference between a prehistoric mammoth and Monday morning traffic, it takes for granted that the mobilized energy was spent killing the mammoth or fleeing from it, and thus gives the order to eat quickly to shore up our energy reserves. In the case of the mammoth, prehistoric humans did expend the mobilized energy one way or the other. A modern person stuck at the wheel of a car, however, does not, so all the extra fats and sugars build up in the abdomen, eventually resulting in abdominal obesity.

So get rid of the energy!

It's a fact that when we are stressed we should do as much exercise as possible. Why? Because in times of stress, the body mobilizes a massive amount of energy to fight or flee the threat. But we must use up this energy; if not, it will begin to cause chronic stress.

Once while giving a public lecture that my neighbor attended, I made the mistake of mentioning that when I am very stressed, I go jogging. From then on, whenever I was coming back from a jog, my neighbor asked me what was stressing me!

A study by Dr. Ulrike Rimmele of the University of Zurich in Switzerland studied the effect of sports on stress reactions. The researchers exposed a group of elite athletes, a group of amateur athletes and a group that didn't participate in any sports activities to a psychological stressor. The results showed that the elite athletes had a lower stress hormone response than the participants who did no sports at all. The stress hormone level for the amateur athletes was between that of the other two groups. These results demonstrate that playing sports regularly has a significant impact on our reactivity to stress, and that you don't have to be an elite athlete to benefit from the positive effects of exercise on your stress response.

If you're a teacher with 30 students in your class, it's quite likely that some of these students are growing up in difficult family situations with a lot of parental conflict, neglect or even abuse. These children mobilize massive amounts of energy to fight or flee the threat they live with on a daily basis. When they get to school, they are literally like ticking time bombs. Their bodies have mobilized energy that remains unspent, since they cannot usually engage in fist fights with their parents. We then expect them to sit down at a desk and stay quiet for several hours. We offer them one or two hours of physical education per week, and are surprised when they act out aggressively, disrupt the class or develop abdominal obesity.

It's imperative that these children expend the energy they have mobilized. Their classmates who are growing up in healthy family situations need exercise as well, but not to the same degree. Using their pent-up energy will allow the stress response of the at-risk children to return to normal, preventing them from developing a chronic stress problem and increasing their ability to pay attention in the classroom.

A recent study conducted by Dr. Henning Budde and his colleagues at Humboldt University in Germany measured stress hormones and memory performance in two groups of children: a group that exercised and a group that did not. The first group of children had to stay quietly seated for 15 minutes. The second group ran around outside for 15 minutes. The results demonstrated a reduction in stress hormones and a significant improvement in memory performance among the children who had played outside in comparison with those who had remained seated in the classroom. The researchers also demonstrated that this effect was heightened in children who had performed poorly in the memory test before exercising. These findings are absolutely phenomenal, and I hope that they will persuade some teachers that an unruly group of students would gain more from a quick 15-minute run outside than they would "lose" by having their math period shortened by the same amount of time.

I'll even go a step further and say that education departments should really reconsider how much time is allocated to physical education classes for children and adolescents. We've already seen how today's children and teens are faced with just as many stressors as their prehistoric counterparts, but aren't likely to have the same opportunities to use up the energy they've mobilized. We need to act swiftly to get our children off the couch and moving around, so that we can avoid creating chronic stress and all the physical and mental problems that go with it. By lowering stress hormone production through physical exercise during the school day, we'll also increase their capacity to learn.

My last suggestion regarding physical activity is addressed directly to physical education teachers in schools. I'm basing this specific request on my own experience as well as that of my friends, my daughter and her friends, and many teenage girls I met during the DeStress for Success program. Ladies and gentlemen, teachers of physical education, here is what I ask of you: most of us girls hate dodgeball! Many of the activities that make up phys-ed classes (soccer, dodgeball, etc.) are much more appealing to boys than to girls, maybe because they are based on the fight/flight response that males love. However, as we saw in Chapter 9, girls have a tendency to form connections rather than fight or flee when under stress. This may be why so many girls can be found congregating and talking about fashion or boys during phys-ed class rather than chasing a ball.

However, one way of getting our girls to expend energy (whether mobilized or not) is by offering an activity that attracts them—for example, dancing. Since the dawn of time, women have always loved to dance. When people dance, they burn a lot of energy. This could be an excellent way for girls to use up the energy mobilized under stress while doing exercise that appeals to them. A teacher told me once that he was afraid that playing pop music in gym class would make the girls more uncontrollable. But have you ever tried? I predict an increase in the dancers' energy for the first 15 minutes, followed by a gradual reduction. I also predict that these girls (and boys who also want to dance) will perform better in their next class!

Ladies, this means you too. When you're under stress, there's nothing better than to put on your favorite pop music and dance until you're out of breath. In my family we often do this to reduce our stress levels. We end up doing the tango, jumping to disco or gyrating to hip-hop, all the while laughing ourselves silly. It's a great way to get rid of the energy we've mobilized during a stressful time.

Laughing at Stress

One morning when I was walking my dog,[1] I asked myself a strange question. You'll remember from Chapter 3 that the stress response begins when the brain detects a threat, causing the body to produce stress hormones. As we saw, the production of stress hormones is the result of a chain reaction that starts in the hypothalamus area of the brain. I wondered what would happen if someone had a lesion of their hypothalamus. Was it possible that he or she would never suffer from stress again? That would be an idea worth patenting, I said to myself.

When I got back home, I checked the scientific literature on the subject and found something very interesting. Clinical studies have shown that when someone has a lesion of the hypothalamus, they suffer from—believe it or not—pathological laughter! This laughter has two notable characteristics: it occurs in the absence of any funny stimulus, and the person cannot control it. I found this fascinating, because I now understood that the same region of the brain that can cause a stress response is involved with laughter.

Have you ever returned home after a very stressful day at the office and started laughing uncontrollably with your spouse about a trivial joke or remark? I sometimes think this results from the short circuit that happens between the "stress role" and the "laughter role" of the hypothalamus.

If the same area of the brain controls both the stress response and laughter, you have to wonder if laughter reduces the production of stress hormones. As it turns out, it does. A study by Dr. Lee Berk and his team at Loma Linda University in California measured the cortisol stress hormone in a group of participants before and after they watched a funny movie and in another group that stayed quiet and didn't watch the movie. The results showed that the production of stress hormones went down significantly in the group that watched the funny movie, but not in the other group.

There's no age limit on laughter. A recent study showed that elderly people with high scores on a questionnaire that measured their sense of humor had lower concentrations of stress hormones than those in the same age group without a sense of humor.

As we've seen, when we have an acute response to stress we tend to feel angry or even furious. Given the effect laughter has on the production of stress hormones, it's when we're under stress that laughter should have the most beneficial effect. So instead of giving the kids a bath when you come home all stressed out, it would be worth considering officially canceling the bath and organizing a tickling session instead, with laughter guaranteed!

Don't Be Afraid of Stress

Reading this book might make you think that the best thing to do to prevent the potentially negative effects of stress on your physical and mental health would be to avoid at all costs any situation that could lead to a stress response in you and your children. But that wouldn't be a good solution.

Remember that to be effective, a vaccine must contain a tiny dose of a virus or bacteria, because this is how the immune system is activated to defend itself against the invader. It's the same thing with stress. Researchers call this "inoculation by stress." If an organism is never exposed to a stressor, it will be more difficult for it to develop resistance to stress.

Dr. David M. Lyons of Stanford University in California is a pioneer in the study of stress inoculation. This researcher has studied the mechanism of stress inoculation in young monkeys that are still being cared for by their mothers. A first group of monkeys is left with the mother full-time, while a second group is taken away from the mother for short periods several times during their development. When the monkey is removed from its mother's care, it's placed with other monkeys and must interact with them. Clearly these interactions often generate a stress response in the young monkeys.

Later, when the monkeys are mature, Dr. Lyons measures their reactivity to stress as adults. The results of these studies show that the monkeys who were exposed to moderate stressors when they were young produce lower levels of stress hormones when they are exposed to a stressful situation as adults. Conversely, monkeys that were not exposed to moderate stressors while young show a greater stress response as adults.

When they appeared in the scientific literature, these results were criticized on the basis that it was possible that the improved stress resistance observed in monkeys that had been exposed to stress while young could be explained by the behavior of the mothers when their offspring were returned to them rather than the fact that the young monkeys had been exposed to stressors. Indeed, some studies done with rats demonstrated that when a young rat was separated from its mother for short periods of time, the mother tended to increase the care she gave when her offspring was returned to her. Thus, it would be the behavior of the mother that would increase the offspring's stress resistance more than the early exposure to stress.

In an attempt to verify this hypothesis, Dr. Karen Parker and her team, also from Stanford, conducted another study. The first group of young monkeys were separated from their mothers and exposed to mild stress. In a second group, the young monkeys and their mothers were both exposed to mild stress, and in a third group, the young monkeys were left with their mothers. The results demonstrated that mothers exposed to stress at the same time as their offspring provided less care to them than mothers who were not exposed to stress at the same time as their offspring. However, both groups of young monkeys that were exposed to stress when they were young (those whose mothers increased their care and those whose mothers did not) demonstrated resistance to stress as adults.

Through this research, Dr. Parker demonstrated that it wasn't the care given by the mother to her offspring after exposure to a stressor that predicted the stress resistance of a young monkey. It really was the fact of having been exposed to mild stressors while young that predicted the development of stress resistance during adulthood. These results confirm that exposure to mild stressors during maturation leads organisms to develop resistance to stressors they experience as adults.

In today's world, we have a tendency to overprotect our children. By constantly watching over them, we reassure ourselves that they will not be kidnapped by a sexual predator or hit by a car. However, when I was young, parents did not have this tendency to overprotect. I remember going into the forest alone to pick blueberries and constantly being afraid of being attacked by a bear. Despite this genuine fear, which was normal where I come from, I continued to pick blueberries. Every time I went, I must have produced quite a lot of stress hormones at the very idea of encountering a bear, but I came out with baskets full of purple fruit and not a scratch on me. It's possible that the parenting practices of that time allowed children to develop a resistance to stress that no longer exists. By overprotecting our children, it's possible that we prevent them from developing resistance to stress that could help them over the long term.

I know, I know. Easier said than done. I myself have told my husband that I wouldn't allow our children to play alone in the park until they were 17, and I would still follow them using GPS! Still, these clear scientific data have persuaded me to give my children a little more space to allow them to experience a bit of stress in their surroundings.

You may be tempted to respond that children nowadays have plenty of stress in their everyday lives and we don't need to add to it. As we saw in other chapters, it's true that our children are exposed daily to a lot of new and unpredictable situations, threats to their egos and a low sense of control. However, there's a big difference between being exposed to a stressor that's forced on us and choosing a stress that we can fight. Choosing to be exposed to a situation that is potentially stressful but stimulates us (like picking blueberries in a forest full of imaginary bears, or playing a game of tennis with Jim even if it's a threat to our ego) allows us to develop more effective resistance to stress that afterward will help us in fighting stress that we *don't* choose.

Heaven Helps Those Who Help Themselves?

It might seem strange or even contradictory to suggest exposing ourselves to mild stressors to improve our resistance to stress. We have this fear of stress because for many years self-help books have described stress as being extremely toxic, something to be avoided at all costs.

In the United States, books on subjects like stress, emotions and so on account for $8.6 billion in sales annually. Customers for these books come from all levels of society, although women tend to buy more of them than men. These publications can be divided into two major categories.

The first category consists of books that create a sense of *victimization*—to help the reader, of course. They'll tell you that the situation you're in is not your fault but is caused by your childhood, your experiences or the manipulative people who constantly surround you. In the second category are books that use an *empowerment* approach. According to these books, all the strengths and qualities you need to become what you want to be already lie within you, and all you need to do is follow a particular method (the one put forward in the book, of course) to succeed. In general, a reader who finds one of these two approaches appealing will only buy books recommending that approach.

I've been collecting self-help books on stress for several years. Most of these books present stress as being an extremely harmful state that we should avoid at all costs. We're told that the best way to manage our stress is to do yoga or meditation, not think about anything, go to the spa or do something to take our mind off things.

I wondered whether all these books had a positive impact on our stress level. After all, you'd think that by reading all these books on personal development, we'd succeed in controlling our stress response. To this day, the only thing I know for sure about these books is that the reader who buys one has bought another one in the previous 18 months. But if these books really worked, the reader wouldn't have to buy any more, right?

On the basis of this observation, I wondered whether consumers of this type of book are less reactive to stress than nonconsumers. If these self-help books are at all useful in lowering the reader's stress, this ought to be the case.

So I did a study (of course!) to find the answer to this question. My team and I recruited about 60 participants. Half of them were avid readers of self-help books and the other half never read them. We exposed both groups to psychological stress and measured the participants' stress hormones before and after the exposure. The results showed that the readers of self-help books produced four times more stress hormones than the nonreaders when faced with a stressful situation. From this result it's impossible to know whether reading these books increases one's reactivity to stress or whether vulnerability to stress causes these individuals to read the books in the first place. However, the study does show that we need to ask some serious questions about the positive effects that these books are supposed to have.

I don't need to tell you that the book you are holding in your hands is not a self-help book.

This book has summarized the scientific basis for the study of human stress. I have shared with you 20 years of scientific research on the stress response—a phenomenon that is at once dangerous and marvelous. Just as wine must be drunk in moderation to have health benefits, so must stress be experienced in moderation to allow us to withstand the biggest mammoths in our lives.

I'll never know whether this new knowledge you have acquired will have beneficial and measurable effects on your stress response. However, I do know that in writing this book, I've summarized, with all the rigor and objectivity I can muster, the current state of scientific knowledge on human stress.

I've done this so you can stop being afraid of stress.

History of the Science of Stress

In the development of the body of knowledge we now think of as the science of stress, two periods stand out: the two world wars. The wars were catalysts in advancing knowledge of stress for a number of reasons.

First, observing that in addition to physical injuries many soldiers in these conflicts exhibited traumatic shock, military physicians asked researchers in physiology and psychology to help them better understand this phenomenon. At that time, there was no collaboration between researchers interested in physiology (study of physiological mechanisms at the base of life) and those interested in psychology (study of people's mental state), so there was no multidisciplinary research on the subject. Researchers were isolated in their own areas of study and tried to explain everything through their own methods of analysis. The result was a major split between the physiological and psychological aspects of the study of stress.

Second, during World War II, many European researchers decided to leave the continent to avoid being caught up in the war and to be able to continue their work. The vast majority of these researchers came to North America, and quite a few of those settled in Montreal, where a number of scientists had already achieved worldwide recognition for their studies of stress—notably Professor Hans Selye, who had first described the physiological response to stress in 1936.

How "Looking Sick" Led to the Concept of Stress

Stress as a field of study thus started in Montreal. Dr. Selye, an Austrian physician, had taken up a medical internship in Montreal in 1932. In his autobiography, he recounted that when studying medicine at the University of Prague, he and his peers accompanied the department head on visits to patients suffering from a variety of medical conditions to observe the symptoms related to each condition. After closely examining the characteristics of patients with various diseases, the future doctor could then recognize the same symptoms in another patient and thus make a diagnosis.

Dr. Selye found this activity very tedious. Nevertheless, one thing puzzled him greatly. He had observed during these visits that no matter what they each suffered individually, the patients all had one thing in common: they all *looked sick*. For example, a patient afflicted with jaundice would have a yellowish tint while one with a lung condition would be short of breath. But despite their very different symptoms, both patients would have the same look of being sick. In addition, he noted that these two patients, even though they suffered from two completely different diseases, displayed common physical features such as a thick and whitish tongue, and both complained of joint pain and intestinal problems accompanied by loss of appetite.

This observation convinced Dr. Selye that there had to be a process that gave patients that sickly look, and that this process was the same no matter what condition the patient was suffering from. He began to think that this physical reaction demonstrated "the non-specific response of the body to any demand placed upon it."[1]

Elaborating on this idea, he observed that when we are exposed to cold, our body responds by shivering (to generate heat), and the blood vessels in the skin contract (to reduce heat loss). The body thus provides two specific responses. If we are exposed to heat, we sweat so that the evaporation of water produces a cooling effect. This is yet another very specific bodily response. When a disease attacks the body, however, the body seems to produce a nonspecific response in that it is similar for all conditions. This includes a sickly appearance, thick tongue, muscle pains and intestinal cramps. What could be the mechanism underlying this nonspecific response?

Putting this observation on the back burner, Dr. Selye decided to pursue a career in research after completing his medical studies. He started researching hormones, the substances produced by the body's glands (ovaries, adrenal glands, thyroid, etc.) that have a wide variety of effects on the body. In 1934, while pursuing his research in the biochemistry department at McGill University, the 28-year-old Dr. Selye discovered, somewhat by accident, what he later called the *biological response to stress.*

At that moment in medical history, a number of laboratories in different parts of the world were busy trying to discover new hormones, with researchers working at top speed. One of the methods used most frequently to find new hormones was to inject the extract of any gland (for example, extracts from ovaries) into a laboratory animal and then measure the reaction. To obtain such an extract, the gland was removed from an animal and pulverized: the result constituted the extract. Unaware of the precise content of the ovarian extract that he injected, Dr. Selye and his colleagues decided that if injecting the extract produced an effect on the animal receiving it, they would conclude that the ovarian extract contained a hormone (as yet unidentified) that had induced the observed effects on the animal.

In his first experiments, Dr. Selye injected ovarian extracts into rats and observed that the rats developed a myriad of reactions, including enlargement of the adrenal glands (the two small glands that are located above the kidneys), shrinking of the thymus (a glandular organ located in the lower neck) and the lymph nodes, and ulcers in the lining of the stomach and duodenum (the beginning of the small intestine). He was surprised by this discovery and realized later that the magnitude of these reactions could be increased or decreased in proportion to the volume of injected ovarian extracts. This discovery galvanized Dr. Selye, who was convinced that he had discovered a new hormone before he had even turned 30.

His euphoria was short-lived, however. When he began injecting extracts from other glands (placenta, pituitary, etc.) into other rats, to his amazement he observed the same effects on the bodies of these animals. How could extracts of different glands give rise to the same effect on the body? It was impossible that the same hormone could be hidden in all these glands. Rather than give up, Dr. Selye continued his search, and this time injected rats with extracts of organs that were not glands, and therefore could not produce hormones: kidney, spleen and other body parts. Once more, he was amazed to observe the same effects on the body, such as enlargement of the adrenal glands and stomach ulcers. The mystery deepened.

Perseverance is the first quality required of any scientist, and Dr. Selye was well endowed with this quality. He decided to inject rats with formalin, a synthetic substance (that is, not produced by the body) used in the laboratory for the preparation of tissues to be studied under a microscope. Once again, he observed the same effects on the bodies of the injected rats. Given this incomprehensible result, Dr. Selye had two options. He could drop this area of research and turn to other scientific concerns. He knew very well that many laboratories around the world were engaged in fierce competition to discover new hormones. This was a daunting task fraught with pitfalls, not to mention personal and professional clashes among researchers.[2] On the other hand, he could choose to continue studying this curious and incomprehensible result to try to understand what was happening. This was the option he chose, and it proved successful.

At this point, Dr. Selye recalled the observations he had made among the patients he had seen during his internship: that no matter what the patients were suffering from, they all showed common features such as looking sick. He understood then that this observation was similar to what he had noticed in the rats, where injections of extracts of glands and organs and even drugs had all produced the same effects on their bodies. This was an astonishing parallel, and he decided to pursue his research. This time, instead of injecting rats with extracts of glands or organs, he submitted them to various adverse conditions, such as a sharp increase or drop in temperature, and analyzed the impact on their bodies. To his great surprise he found that in every one of these experiments, without exception, he observed exactly the same array of symptoms in the animals as he had in previous experiments!

Dr. Selye was therefore forced to conclude that far beyond the specific disease that affected a given individual or the adverse conditions to which he or she was subjected, the body generates a nonspecific response to disease or external attacks. Worse yet, he discovered that this reaction could in itself kill the subject if not controlled. The researcher had discovered what he called at the time the general adaptation syndrome: the typical, although not specific, response the body produces when exposed to adverse conditions such as disease.

A little later in his career, around 1936, Dr. Selye borrowed the term *stress* from the engineering profession and coined the term *stress response* to describe the body's initial response to various attacks (diseases, extracts of glands or organs, etc.). He emphasized that stress was the specific response of the body to nonspecific conditions. This meant that regardless of the nature of the attack on a body, it would react with a very specific response (the stress response or general adaptation syndrome), which includes a sickly demeanor, thickening of the tongue, abdominal pain and stomach ulcers.

In 1936, Dr. Selye published a short article in the journal *Nature* describing the results of his research and the general adaptation syndrome. Although these observations were interesting, they were not enough to draw conclusions about the precise nature of the mechanism that generated this stress response or, more importantly, about the physiological process through which this reaction could become harmful to the body. In scientific terms, Dr. Selye's discovery offered merely an empirical finding: a result obtained by observing the effects of different conditions on the body.

For science to advance, however, we must also understand the exact mechanism through which a particular state occurs. What is the substance produced by the body during illness or external attacks that results in the development of this nonspecific response? And why does the body produce this nonspecific response? Does it protect the body or help destroy it?

Faced with these questions, Dr. Selye decided to continue his research. At this point in his career, he accepted a position at the Université de Montréal, which offered to set up a medical institute that would specialize in the study of stress. His reputation had grown, and many students around the world jostled for the privilege of studying under him.

To begin his quest to understand how the stress response was produced, as a way of keeping things simple, he decided to focus on just one manifestation of the nonspecific physical response. He asked what could induce thymic atrophy (atrophy of the small gland at the base of the neck) in rats that were subjected to stressful conditions.

He conducted the following experiment. He subjected rats to physical stresses such as cold and heat (which he called *stressors*) and observed that their bodies produced the typical response: atrophy of the thymus (a feature of the physiological stress response). He figured he could discover the origin of this atrophy if he systematically removed various glands from the animal's body and observed the result. If the body's response to the attack of cold or heat came from a message sent by a gland, then removal of this gland should prevent atrophy of the thymus. After several attempts, he observed that when the animal had undergone removal of the adrenal glands, atrophy of the thymus no longer occurred when the animal was subjected to adverse conditions.

With this result, he proved beyond a doubt that the basic message that caused the atrophy of the thymus was coming from the adrenal glands. This result was consistent with the enlargement of these glands that was also observed when the animals were subjected to adverse conditions—any gland that produces substances in large quantities will grow.

He therefore concluded that the adrenal glands must be producing a substance or a hormone that induces the negative effect on the thymus. To test his hypothesis, he injected adrenal gland extracts into the animals and again saw the typical changes observed in the thymus. Clearly, the adrenal gland contained a substance that induces these changes.

At this stage in his research, an obvious question arose. How does the adrenal gland know when there is a stressful condition and, therefore, a need to produce this substance? In other words, where does the message come from that tells the adrenal glands to produce the substance that has so many adverse effects on the body? At this time, the search for new hormones had led researchers to understand that the pituitary gland, a tiny gland at the base of the brain, produces hormones. With this information, Selye decided to remove the pituitary gland to see if he could still induce thymic atrophy in conjunction with adverse conditions.

He discovered that when the pituitary gland was absent and the animal was subjected to adverse conditions, there was no effect on the thymus. Conversely, when he injected the hormone produced by the pituitary gland (ACTH), he could produce the effects on the thymus. He had discovered that to produce the substance that caused the stress response, the adrenal gland had to receive a message from the hormone ACTH, produced by the pituitary gland.

A few years later a former student of Dr. Selye's, Dr. Roger Guillemin, and his fierce rival Dr. Geoffrey Harris both discovered that to produce ACTH, the pituitary gland had to receive a message from another gland called the hypothalamus. Located in the central part of the brain, this gland produces a hormone called CRF. When there is an adverse condition, the hypothalamus produces CRF, which travels to the pituitary gland to enable the production of ACTH. The

ACTH produced by the pituitary gland then travels through the blood to activate the adrenal glands that produce the substance that creates the adverse effects Dr. Selye had described. The exact mechanism of the chain of events that occur during exposure to adverse conditions had been discovered. But there remained one very important unknown. What was the substance produced by the adrenal gland that led to the adverse effects described by Dr. Selye in conditions of stress?

The Discovery of Stress Hormones

Let's go back a little further in history. In 1849, a physician named Thomas Addison observed that several of his patients presented with a very bizarre syndrome. These patients complained of extreme fatigue, they had suffered a significant loss of muscle strength and their *skin was very dark brown* (hence the original name of "*dark skin disease*" given to this syndrome before it was changed to Addison's disease). They also experienced loss of appetite, followed by exhaustion and then death. Dr. Addison performed autopsies on three patients and observed that in all cases there was atrophy (a decrease in the volume) of the adrenal glands. Another doctor, Charles-Édouard Brown-Séquard, immediately began experiments on animals in which he removed the adrenal gland. Each time he did this, the animals began to show symptoms similar to those of Dr. Addison's patients and subsequently died. Dr. Brown-Séquard therefore concluded that this small gland contained a substance that is necessary for life.

In studying this gland, researchers found that it contains two distinct parts, which they called the medulla (the center of the gland) and the cortex (the periphery). In 1901, researchers isolated a substance in the medulla they called adrenaline and discovered that adrenaline was a hormone. They then began to study its effects on the body.

It was in 1919, through a series of extraordinary events, that Dr. Walter Cannon discovered the role of adrenaline in the body. He began his career studying how the digestive system functions. While he was engaged in an experiment, he observed that when an animal was subjected to conditions that could scare it or make it uncomfortable (such as pain), peristalsis (waves of contraction) of its stomach stopped precipitously. He began to study this further and observed that in adverse conditions, the animal also produced adrenaline.

By studying the conditions under which adrenaline is produced, he demonstrated that the medulla of the adrenal gland produced adrenaline when the subject was faced with an immediate danger (this occurred through the activation of a complex system called the sympathetic nervous system). The hormone is produced to help the body mobilize enough energy to either fight the danger or flee it if it is too great, thus ensuring the individual's survival. He developed his theory that exposure to intense emotion, such as fear or danger, leads to production of adrenaline, which allows the individual to mobilize the energy to fight or flee the threat. Dr. Cannon thus formulated the concept of the "fight-or-flight response."

After the outbreak of World War I in 1914, British Army doctors began to observe the phenomenon of shell shock among soldiers. Shell shock leads to a sharp decrease in blood pressure, which can be fatal. The British Army asked Dr. Cannon to help it better understand the septic shock observed in soldiers. Dr. Cannon spent several years on the battlefield (in spite of a wife and five children at home) trying to understand this state of shock and treat it. He observed that when an individual is in shock there is a significant decrease in blood circulation; when blood circulation is brought back into balance, death can be prevented. This knowledge helped Dr. Cannon develop the concept of homeostasis on his return from the war. He described it as the body's way of regulating itself to maintain a stable condition. For example, an abrupt decline in blood glucose is corrected by the production of other substances that help restore glucose balance. Without this balance, the body cannot function and will die.

Who Coined the Term *Stress*?

This is the debate of the century in stress science! Most writers attribute the origin of the term stress to Hans Selye, who first described it in 1936. However, in 1934, Walter Cannon also discussed "stress" in his research, and so many others attribute authorship of the term to Cannon.

There was a major difference between the two scientists' definitions of "stress." Cannon used the term stress to refer to any external condition that can affect homeostasis and induce the production of adrenaline. Thus, for Cannon, stress was just a word to describe the various conditions (intense heat or cold, fear, adverse conditions, etc.) that would produce a negative

(continued)

response in the body. Selye, however, was the first to identify the body's nonspecific physiological response to any outside attack, which he called stress. As mentioned earlier, he borrowed the term from engineering, where it had first been used around 1935. In the aircraft industry, for example, one can "stress" metal to the point that it would shatter like glass. For Selye, this engineering terminology fit what he was trying to describe. Through Selye's appropriation of the term, stress moved from the exclusive domain of engineering to that of medicine, and then on to common language.

Having been the first to use the word stress to denote a nonspecific physical reaction, rather than the external agent that can induce that reaction, Selye would then say that he had discovered stress. Cannon never described any "stress theory" and spent his entire career working on the fight-or-flight response, which, as we'll see, forms part of the new stress models. To mark the distinction between stress as the external agent that attacks the body and stress as the body's response, Selye capitalized the word Stress in all his articles and books. Selye's Stress thus became a concept in itself. Today, the concepts developed by both Cannon and Selye are used in research. We speak of "stressors" to describe the adverse conditions that can lead to a "stress response," which is the production of stress hormones that can affect the body and brain.

However, in the seventeenth century, long before Cannon and Selye started discussing stress, the term was already being used to describe the various trials of life. During the eighteenth and nineteenth centuries, its meaning evolved to reflect concepts such as pressure and the tension that a person experiences in life. From there, it was appropriated by the engineering field and then subsequently used by proponents of the psychological approach to stress.

Let's go back to the work of Dr. Addison and Dr. Brown-Séquard, which demonstrated that the adrenal gland should contain a substance that is necessary for life. By studying this gland, researchers found that its central portion, the medulla, produces adrenaline, the hormone involved in the fight-or-flight response. But was it this hormone that is necessary for life?

Research continued on the various hormones produced by the adrenal glands, and special attention was now focused on the second part of the adrenal gland, the cortex. The researchers quickly found that unlike the medulla hormones, the hormones in this part of the gland were very difficult to extract from the tissue. To be able to extract large quantities of substances from the adrenal gland for study purposes, scientists worked on the adrenal glands of cattle, which could be obtained in large quantities from surrounding farms and slaughterhouses.

At that time, the Mayo Clinic published research in which the authors claimed that an extract from the cortex of a cow's adrenal glands could keep patients with Addison's disease alive. What a discovery! Very quickly, patients with this disease were given large doses of extracts from the adrenal glands of cattle. Subsequently, animal studies showed that if an animal's adrenal glands are removed, it can be kept alive by these extracts from the adrenal glands of cattle. These experiments again demonstrated that a substance present in the cortex of the adrenal glands can enable an individual to stay alive.

However, extracting large quantities of these substances would require a daunting number of cattle adrenal glands. It was therefore necessary to identify and isolate the exact substance that could sustain life in patients with Addison's disease. This work was undertaken by Dr. Edward C. Kendall, who between 1930 and 1940 isolated four hormones from the cortex of the adrenal gland, which he named A, B, E and F. Later, researchers discovered that compound E (now called cortisol) was the active element in the stress response and the survival of the animal. So that was the source of the positive effects the cattle's adrenal glands were having on patients suffering from Addison's disease.

At that point, World War II broke out in Europe. From the beginning, European research institutions decided to mobilize researchers to try to help the soldiers who had gone to the front. The adrenal glands of cattle and their potential life-saving virtues were in fashion in the scientific world. Thus, a rumor that Germany had procured large quantities of cattle adrenal gland in South America to make extracts that could be administered to its soldiers caused the Allied forces great concern. Presumably, these extracts would be used to prevent hypoxia (an oxygen deficiency that can cause the brain to stop working within 20 to 30 seconds) in German pilots, allowing them to fly at higher altitudes. In addition, these extracts were said to be useful in preventing wounded soldiers from going into septic shock, a dangerous consequence of bacterial toxins in the blood.

A vast military effort was therefore undertaken to test whether the extracts could produce resistance to hypoxia and shock in Allied soldiers. However, these studies were all negative and were of no use to the military. Therefore, by 1944, toward the end of the war, almost all the researchers had stopped working on this question. Only two research groups persisted: at the Mayo Clinic and at the Merck pharmaceutical company.

Since Dr. Kendall had succeeded in isolating and purifying the hormones of the adrenal glands, a special military committee asked him to create synthesized samples of these hormones in the laboratory. To synthesize a substance in the laboratory, one must first know exactly how the substance is made, its chemical structure and its composition. This was the first part of Dr. Kendall's work in collaboration with researchers at the Mayo Clinic and Merck. By December 1944, researchers at Merck were able to prepare a few milligrams of compound E.

The people at Merck then contacted Dr. Kendall to let him know they had a small quantity of synthesized compound E, and given the lack of interest in it within the research community, they did not plan to produce more. So if Dr. Kendall and his colleagues wanted to test the effects of the synthetic substance under specific conditions, it was now or never.

The Discovery of a Wonder Drug

Dr. Philip S. Hench, a doctor at the Mayo Clinic, observed that patients suffering from rheumatoid arthritis often went into remission when they caught jaundice, and some women saw their arthritis get better when they were pregnant. He postulated that there must be a substance produced during jaundice or pregnancy that would cause this remission. Dr. Hench and Dr. Kendall discussed this hypothesis and decided to test the potential effects of compound E on the symptoms of rheumatoid arthritis. There was no reason to think this would work, but since they had got hold of the substance in question, why not test the effects on these patients?[3]

In September 1948, compound E was injected into a woman suffering from rheumatoid arthritis. The woman's symptoms soon disappeared. Using a larger number of patients suffering from various inflammatory disorders, Dr. Hench and Dr. Kendall observed that nearly every patient went into remission following injection of compound E. But they also discovered that they had to keep administering the compound or the symptoms would reappear. Hench and Kendall had just discovered the anti-inflammatory properties of compound E.

The excitement was palpable, even among the researchers, but they remained cautious about their discovery, waiting nearly seven months before announcing the results of their study publicly. In 1949, the positive benefits of compound E for patients with inflammatory disorders were finally announced. What doctors would later call a wonder drug had just been discovered. To simplify the lives of researchers and clinicians, Dr. Hench chose the name *cortisol* for the natural structure of compound E (produced naturally by the human body), while he called its synthetic form (produced in laboratories) *cortisone*. In 1950, Dr. Hench and Dr. Kendall, along with a collaborator, Dr. Tadeus Reichstein, won the Nobel Prize in medicine for this chance discovery!

But let's get back to Dr. Selye. After this discovery, knowing now that the adrenal gland produced a hormone called "cortisol," Dr. Selye tested its effects on rats to see whether this hormone, when produced by the cortex of the adrenal gland, was actually what induced the body's nonspecific response. It was quite a surprise for him to discover that this was indeed the case: this hormone was at the origin of the biological stress response he had been observing for many years. Knowing now that cortisol hormone was a substance derived from several others (compounds A, B and F), he categorized cortisol and its derivatives as *glucocorticoids*. This was the missing link. Dr. Cannon had demonstrated the role of adrenaline (from the medulla of the adrenal gland) in the fight-or-flight response, and Dr. Selye had demonstrated the role of cortisol (from the cortex of the adrenal gland) on the body's nonspecific response to stress.

The Wonder Drug's Side Effects

The adrenal gland substance that helped cure inflammations had just been discovered. Cortisone soon became very popular for the treatment of various inflammatory disorders such as rheumatoid arthritis, asthma, ulcerative colitis and other ailments. Dr. Hench had observed that the therapeutic effects of cortisone on inflammation required continuous treatment. And so at that point, most doctors treated patients with large doses of cortisone over very long periods of time.

But two years after cortisone was introduced as an anti-inflammatory treatment, the enthusiasm it stirred was deflated by new scientific and clinical data showing that long-term cortisone treatment caused very serious side effects, especially on the ability to learn, memorize and pay attention (affect and cognition). The first case study on the side effects of cortisone treatment was published in 1951 by Dr. M. C. Borman, who reported a case of suicide after administration of cortisone. A year later, three more scientific articles were published, in which the authors reported serious mental disorders when cortisone was taken on a long-term basis.

The side effects of cortisone treatment on affect and cognition were numerous, and they resembled a psychosis. Patients treated with cortisone presented thought disorders, sharp mood swings from euphoria to depression, and hallucinations. Since cortisone is part of the steroid family, researchers called this syndrome caused by cortisone therapy *steroid psychosis*. Researchers noted that the clinical presentation of steroid psychosis was very similar to the symptoms observed among patients suffering from Cushing's syndrome, in which a pituitary gland tumor leads to high cortisol concentrations through ACTH hormone.

But the question remained: how could cortisol, a hormone produced by the adrenal gland, located above the kidneys, produce such substantial psychotic and mental effects? It had long been known that mental disorders emerge mainly from chemical disturbances in the brain. At that time, it was thought that hormones produced outside the brain, such as cortisol, did not reach the brain.

This made little sense, however, because cortisone, a synthetic form of the cortisol hormone produced by the adrenal glands, could cause psychoses in humans. That meant this hormone could reach the brain. There was no other possible explanation.

It Becomes Known that the Brain Reacts to Stress Hormones

For 15 years following the discovery of steroid psychosis, researchers set out to see whether cortisol could reach the brain in some way or other. This area of research became very prolific. In 1968, Dr. Bruce McEwen of Rockefeller University in New York discovered that the brain contained receptors capable of recognizing cortisol. For any bodily substance to be able to have an effect, it must have a receptor—a protein that allows that substance, and only that substance, to be recognized. Thus, for each substance produced by our body and our brain, there is a receptor specific to that substance. The discovery in 1968 that there were cortisol receptors in the brain made it possible to understand how cortisone treatment could induce mental effects. When produced by the adrenal gland, cortisol hormone—or its synthetic form, cortisone—reaches the brain through the blood, passing through the brain's natural blood barrier to activate the cortisol receptors.

Another discovery by Dr. McEwen led to a better understanding of the mechanism through which cortisone could induce effects on affect and cognition. At the time of his 1968 discovery, Dr. McEwen also noted that cortisol receptors were located mostly in a very specific area of the brain, called the hippocampus because of its seahorse shape. It had been known since 1956 from work by Dr. Wilder Penfield and Dr. Brenda Milner at the Montreal Neurological Institute that the hippocampus was a key area of the brain for memory. When the hippocampus had to be removed from a patient to treat intractable epilepsy, the patient was found to have general amnesia. Through these experiments, Dr. Penfield and Dr. Milner showed the hippocampus's major role in memory. We know today that there are also cortisol receptors in the frontal lobe and the amygdaloid nucleus, two highly important areas of the brain for regulating emotions and affect.

The affect and cognition disorders shown by patients receiving high doses of cortisone for long periods were thus due to the fact that cortisone, when administered chronically, reaches the brain and, more particularly, the areas of the brain involved in affect (frontal lobe and amygdaloid nucleus) and memory (hippocampus). Chronic activation of these receptors would disturb the functioning of these areas, leading to the disorders observed among patients under cortisone therapy.

Of course, on the basis of these results, researchers set out to synthesize another substance that would act like cortisone but without the side effects, and they succeeded. Today patients most often receive nonsteroidal anti-inflammatory drugs: substances with properties similar to those of cortisone but not presenting the same side effects.

Meanwhile, researchers began asking another important question. If synthetic cortisone could have these sorts of harmful effects on the brain, could natural cortisol, produced by the body in stress situations, be having the same effects? They recalled that for cortisone treatment to have harmful effects on affect and cognition, the drug had to be given chronically. Linking this element to cortisol stress hormone, researchers began asking whether an individual's exposure to chronic stress could harm the brain. This was a powerful hypothesis: if confirmed, it would lead to a better understanding of why stress in life can cause various disorders such as memory loss, depression and so on.

A major research effort began. Between 1970 and 1990, a sizable number of animal studies showed that when an animal is subject to chronic stress, it develops memory and behavioral disorders as well as atrophy of the hippocampus. In the early 1990s, researchers attempted to see whether these results could apply to humans.

A major problem arose here. Under strict ethical rules, researchers can subject a rat to chronic stress (being held in the same spot, heat, cold, etc.) and check the effects on its brain. They can't do the same with humans—without ending up in jail! Therefore, to study the effects of chronic stress on humans, researchers used what they called "natural experiments." That is, they studied populations that were routinely subjected to chronic stress, such as people living in war zones, patients suffering from depression or post-traumatic stress disorder (a mental disorder arising after intense trauma), maltreated children, chronically stressed elderly people and so on. Researchers measured the cortisol (and sometimes the adrenaline) levels among these various groups to try to confirm the results of animal studies.

In studying these groups, researchers showed that under all these conditions, individuals reporting chronic stress produced abnormal cortisol concentrations as well as atrophy of the hippocampus and affect and cognition disorders.

Putting all the discoveries in the nineteenth and twentieth centuries together, scientists now understood that when an organism is subjected to adverse conditions, it produces adrenaline to induce the fight-or-flight response, enabling it to rally the energy needed for either of these actions. At the same time, the body also produces cortisol, which has the phenomenal property of reaching the brain and acting on the areas involved in affect and memory. This was an ecstatic moment for scientists.

But once again, a new question arose. What causes someone to produce adrenaline and cortisol in the first place? What are the conditions in the environment that result in an individual producing large quantities of these stress hormones, while someone else may produce only normal concentrations? What is the departure point for this chain of events? To answer this question, we need to go back to World War II and introduce the psychological approach to stress.

Psychology Takes Over the Notion of Stress

It's 1944, near the end of World War II, and physiologists' research on the potential benefits of cattle adrenal glands for treating septic shock and hypoxia are not generating positive results.

However, the war has produced many victims, and returning soldiers are suffering from traumatic shock (a psychological shock that we now call post-traumatic stress disorder). Military doctors wanted to be able to keep helping these soldiers, and physiologists weren't being of much use. So they turned to psychologists, hoping their research expertise could provide the answer to war's ravages on the brain. The return of soldiers from World War II and the war's effects on their mental health gave rise to the field of stress psychology.

In 1953, the U.S. Army held the first symposium on psychological stress in Washington, DC. Military staff saw the study of psychological stress as a way of maximizing the effectiveness of the armed forces in wartime. The growing need for the U.S. Army to conduct psychological research on stress resulted in this type of research moving from Montreal to the United States. The majority of psychological stress theorists still come from the United States. The military fascination with the study of psychological stress reached the point where, in 1976, nearly a third of all top researchers working on psychological stress were based at U.S. military institutions.[4]

Researchers specializing in the psychology of stress of course knew nothing about the work conducted by researchers studying physiological stress response (and vice versa). They had to go back to some of the concepts developed by Dr. Selye and apply a psychological approach to them. Psychologists also went back to meanings given to stress in the eighteenth and nineteenth centuries, when people spoke of stress as mental tension, perceived pressure or general unease. The physiological stress syndrome described by Dr. Selye was referred to as a negative psychological experience felt by an individual. This psychological experience would have to be measured, but how? Psychological researchers decided that the best way to measure individuals' psychological stress was to quantify the psychological stressors someone was subjected to over a given period.

The first stress questionnaire was developed in 1967 by two psychologists, Dr. Thomas H. Holmes and Dr. Richard H. Rahe. Their "life events" questionnaire measured the number of stressful events experienced by an individual over a period of several months.

Dr. Holmes and Dr. Rahe postulated that the more someone was exposed to stressful events, the higher the subjective stress level (perceived stress) would be, as measured by the questionnaire. The questionnaire asked questions such as "Have you recently been divorced?" or "Have you recently been in mourning?" The researchers then linked the number of stressful events experienced by a person to various physical and mental disorders such as hypertension, diabetes, colds and even accidents among children.

Psychologists greeted these questionnaires with great enthusiasm. They were easy to use in clinics with patients who said they suffered from psychological distress, and they generated substantial research in the 1970s. Widely used in clinics, the questionnaires also had the effect of bringing the notion of stress into the public domain. People who were not part of the scientific community got a better understanding of the notion of stress from filling out a questionnaire than from hearing a talk about biology. With these questionnaires, people began to see stress as a tension and a negative pressure related to difficult events in life. The development of the psychological approach guaranteed the popularity of the term *stress*. This was a highly positive aspect of this line of thinking.

However, in the late 1970s, work on "life events" questionnaires was broadly discredited by two major facts. First, researchers began criticizing the nature of events described in these questionnaires as potentially stressful. After all, who are researchers to decide that a divorce is stressful and should be categorized as such? If you never loved your husband and he tells you he wants a divorce, it's possible you would jump for joy rather than feel stressed! The questionnaires failed to take account of differences between individuals and between life experiences among the people who were responding to them.

Second, in suggesting that all people react with the same stress intensity to all stressful events, these questionnaires failed to take into account the nature of the relationship between a person and an event. It's quite plausible that different people will handle various situations in different ways (for instance, in the case of divorce just mentioned). The questionnaires thus failed to consider individual differences in how we respond to adverse events in life.

In response to these criticisms, people doing research on the psychology of stress developed new tools to take these factors into account. This led to the appearance of psychological questionnaires such as the "social readjustment questionnaire" measuring the significance given by individuals to stressful events in life, and the "daily hassle scale" measuring the accumulation of minor day-to-day troubles as stressful events. Over a 10-year period, from 1970 to 1980, more than a hundred psychological questionnaires were developed, and their results were correlated with physical and mental disorders. It was found that daily hassles are associated with diabetes. It was also found that a lack of social readjustment is an indicator of possible illness, and negative life events are associated with depression.

But at that point, it was recognized that not everyone with high scores on these questionnaires ended up with physical or mental illnesses. Researchers then wondered whether there could be personality traits that could increase some people's vulnerability (or resistance) to illness. They then rediscovered an old scientific article written in 1892 by the Canadian researcher Dr. William Osler describing how most of the patients he treated for heart problems had similar personalities, characterized by brusqueness and ambition. This question was taken up again in the 1950s by two doctors, Meyer Friedman and Ray Rosenman, who confirmed that the patients they treated for heart problems all shared a set of emotional reactions, which they described as Type A personality.

People with Type A personality were characterized by intense ambition, a strongly competitive spirit, hostility toward others, a constant concern with deadlines and a sense of urgency. Dr. Friedman and Dr. Rosenman referred to anyone who didn't show the pattern of Type A personality traits as a Type B personality. On the basis of these studies, the researchers concluded that people who demonstrate a Type A personality are those most likely to suffer from heart problems. This result was very popular among psychologists, who took up the concept of Type A and Type B personalities (later adding other personality types) and associated it with scores on psychological questionnaires such as the life events or daily hassles questionnaires. The overall results from these studies showed significant links between Type A personality and stress questionnaire scores. In 1991, however, after nearly 40 years of research on Type A personality and its link with heart problems, the concept fell into disuse as a result of new scientific data. (This is discussed at greater length in Chapter 8 on the link between personality and stress.)

Although research on the psychology of stress has provided worthwhile findings on the connection between life events, personality and the risk of developing physical and mental illnesses, there were two basic problems with this type of research. First, none of the stress questionnaires developed by psychologists took account of how an individual dealt with the stress experienced in an event. Thus, each event was seen as stressful for everyone, regardless of the differences inherent to each of us.

The second problem was that although the overall work conducted on the psychology of stress showed a clear link between exposure to stressful events and certain illnesses, no psychological researcher had managed to describe the exact mechanism through which interpretation of a potentially stressful event could make someone sick. Discovery of the missing link between the psychology of stress and the biology of stress would have to await the arrival of two key researchers, Dr. Richard Lazarus and Dr. John Mason.

Each Person Handles Stressors Differently

Dr. Lazarus undertook his research at the end of World War II after serving in the army. He soon observed that the way someone reacted to a stressful situation could be quite different from the way someone else reacted to a similar situation. However, most psychological studies of stress failed to take this into account.

Dr. Lazarus attributed this failure to the assertion by the behaviorist movement at the time that all behavior could be understood by the presence of a stimulus (S) and an appropriate response (R). Each stimulus always led to the same response. Dr. Lazarus rejected this idea. He suggested instead that between the stimulus (S) and the response (R), there is an organism (O) that has a life history, a personality and emotions. As a result of all these factors, any individual, when confronted with a stimulus, will first appraise the stimulus based on his or her life history, personality and emotions. Accordingly, the resulting response will not necessarily be the same for all individuals. To understand stress better it was necessary to understand the variables forming the basis of this transaction between the individual and the environment. He called this the "stress appraisal model."

Dr. Lazarus started from the premise that stress is a response that's specific to each of us, depending on our capacity to deal with a particular stressor. Dr. Lazarus saw stress as a "transaction" between an individual and a situation—a little bit like people lining up to use the same ATM but for different operations: deposits, withdrawals, updates and so on. Each person interprets whether or not a situation is stressful on the basis of their personal history, personality and emotions. Dr. Lazarus thus defined stress as the appraisal of a given situation based on each person's own characteristics (resources). In handling a situation, an individual will make an unconscious primary appraisal: is the situation threatening? If it is, the individual moves on to a secondary appraisal: do I have the resources to cope with this demand? An individual who concludes that he or she lacks the ability will then feel psychological stress.

In his years of research, Dr. Lazarus extended his area of study to find out about the extent to which coping mechanisms could have an impact on the emotions felt in adverse situations. During the 1960s, he undertook a set of studies in which he showed participants a film on a negative theme and measured individuals' stress perception. One of these films showed the circumcision of a young man during a rite of passage in a primitive society. In studying the subjective stress experienced by a participant, Dr. Lazarus showed that the level of stress experienced depended on the strategy the participant used to "cope" with this hard-to-watch film.

For example, he observed that the subjective stress response was lower when participants used a denial strategy, telling themselves that the young man in the film was happy to go through this rite of passage. The same effect was observed when participants made an effort to detach themselves from the film's content (which is what most of us do naturally when we cover our eyes with our hands while watching a horror movie!). Through this type of study, Dr. Lazarus showed that the way individuals interpret a situation will have a clear impact on their perception of a situation as stressful and on their capacity to cope with this situation.

Dr. Lazarus's studies were the most important in the history of the psychology of stress. His model helped move beyond simple questionnaires that saw stress as universal and thought it could be quantified through simple life events. Lazarus's model led to an understanding that between an adverse situation and a stress response there is an individual coping with this situation based on his or her life history, personality and emotions.

However, although highly regarded in the field of psychology, Dr. Lazarus's model was also criticized by many researchers. The first criticism of the proposed model was that Dr. Lazarus seemed to think people are aware of their behavior when they cope with a stressful situation, wondering whether they have the resources to deal with it. We know through experience that this isn't always the case and that we can undergo a powerful stress response without really knowing what's stressing us.

The second criticism is that although Dr. Lazarus strongly criticized stress questionnaires, he himself devised and use a broad array of psychological questionnaires intended to measure individuals' coping abilities. These questionnaires are highly complex and measure many different concepts related to the notion of coping. It's not clear to what extent they can really provide a better understanding of what induces an initial stress response.

The final criticism of Dr. Lazarus's model is that although it contributed greatly to showing that an understanding of stress requires taking into account individual differences in the capacity to cope with each adverse situation, it never provided an indication of the mechanism through which a negative interpretation of a situation could produce a stress response and how this stress response could lead to physical or mental disorders, or both. Demonstrating this would require yet another researcher—one who, for the first time in the history of stress science, was able to put biological stress data together with psychological data.

The Crossroads: Psychology Meets Biology

This brings us to the early 1970s. Stress research is advancing along two different tracks. On one side, researchers specializing in the biology of stress are showing that when an animal is subjected to adverse conditions such as intense heat or cold, two stress hormones, adrenaline and cortisol, are produced. At the same time, researchers specializing in the psychology of stress are showing that, to feel subjective stress as assessed on a questionnaire, an individual has to deal with a situation as being potentially threatening. The two areas of research are completely separate from each other, and results from one area are never transmitted to the other.

However, one researcher, Dr. John Mason, set out to learn about both of these scientific fields and draw links between them. Dr. Mason understood that the weakness of the psychological approach to stress lay in the absence of objective measurement of the stress response. As a researcher working in the biology of stress, Dr. Mason knew about hormonal measurement. At that point, stress hormones, especially cortisol, could easily be measured in urine.[5] He also knew that according to Dr. Selye's model any adverse condition should lead to production of cortisol—what he called the body's nonspecific response. Dr. Mason wondered whether this was really the case.

Dr. Selye had always used physical stressors (heat, intense cold, shocks and so on) in his experiments and never thought of testing the power of psychological stressors on the physiological stress response. Dr. Mason noted that it's extremely difficult to subject animals to adverse physical conditions such as heat or intense cold without these conditions also inducing concomitant psychological effects such as pain, fear or discomfort in the animal. Given this, might it be possible that the results obtained by Dr. Selye and his colleagues could be linked to the psychological aspect of the adverse conditions to which they subjected their animals rather than to the purely physical aspect? Looking at some of the principles in Dr. Lazarus's transactional model, Dr. Mason began to wonder whether the stress response is really so nonspecific to any form of stimulation. In other words, could it be, as Dr. Lazarus suggested, that the stress response could be specific to certain psychological conditions or characteristics of a situation?

At this point, Dr. Mason remembered a set of experiments he had conducted with monkeys many years earlier. In those experiments, Dr. Mason had studied the effects of hunger on monkeys' stress response. Pushing his research further, he chose eight monkeys and stopped feeding two of them, without changing their environment. The animal-care worker entered the area reserved for the monkeys several times a day to feed the six monkeys in the control group and did not feed the two other monkeys being experimented on (hunger effect). As expected, Dr. Mason observed that the two monkeys he had deprived of food showed a rise in cortisol, which he attributed to the adverse condition of hunger.

However, he also observed that the behavior of the monkeys deprived of food changed dramatically when the animal-care worker entered the reserved area in the cages to feed the other six monkeys. The monkeys deprived of food seemed to become uncomfortable and produced loud vocal sounds.

He then decided to repeat his initial experiment, but this time he placed the monkeys deprived of food in a different room, where they couldn't see the animal-care worker feed the monkeys in the control group. To his great surprise, he found that, in this case, the monkeys deprived of food didn't show a rise in cortisol! Thus, his earlier attribution of the rise in cortisol to the adverse condition of hunger (physical stress) was an erroneous conclusion. In fact, this rise was due to the "psychological" aspect of the situation—the monkeys deprived of food seeing their fellow creatures being fed while they themselves were not.

Following this discovery, Dr. Mason and his colleagues undertook a set of experiments in an effort to discover which psychological characteristics of a situation would induce a biological stress response. The fusion of the two approaches to stress was born.

From 1960 to 1980, an impressive number of experiments were undertaken with animals and humans to seek a better understanding of the psychological aspects of a situation that can induce a biological stress response. Stress hormone levels were measured in all sorts of life or work conditions that could potentially be stressful. For example, researchers studied stress hormones among air traffic controllers, police officers, air force pilots, people in a weightless state, students the day before an exam, people who would be undergoing an operation and on and on and on!

I like to describe one of these experiments in particular because I see it as highly revealing of the fusion of the two approaches and the phenomenal discoveries this has generated. When you learn about this study, you'll slowly begin to put the pieces of the puzzle together and understand better what generates biological stress response among humans.

As part of the study, the researchers set out to measure stress hormones in people who would be skydiving for the first time in their lives to gain a better understanding of what, in jumping with a parachute, can induce cortisol production. They began the study by measuring the cortisol in participants' urine several minutes before their first jump. Cortisol levels at that point were found to be very high. They concluded that skydiving was a stressor because it led to an increase in cortisol. However, the researchers had the sensible idea of measuring cortisol levels among the novices' trainers, who would also be jumping several minutes later. They found that the trainers showed no increase in cortisol before skydiving. A problem. It could not be concluded that skydiving was stressful because, although the novices showed an increase in cortisol just before the jump, this was not observed in the trainers.

They then decided to continue the study, and they measured the novices' stress hormones 24 hours before their first parachute jump.

They found no increase in cortisol. However, when they measured stress hormones in the novices' trainers 24 hours before the jump, they found that the trainers showed an increase in stress hormones.

Through this experiment, the researchers had shown that the different characteristics of both a situation and an individual would result in that individual producing, or not producing, a stress response in a *potentially* adverse condition. The word *potentially* is very important in this context. Dr. Selye and his colleagues in the field of biology believed that any adverse condition would produce a stress response. Dr. Mason proved the contrary, using Dr. Lazarus's model. He showed that a situation will induce a stress response if, and only if, the individual sees a characteristic in this situation that can be interpreted as adverse or threatening. Thus, no situation is adverse in and of itself. It's our interpretation of it that can make it adverse or not. But what, in a particular situation, results in our interpreting the situation as adverse or not adverse?

Dr. Mason came up with the answer. By reading every study in which stress hormones were measured under various conditions. Dr. Mason made one of stress science's most important discoveries of the twentieth century. Examining the stress responses noted in all these studies, he found a common denominator in all instances where researchers reported a rise in stress hormones. These situations had to involve at least one of four characteristics. This led him to discover the four psychological characteristics of a situation that— regardless of who you are, regardless of your gender, age or job—will result in your producing a biological stress response (production of stress hormones) in every instance.

In every instance! He also observed that a situation doesn't necessarily have to include all four characteristics to induce a stress response, but that the more these characteristics are involved in a situation, the higher the production of stress hormones.

That moment in history was the starting point for this book. Now you know the rest. However, if you've decided to start with this history of stress science, I wish you happy reading!

Appendix 2
References

Chapter 1: Do You Know the Meaning of Stress?

Lupien SJ, McEwen BS, Gunnar MR, Heim C (2009). Effects of stress throughout the lifespan on the brain, behaviour and cognition. *Nat Rev Neurosci* 10: 434–445.

Lupien SJ, Pilgrim K (2005). Conceptions and misconceptions of stress. *Internal Reports of the Centre for Studies on Human Stress:* 1–14.

Chapter 3: Acute Stress to Help Us Survive

Lupien SJ, Ouellet-Morin I, Hupbach A, Walker D, Tu MT, Buss C, Pruessner J, McEwen BS (2006). Beyond the stress concept: Allostatic load—a developmental biological and cognitive perspective. In: *Developmental psychopathology* (Cicchetti D, Cohen DJ, eds.), pp. 784–809. New York: Wiley.

McEwen BS, Wingfield JC (2003). The concept of allostasis in biology and biomedicine. *Hormones and Behavior* 43: 2–15.

Chapter 4: The Long and Winding Road to Chronic Stress

Aerni A, Traber R, Hock C, Roozendaal B, Schelling G, Papassotiropoulos A, Nitsch RM, Schnyder U, de Quervain DJ (2004). Low-dose cortisol for symptoms of posttraumatic stress disorder. *Am J Psychiatry* 161: 1488–1490.

Anagnostis P, Athyros VG, Tziomalos K, Karagiannis A, Mikhailidis DP (2009). Clinical review: The pathogenetic role of cortisol in the metabolic syndrome: A hypothesis. *J Clin Endocrinol Metab* 94: 2692–2701.

Cohen S, Tyrrell DA, Smith AP (1991). Psychological stress and susceptibility to the common cold. *New England Journal of Medicine* 325: 606–612.

Dallman MF, la Fleur SE, Pecoraro NC, Gomez F, Houshyar H, Akana SF (2004). Minireview: glucocorticoids—food intake, abdominal obesity, and wealthy nations in 2004. *Endocrinology* 145: 2633–2638.

Epel ES, McEwen B, Seeman T, Matthews K, Castellazzo G, Brownell KD, Bell J, Ickovics JR (2000). Stress and body shape: stress-induced cortisol secretion is consistently greater among women with central fat. *Psychosom Med* 62: 623–632.

Lesperance F, Frasure-Smith N (2000). Depression in patients with cardiac disease: A practical review. *J Psychosom Res* 48: 379–391.

McEwen BS (1998). Stress, adaptation, and disease: Allostasis and allostatic load. *Ann NY Acad Sci* 840: 33–44.

McEwen BS (2003). Mood disorders and allostatic load. *Biol Psychiatry* 54: 200–207.

Pruessner JC, Hellhammer DH, Kirschbaum C (1999). Burnout, perceived stress, and cortisol responses to awakening. *Psychosom Med* 61: 197–204.

Pruessner M, Hellhammer DH, Pruessner JC, Lupien SJ (2003). Self-reported depressive symptoms and stress levels in healthy young men: Associations with the cortisol response to awakening. *Psychosom Med* 65: 92–99.

Sachar EJ, Hellman L, Roffwarg HP, Halpern FS, Fukushima DK, Gallagher TF (1973). Disrupted 24-hour patterns of cortisol secretion in psychotic depression. *Archives of General Psychiatry* 28: 19–24.

Soravia LM, Heinrichs M, Aerni A, Maroni C, Schelling G, Ehlert U, Roozendaal B, de Quervain DJ (2006). Glucocorticoids reduce phobic fear in humans. *Proc Natl Acad Sci USA* 103: 5585–5590.

van Raalte DH, Ouwens DM, Diamant M (2009). Novel insights into glucocorticoid-mediated diabetogenic effects: towards expansion of therapeutic options? *Eur J Clin Invest* 39: 81–93.

Wallerius S, Rosmond R, Ljung T, Holm G, Bjorntorp P (2003). Rise in morning saliva cortisol is associated with abdominal obesity in men: A preliminary report. *J Endocrinol Invest* 26: 616–619.

Chapter 5: Measuring the Weight of Chronic Stress: The Allostatic Load Battery

Evans GW (2003). A multimethodological analysis of cumulative risk and allostatic load among rural children. *Developmental Psychology* 39: 924–933.

Evans GW, Kim P, Ting AH, Tesher HB, Shannis D (2007). Cumulative risk, maternal responsiveness, and allostatic load among young adolescents. *Dev Psychol* 43: 341–351.

Felitti VJ, Anda RF, Nordenberg D, Williamson DF, Spitz AM, Edwards V, Koss MP, Marks JS (1998). Relationship of childhood abuse and household dysfunction to many of the leading causes of death in adults: The Adverse Childhood Experiences (ACE) Study. *American Journal of Preventive Medicine* 14: 245–258.

Juster RP, McEwen BS, Lupien SJ (2010). Allostatic load biomarkers of chronic stress and impact on health and cognition. *Neurosci Biobehav Rev* 35: 2–16.

Juster RP, Sindi S, Marin MF, Perna A, Hashemi A, Pruessner JC, Lupien SJ. A clinical allostatic load index detects burnout physiology and symptomatology in health workers. *Psychoneuroendocrinology* 36: 797–805.

Karlamangla AS, Singer BH, McEwen BS, Rowe JW, Seeman TE (2002). Allostatic load as a predictor of functional decline: MacArthur studies of successful aging. *Journal of Clinical Epidemiology* 55: 696–710.

Kinnunen MJ, Kaprio J, Pulkkinen L (2005). Allostatic load of men and women in early middle age. *Journal of Individual Differences* 26: 20–31.

Seeman T, Glei D, Goldman N, Weinstein M, Singer B, Lin YH (2004). Social relationships and allostatic load in Taiwanese elderly and near elderly. *Soc Sci Med* 59: 2245–2257.

Seeman TE, McEwen BS, Rowe JW, Singer BH (2001). Allostatic load as a marker of cumulative biological risk: MacArthur studies of successful aging. *Proc Natl Acad Sci USA* 98: 4770–4775.

Seeman TE, Singer BH, Rowe JW, Horwitz RI, McEwen BS (1997). Price of adaptation—allostatic load and its health consequences: MacArthur studies of successful aging. *Archives of Internal Medicine* 157: 2259–2268.

Chapter 6: When Stress Affects Our Memory

Coates JM, Gurnell M, Sarnyai Z (2010). From molecule to market: Steroid hormones and financial risk-taking. *Philos Trans R Soc Lond B Biol Sci* 365: 331–343.

Coates JM, Herbert J (2008). Endogenous steroids and financial risk taking on a London trading floor. *Proc Natl Acad Sci USA* 105: 6167–6172.

Lupien SJ, Brière S (2000). Stress and memory. In: *The Encyclopedia of Stress* (Fink G, ed.), pp. 721–728. San Diego, CA: Academic Press.

Lupien SJ, Fiocco A, Wan N, Maheu F, Lord C, Schramek T, Tu MT (2005). Stress hormones and human memory function across the lifespan. *Psychoneuroendocrinology* 30: 225–242.

Lupien SJ, Gillin CJ, Hauger RL (1999). Working memory is more sensitive than declarative memory to the acute effects of corticosteroids: A dose-response study in humans. *Behavioral Neuroscience* 113: 420–430.

Lupien SJ, Lecours AR, Lussier I, Schwartz G, Nair NP, Meaney MJ (1994). Basal cortisol levels and cognitive deficits in human aging. *Journal of Neuroscience* 14: 2893–2903.

Lupien SJ, Ouellet-Morin I, Hupbach A, Walker D, Tu MT, Buss C, Pruessner J, McEwen BS (2006). Beyond the stress concept: Allostatic load—a developmental biological and cognitive perspective. In: *Developmental psychopathology* (Cicchetti D, Cohen DJ, eds.), pp. 784–809. New York: Wiley.

Maheu FS, Lupien SJ (2003). La mémoire aux prises avec les émotions et le stress: Un impact nécessairement dommageable? [Memory in the grip of emotions and stress: A necessarily harmful impact ?]. *Med Sci* (Paris) 19: 118–124.

Nyman A, Taskinen T, Grönroos M, Haataja L, Lahdetie J, Korhonen T (2010). Elements of working memory as predictors of goal-setting skills in children with attention-deficit/hyperactivity disorder. *J Learn Disabil* 43(6): 553–562.

Pilgrim K, Marin MF, Lupien SJ (2010). Attentional orienting toward social stress stimuli predicts increased cortisol responsivity to psychosocial stress irrespective of the early socioeconomic status. *Psychoneuroendocrinology* 35: 588–595.

Pollak SD, Cicchetti D, Hornung K, Reed A (2000). Recognizing emotion in faces: developmental effects of child abuse and neglect. *Developmental Psychology* 36: 679–688.

Pollak SD, Sinha P (2002). Effects of early experience on children's recognition of facial displays of emotion. *Developmental Psychology* 38: 784–791.

Pollak SD, Tolley-Schell SA (2003). Selective attention to facial emotion in physically abused children. *Journal of Abnormal Psychology* 112: 323–338.

Chapter 7: Why Are We So Stressed These Days?

Friedman SB, Chodoff P, Mason JW, Hamburg DA (1963). Behavioral observations on parents anticipating the death of a child. *Pediatrics* 32: 610–625.

Friedman SB, Mason JW, Hamburg DA (1963). Urinary 17-hydroxy-corticosteroid levels in parents of children with neoplastic disease: A study of chronic psychological stress. *Psychosom Med* 25: 364–376.

Lupien SJ (2009). Brains under stress. *Can J Psychiatry* 54: 4–5.

Lupien SJ, Maheu F, Tu M, Fiocco A, Schramek TE (2007). The effects of stress and stress hormones on human cognition: Implications for the field of brain and cognition. *Brain Cogn* 65: 209–237.

McEwen BS, Wingfield JC (2003). The concept of allostasis in biology and biomedicine. *Hormones and Behavior* 43: 2–15.

Schreir A, Evans GW (2003). Adrenal cortisol response of young children to modern and ancient stressors. *Current Anthropology* 44: 306–309.

World Health Organization (2001). *The World Health Report 2001—Mental Health: New Understanding, New Hope.* Geneva, Switzerland: Author.

Chapter 8: Stress to Match Each Personality

Burns JW, Evon D, Strain-Saloum C (1999). Repressed anger and patterns of cardio-vascular, self-report and behavioral responses: effects of harassment. *J Psychosom Res* 47: 569–581.

Burns JW, Higdon LJ, Mullen JT, Lansky D, Wei JM (1999). Relationships among patient hostility, anger expression, depression, and the working alliance in a work hardening program. *Ann Behav Med* 21: 77–82.

Chida Y, Hamer M (2008). Chronic psychosocial factors and acute physiological responses to laboratory-induced stress in healthy populations: A quantitative review of 30 years of investigations. *Psychol Bull* 134: 829–885.

Friedman HS, Booth-Kewley S (1987). The "disease-prone personality": A meta-analytic view of the construct. *Am Psychol* 42: 539–555.

Friedman M, Rosenman RH (1959). Association of specific overt behavior pattern with blood and cardiovascular findings; blood cholesterol level, blood clotting time, incidence of arcus senilis, and clinical coronary artery disease. *J Am Med Assoc* 169: 1286–1296.

Kirschbaum C, Prussner JC, Stone AA, Federenko I, Gaab J, Lintz D, Schommer N, Hellhammer DH (1995). Persistent high cortisol responses to repeated psychological stress in a subpopulation of healthy men. *Psychosom Med* 57: 468–474.

Lemogne C, Nabi H, Zins M, Cordier S, Ducimetiere P, Goldberg M, Consoli SM (2009). Hostility may explain the association between depressive mood and mortality: Evidence from the French GAZEL cohort study. *Psychother Psychosom* 79: 164–171.

Malarkey WB, Kiecolt-Glaser JK, Pearl D, Glaser R (1994). Hostile behavior during marital conflict alters pituitary and adrenal hormones. *Psychosom Med* 56: 41–51.

Pruessner JC, Baldwin MW, Dedovic K, Renwick R, Mahani NK, Lord C, Meaney M, Lupien S (2005). Self-esteem, locus of control, hippocampal volume, and cortisol regulation in young and old adulthood. *Neuroimage* 28: 815–826.

Pruessner JC, Lord C, Meaney M, Lupien S (2004). Effects of self-esteem on age-related changes in cognition and the regulation of the hypothalamic-pituitary-adrenal axis. *Ann NY Acad Sci* 1032: 186–194.

Ranjit N, Diez-Roux AV, Sanchez B, Seeman T, Shea S, Shrager S, Watson K (2009). Association of salivary cortisol circadian pattern with cynical hostility: Multi-ethnic study of atherosclerosis. *Psychosom Med* 71: 748–755.

Shekelle RB, Gale M, Ostfeld AM, Paul O (1983). Hostility, risk of coronary heart disease, and mortality. *Psychosom Med* 45: 109–114.

Chapter 9: Two Sexes, Two Types of Stress?

David DH, Lyons-Ruth K (2005). Differential attachment responses of male and female infants to frightening maternal behavior: Tend or befriend versus fight or flight? *Infant Ment Health J* 21: 1–18.

Ditzen B, Neumann ID, Bodenmann G, von Dawans B, Turner RA, Ehlert U, Heinrichs M (2007). Effects of different kinds of couple interaction on cortisol and heart rate responses to stress in women. *Psychoneuroendocrinology* 32: 565–574.

Flinn MV, England BG (1997). Social economics of childhood glucocorticoid stress response and health. *American Journal of Physical Anthropology* 102: 33–53.

Heinrichs M, Baumgartner T, Kirschbaum C, Ehlert U (2003). Social support and oxytocin interact to suppress cortisol and subjective responses to psychosocial stress. *Biol Psychiatry* 54: 1389–1398.

Heinrichs M, Neumann I, Ehlert U (2002). Lactation and stress: Protective effects of breast-feeding in humans. *Stress* 5: 195–203.

Kirschbaum C, Klauer T, Filipp SH, Hellhammer DH (1995). Sex-specific effects of social support on cortisol and subjective responses to acute psychological stress. *Psychosom Med* 57: 23–31.

Kirschbaum C, Kudielka BM, Gaab J, Schommer NC, Hellhammer DH (1999). Impact of gender, menstrual cycle phase, and oral contraceptives on the activity of the hypothalamus-pituitary-adrenal axis. *Psychosom Med* 61: 154–162.

Lupien SJ, King S, Meaney MJ, McEwen BS (2000). Child's stress hormone levels correlate with mother's socioeconomic status and depressive state. *Biol Psychiatry* 48: 976–980.

Ray S, Mishra SK, Roy AG, Das BM (2010). Menstrual characteristics: A study of the adolescents of rural and urban West Bengal, India. *Ann Hum Biol* 37(5): 668–681.

Smith AM, Loving TJ, Crockett EE, Campbell L (2009). What's closeness got to do with it? Men's and women's cortisol responses when providing and receiving support. *Psychosom Med* 71: 843–851.

Stroud LR, Salovey P, Epel ES (2002). Sex differences in stress responses: Social rejection versus achievement stress. *Biol Psychiatry* 52: 318–327.

Taylor SE, Klein LC, Lewis BP, Gruenewald TL, Gurung RA, Updegraff JA (2000). Biobehavioral responses to stress in females: Tend-and-befriend, not fight-or-flight. *Psychol Rev* 107: 411–429.

Tu MT, Lupien SJ, Walker CD (2006). Multiparity reveals the blunting effect of breast-feeding on physiological reactivity to psychological stress. *J Neuroendocrinol* 18: 494–503.

Chapter 10: Your Social Status, Your Stress

Craig W (2004). Bullying and fighting. In: *Young people in Canada: Their health and well-being* (Boyce W, ed.), pp. 87–96. Health Canada/Health Behaviour in School-Aged Children, a World Health Organization Cross-National Study.

Craig WM, Harel Y (2004). Bullying, physical fighting and victimization. In: *Young People's Health in Context: Health Behaviour in School-Aged Children (HSBC) study: International Report from the 2001/2002 survey* (Currie C, Roberts C, Morgan A, Smith R, Settertobulte W, Samdal O, Rasmussen VB, eds.), pp. 133–144. Copenhagen, Denmark: World Health Organization Regional Office for Europe.

Gruenewald TL, Kemeny ME, Aziz N (2006). Subjective social status moderates cortisol responses to social threat. *Brain Behav Immun* 20: 410–419.

Hansen AM, Hogh A, Persson R, Karlson B, Garde AH, Orbaek P (2006). Bullying at work, health outcomes, and physiological stress response. *J Psychosom Res* 60: 63–72.

Hellhammer DH, Buchtal J, Gutberlet I, Kirschbaum C (1997). Social hierarchy and adrenocortical stress reactivity in men. *Psychoneuroendocrinology* 22: 643–650.

Johnson NJ, Klee T (2007). Passive-aggressive behavior and leadership styles in organizations. *Journal of Leadership & Organizational Studies* 14: 130–142.

Kliewer W (2006). Violence exposure and cortisol responses in urban youth. *Int J Behav Med* 13: 109–120.

Kunz-Ebrecht SR, Kirschbaum C, Steptoe A (2004). Work stress, socioeconomic status and neuroendocrine activation over the working day. *Soc Sci Med* 58: 1523–1530.

Lupien SJ, King S, Meaney MJ, McEwen BS (2001). Can poverty get under your skin? Basal cortisol levels and cognitive function in children from low and high socioeconomic status. *Development & Psychopathology* 13: 651–674.

Marmot MG (2003). Understanding social inequalities in health. *Perspect Biol Med* 46: S9–23.

Safaei J (2006). Is democracy good for health? *Int J Health Serv* 36: 767–786.

Sapolsky RM (2005). The influence of social hierarchy on primate health. *Science* 308: 648–652.

Steptoe A, Kunz-Ebrecht S, Owen N, Feldman PJ, Willemsen G, Kirschbaum C, Marmot M (2003). Socioeconomic status and stress-related biological responses over the working day. *Psychosom Med* 65: 461–470.

Tangri PR (2003). *What stress costs.* Halifax, NS: Chrysalis Performance Strategies.

Vaillancourt T, Duku E, Decatanzaro D, Macmillan H, Muir C, Schmidt LA (2008). Variation in hypothalamic-pituitary-adrenal axis activity among bullied and non-bullied children. *Aggress Behav* 34: 294–305.

West P (1997). Health inequalities in the early years: Is there equalization in youth? *Soc Sci Med* 44: 833–858.

West P, Sweeting H, Young R, Kelly S (2010). The relative importance of family socio-economic status and school-based peer hierarchies for morning cortisol in youth: An exporatory study. *Soc Sci Med* 70: 1246–1253.

Chapter 11: Recognizing When You're Stressed
Kinnunen MJ, Kaprio J, Pulkkinen L (2005). Allostatic load of men and women in early middle age. *Journal of Individual Differences* 26: 20–31.

Lundberg U (1999). Coping with stress: Neuroendocrine reactions and implications for health. *Noise Health* 1: 67–74.

McEwen BS (1998). Stress, adaptation, and disease: Allostasis and allostatic load. *Ann NY Acad Sci* 840: 33–44.

McEwen BS (2000). The neurobiology of stress: From serendipity to clinical relevance. *Brain Research* 886: 172–189.

McEwen BS (2003). Mood disorders and allostatic load. *Biol Psychiatry* 54: 200–207.

McEwen BS, Stellar E (1993). Stress and the individual: Mechanisms leading to disease. *Archives of Internal Medicine* 153: 2093–2101.

Chapter 12: To Kill a Mammoth, You First Have to Know Where to Find It
Abelson JL, Khan S, Liberzon I, Erickson TM, Young EA (2008). Effects of perceived control and cognitive coping on endocrine stress responses to pharmacological acti-vation. *Biol Psychiatry* 64: 701–707.

Abelson JL, Khan S, Young EA, Liberzon I (2010). Cognitive modulation of endocrine responses to CRH stimulation in healthy subjects. *Psychoneuroendocrinology* 35: 451–459.

Are your kids NUTS about school? (2008). *Mammoth Magazine*, Issue 5. Retrieved from: http://www.humanstress.ca/documents/pdf/Mammouth%20Magazine/Mammoth_vol5_EN.pdf

Mason OJ, Brady F (2009). The psychotomimetic effects of short-term sensory depriva-tion. *J Nerv Ment Dis* 197: 783–785.

Merabet LB, Maguire D, Warde A, Alterescu K, Stickgold R, Pascual-Leone A (2004). Visual hallucinations during prolonged blindfolding in sighted subjects. *J Neuroophthalmol* 24: 109–113.

Stress at work (2007). *Mammoth Magazine*, Issue 4. Retrieved from: http://www.humanstress.ca/documents/pdf/Mammouth%20Magazine/Mammoth_vol4_EN.pdf

Vernon J, Marton T, Peterson E (1961). Sensory deprivation and hallucinations. *Science* 133: 1808–1812.

Ziskind E, Augsburg T (1962). Hallucinations in sensory deprivation: Method or mad-ness? *Science* 137: 992–993.

Chapter 13: Addressing NUTS for Adolescents
Lupien S (2008). *Programme DéStresse et Progresse*. Montreal: Centre d'études sur le stress humain.

Lupien S (2008). *DeStress for Success program*. Montreal: Centre for Studies on Human Stress.

Youths . . . the keys to changing MENTAL-ities! (2009). *Mammoth Magazine*, Issue 7. Retrieved from: http://www.humanstress.ca/documents/pdf/Mammouth%20Magazine/ Mammoth_vol7_EN.pdf

Chapter 14: Addressing NUTS for Adult Workers

France (2009). *Arrêté du 23 avril 2009 portant extension d'un accord national inter-professionnel sur le stress au travail*. JORF no. 0105 du 6 mai 2009 page 7632, texte no. 90. Retrieved from: http://www.legifrance.gouv.fr/affichTexte.do?cidTexte=JORFT EXT000020581815

Gabriel P, Liimatainen MR (2000). *Mental health in the workplace: Introduction*. Geneva, Switzerland: International Labour Office.

Korte SM, Koolhaas JM, Wingfield JC, McEwen BS (2005). The Darwinian concept of stress: Benefits of allostasis and costs of allostatic load and the trade-offs in health and disease. *Neurosci Biobehav Rev* 29: 3–38.

Leka S, Griffiths A, Cox T (2003). *Work organisation and stress: Systematic problem approaches for employers, managers and trade union representatives*. Protecting workers' health series no 3. Geneva, Switzerland: World Health Organization. Retrieved from: http://whqlibdoc.who.int/publications/2003/9241590475.pdf

Lupien SJ (2010a). *NUTS questionnaire for adults*. Montreal: Centre for Studies on Human Stress.

Lupien SJ (2010b). *Programme Stress & Compagnie*. Montreal: Centre d'études sur le stress humain.

Lupien SJ (2010c). *Questionnaire CINÉ pour les adultes*. Montreal: Centre d'études sur le stress humain.

Lupien SJ (2010d). *Stress Inc. program*. Montreal: Centre for Studies on Human Stress.

Lupien SJ, Marin MF (2007). Do stressful work environments exist, and if so, what do they look like? *Mammoth Magazine*, Issue 4, pp. 1–4. Retrieved from: http://www.human-stress.ca/documents/pdf/Mammouth%20Magazine/Mammoth_vol4_EN.pdf

Robert Half Finance & Accounting (2010). *Global financial employment monitor*. Retrieved from: http://www.roberthalffinance.com/EmployerFreeResources

Tangri PR (2003). *What stress costs*. Halifax, NS: Chrysalis Performance Strategies.

Chapter 15: Fleeing the Mammoth Can Help Us Control Our Stress

Dallman MF(1993). Adaptation of the hypothalamic-pituitary-adrenal axis to chronic stress. *Trends in Endocrinology and Metabolism* 4: 62–69.

McEwen BS, Wingfield JC (2003). The concept of allostasis in biology and biomedicine. *Hormones and Behavior* 43: 2–15.

Steptoe A, Cropley M, Griffith J, Kirschbaum C (2000). Job strain and anger expression predict early morning elevations in salivary cortisol. *Psychosom Med* 62: 286–292.

Chapter 16: The Power of Others

Cacioppo JT, Hawkley LC (2009). Perceived social isolation and cognition. *Trends Cogn Sci* 13: 447–454.

Cacioppo JT, Hawkley LC, Thisted R (2010). Perceived social isolation makes me sad: 5-year cross-lagged analyses of loneliness and depressive symptomatology in the Chicago Health, Aging,and Social Relations Study. *Psychology and Aging* 25: 453–463.

Charney DC (2004). Psychobiological mechanisms of resilience and vulnerability: Implications for successful adaptation to extreme stress. *Am J Psychiatry* 161: 195–216.

Cohen S (2004). Social relationships and health. *Am Psychol* 59: 676–684.

Cusack O, Smith E (1984). *Pets and the elderly: The therapeutic bond*. NewYork: Haworth Press.

Hawkley LC, Thisted RA, Masi CM, Cacioppo JT (2010). Loneliness predicts increased blood pressure: 5-year cross-lagged analyses in middle-aged and older adults. *Psychology and Aging* 25: 132–141.

Katcher AH, Friedmann E, Beck AM, Lynch J (1983). *New perspectives on our lives with companion animals*. Philadelphia: University of Pensylvania Press.

McClelland DC, Kirshnit C (1988). The effect of motivational arousal through films on salivary immunoglobulin A. *Psychology and Health* 2: 31–52.

Odendaal JS, Meintjes RA (2003). Neurophysiological correlates of affiliative behaviour between humans and dogs. *Vet J* 165: 296–301.

Seeman TE (1996). Social ties and health: The benefits of social integration. *Annals of Epidemiology* 6: 442–451.

Seeman TE, Berkman LF, Kohout F, Lacroix A, Glynn R, Blazer D (1993). Intercommunity variations in the association between social ties and mortality in the elderly: A comparative analysis of three communities. *Annals of Epidemiology* 3: 325–335.

Seeman T, Glei D, Goldman N, Weinstein M, Singer B, Lin YH (2004). Social relationships and allostatic load in Taiwanese elderly and near elderly. *Soc Sci Med* 59: 2245–2257.

Seeman TE, Lusignolo TM, Albert M, Berkman L (2001). Social relationships, social support, and patterns of cognitive aging in healthy, high-functioning older adults: MacArthur studies of successful aging. *Health Psychology* 20: 243–255.

Seeman TE, McEwen BS (1996). Impact of social environment characteristics on neuroendocrine regulation. *Psychosom Med* 58: 459–471.

Seeman TE, Singer BH, Ryff CD, Dienberg Love G, Levy-Storms L (2002). Social relationships, gender, and allostatic load across two age cohorts. *Psychosom Med* 64: 395–406.

Uchino BN, Cacioppo JT, Kiecolt-Glaser JK (1996). The relationship between social support and physiological processes: A review with emphasis on underlying mechanisms and implications for health. *Psychological Bulletin* 119: 488–531.

Viau R, Arsenault-Lapierre G, Fecteau S, Champagne N, Walker CD, Lupien S (2010). Effect of service dogs on salivary cortisol secretion in autistic children. *Psychoneuroendocrinology* 35: 1187–1193.

Chapter 17: Your Body Is Your Most Effective Ally

Berk LS, Tan SA, Fry WF, Napier BJ, Lee JW, Hubbard RW, Lewis JE, Eby WC (1989). Neuroendocrine and stress hormone changes during mirthful laughter. *American Journal of the Medical Sciences* 298: 390–396.

Bernardi L, Piepoli MF (2001). [Autonomic nervous system adaptation during physical exercise]. *Ital Heart J* Suppl 2: 831–839.

Bernardi L, Porta C, Casucci G, Balsamo R, Bernardi NF, Fogari R, Sleight P (2009). Dynamic interactions between musical, cardiovascular, and cerebral rhythms in humans. *Circulation* 119: 3171–3180.

Bernardi L, Porta C, Gabutti A, Spicuzza L, Sleight P (2001). Modulatory effects of respiration. *Auton Neurosci* 90: 47–56.

Bernardi L, Sleight P, Bandinelli G, Cencetti S, Fattorini L, Wdowczyc-Szulc J, Lagi A (2001). Effect of rosary prayer and yoga mantras on autonomic cardiovascular rhythms: comparative study. *BMJ* 323: 1446–1449.

Budde H, Voelcker-Rehage C, Pietrassyk-Kendziorra S, Machado S, Ribeiro P, Arafat AM (2010). Steroid hormones in the saliva of adolescents after different exercise intensities and their influence on working memory in a school setting. *Psychoneuroendocrinology* 35: 382–391.

Dedert EA, Studts JL, Weissbecker I, Salmon PG, Banis PL, Sephton SE (2004). Religiosity may help preserve the cortisol rhythm in women with stress-related illness. *Int J Psychiatry Med* 34: 61–77.

Gerra G, Zaimovic A, Franchini D, Palladino M, Giucastro G, Reali N, Maestri D, Caccavari R, Delsignore R, Brambilla F (1998). Neuroendocrine responses of healthy volunteers to "techno-music": relationships with personality traits and emotional state. *Int J Psychophysiol* 28: 99–111.

Grape C, Sandgren M, Hansson LO, Ericson M, Theorell T (2003). Does singing promote well-being ?: An empirical study of professional and amateur singers during a singing lesson. *Integr Physiol Behav Sci* 38: 65–74.

Hand AE, Lai B, Juster RP, Pilgrim K, Sindi S, Lupien SJ (2007). A psychoneuroendocrine analysis of consumers and non-consumers of self-help books. *Proceedings of the International Society of Psychoneuroendocrinology* 14: 22.

Hebert S, Beland R, Dionne-Fournelle O, Crete M, Lupien SJ (2005). Physiological stress response to video-game playing: the contribution of built-in music. *Life Sci* 76: 2371–2380.

Khalfa S, Bella SD, Roy M, Peretz I, Lupien SJ (2003). Effects of relaxing music on salivary cortisol level after psychological stress. *Ann NY Acad Sci* 999: 374–376.

Kiecolt-Glaser JK, Christian L, Preston H, Houts CR, Malarkey WB, Emery CF, Glaser R (2010). Stress, inflammation, and yoga practice. *Psychosom Med* 72: 113–121.

Kreutz G, Bongard S, Rohrmann S, Hodapp V, Grebe D (2004). Effects of choir singing or listening on secretory immunoglobulin A, cortisol, and emotional state. *J Behav Med* 27: 623–635.

Krul J, Girbes AR (2009). Experience of health-related problems during house parties in the Netherlands: Nine years of experience and three million visitors. *Prehosp Disaster Med* 24: 133–139.

Lai JC, Chong AM, Siu OT, Evans P, Chan CL, Ho RT (2010). Humor attenuates the cortisol awakening response in healthy older men. *Biol Psychol* 84: 375–380.

Lyons DM, Parker KJ (2007). Stress inoculation-induced indications of resilience in monkeys. *J Trauma Stress* 20: 423–433.

Lyons DM, Parker KJ, Katz M, Schatzberg AF (2009). Developmental cascades linking stress inoculation, arousal regulation, and resilience. *Front Behav Neurosci* 3: 32.

Parker KJ, Buckmaster CL, Sundlass K, Schatzberg AF, Lyons DM (2006). Maternal mediation, stress inoculation, and the development of neuroendocrine stress resistance in primates. *Proc Natl Acad Sci USA* 103: 3000–3005.

Parker KJ, Rainwater KL, Buckmaster CL, Schatzberg AF, Lindley SE, Lyons DM (2007). Early life stress and novelty seeking behavior in adolescent monkeys. *Psychoneuroendocrinology* 32: 785–792.

Rimmele U, Seiler R, Marti B, Wirtz PH, Ehlert U, Heinrichs M (2009). The level of physical activity affects adrenal and cardiovascular reactivity to psychosocial stress. *Psychoneuroendocrinology* 34: 190–198.

Salerno S (2005). *SHAM: How the self-help movement made america helpless.* New York: Crown.

West J, Otte C, Geher K, Johnson J, Mohr DC (2004). Effects of Hatha yoga and African dance on perceived stress, affect, and salivary cortisol. *Annals of Behavioral Medicine* 28: 114–118.

Appendix 1: History of the Science of Stress

Cannon W (1920). *Bodily changes in pain, hunger, fear and rage.* Facsimile reprint, 2008. Whitefish, MT: Kessinger.

Cannon W (1929). The wisdom of the body. *Physiological Review* 9: 399–431.

Cooper CL, Dewe P (2005). Stress: A brief history. Boston, MA: Blackwell.

Ingle D (1975). *Edward C. Kendall, 1886–1972: A biographical memoir.* Washington, DC: National Academy of Sciences.

Gaunt R, Eversole WJ (1949). Notes on the history of the adrenal cortical problem. *Ann NY Acad Sci* 50: 511–521.

Mason JW (1968a). A review of psychoendocrine research on the pituitary-adrenal cortical system. *Psychosom Med* 30: 576–607.

Mason JW (1968b). A review of psychoendocrine research on the sympathetic-adrenal medullary system. *Psychosom Med* 30: 631–653.

Mason JW (1971). A re-evaluation of the concept of non-specificity in stress theory. *Journal of Psychiatry Research* 8: 323–333.

Selye H (1936). A syndrome produced by diverse nocuous agents. *Nature* 138: 32.

Selye H (1975a). Confusion and controversy in the stress field. *Journal of Human Stress* 1: 37–44.

Selye H (1975b). Stress and distress. *Comprehensive Therapy* 1: 9–13.

Selye H (1976). *The stress of life.* New York: McGraw-Hill.

Viner R (1999). Putting stress in life: Hans Selye and the making of stress theory. *Social Studies of Science* 29: 391–410.

Wade N (1981). *The Nobel duel.* New York: Anchor Press.

Notes

Chapter 2: Stress Is Really NUTS

1. Any almond-shaped organ can be referred to as "amygdaloid." The amygdaloid nucleus I'm talking about here is a very small structure right in the middle of the brain that plays an important role in fear behavior and the regulation of emotions.

Chapter 3: Acute Stress to Help Us Survive

1. Evolutionary biology is a research field in which scientists seek to understand how the human species has evolved and what factors have led it to evolve in one way rather than another.

2. Animal studies also describe a third possible response to a threat, known as the *freeze response*. Faced with a very serious threat, such as an approaching predator, an animal can "freeze in place"—stop moving and almost stop breathing. This drastic response allows the animal to survive, because the predator thinks the animal is dead and leaves the scene. Although the freeze response is observed in animals, it's not generally included in basic models of physiological stress because it occurs only in conditions that go beyond "normal" stress and are clearly traumatizing for the animal. In addition, if the freeze response were the norm rather than an exception, we would not have survived the mammoth—you've got to admit that it's not very practical to "freeze" in the face of a mammoth coming at you at top speed. Nevertheless, it's interesting to

note that the freeze response is sometimes observed in humans in very intense conditions of stress—in other words, in traumatic conditions.

Chapter 4: The Long and Winding Road to Chronic Stress

1. It's now possible to measure the concentration of stress hormones in saliva. However, stress hormone measurements in saliva are still at the experimental stage and cannot yet be used clinically. People often contact me to ask whether I can measure the stress hormones in their saliva to tell them whether or not they're stressed. Unfortunately, we're not yet in a position to do that. But I hope that by reading this book, you'll learn to recognize when you're stressed—without taking a saliva sample!

2. This discovery was made by my friend Dr. Mary Dallman of the University of California at San Diego. Dr. Dallman is a pioneer in the scientific study of the effects of stress on obesity. Through her studies, she achieved a clear understanding of the mechanism through which chronic stress can lead to abdominal obesity. Now "retired," she still crisscrosses the globe to work with researchers specializing in stress science.

Chapter 6: When Stress Affects Our Memory

1. During pregnancy, a woman doesn't menstruate for at least ten months. Afterward, if the mother breastfeeds her child, menstruation doesn't resume, so that the woman is infertile and can't procreate again during that time. Our grandmothers often used breastfeeding as a method of contraception!

2. Unless, of course, you decide that the information coming out of the meeting is completely irrelevant, in which case you'll perform very well on the BlackBerry!

Chapter 8: Stress to Match Each Personality

1. On the basis of these criteria, I officially announce that I have a Type Double A personality!

2. You've got to admit that it would not look good for a researcher specializing in stress to die of a heart attack! However, we now know that heart attacks have many causes and that genetic factors are as important as psychological ones. I thus claim the right to die of a heart attack with my head held high!

3. And since I don't have this personality trait, my survival is assured!

Chapter 9: Two Sexes, Two Types of Stress?

1. This is no longer the case, since the incidence of cardiovascular disorders in women is now just as high as it is in men.

2. See Appendix 1: History of the Science of Stress.

3. This may explain why a woman will often run to the telephone to call her mother when she's going through a stressful period!

4.   Hence, oxytocin may be administered to a pregnant woman who has reached her due date to "induce labor." Studies have also shown that a woman's orgasm induces increased oxytocin production. Some researchers maintain that oxytocin production during orgasm could explain why a woman who has an orgasm late in pregnancy will sometimes go into labor sooner than expected!

Chapter 10: Your Social Status, Your Stress

1.   At least not very often.

2.   I think that's the moment when I should measure stress hormones in the child's parents!

Chapter 12: To Kill a Mammoth, You First Have to Know Where to Find It

1.   Resilience can be defined as "the capacity to bounce back after trauma."

2.   I once had to work on a Plan U to deal with a situation that I found very stressful.

3.   Here I speak from personal experience.

Chapter 14: Addressing NUTS for Adult Workers

1.   See Chapter 10: Your Social Status, Your Stress.

Chapter 16: The Power of Others

1.   See Chapter 5: Measuring the Weight of Chronic Stress: The Allostatic Load Battery.

2.   Unfortunately, Dr. Viau died while the results of the study were being analyzed. With the help of his colleagues at the MIRA Foundation in Quebec, my team and I finished analyzing the data and published the scholarly article in his name.

Chapter 17: Your Body Is Your Most Effective Ally

1.   Ladies and gentlemen, at this point my publisher has asked me, and I've agreed, to give you the name of this now-famous pooch. His name is Jim and he's an 8-year-old blond Labrador retriever. Last week he broke his leg—no more walks for Jim for two months. But guess what! I still walk every morning and evening, day after day, to deconstruct and reconstruct my stressors. Each time I leave, Jim looks at me with sad eyes. To help him manage his stress, I pat his head! And of course, I'm waiting impatiently for the day when we can walk together once again like the good old human-animal pair we've become.

Appendix 1: History of the Science of Stress

1.   Hans Selye, *Stress without Distress* (Toronto: McClelland & Stewart, 1974).

2.   One of Dr. Selye's students, Dr. Roger Guillemin, later discovered a large number of hormones by analyzing sheep tissues taken from local abattoirs. Dr. Guillemin

competed fiercely with his colleague Andrew Schally—who used pig tissues, also taken from abattoirs—to discover new hormones. This competition bore significant fruit in the form of many new hormones discovered by these two researchers. Ironically, in 1977 the two bitter enemies learned that they had been jointly awarded the Nobel Prize in medicine for their major discoveries. Despite their fierce rivalry in research, they shared the supreme prize for their efforts.

3.   It's no surprise that during World War II, ethical standards for scientific research were not as strict as they are now!

4.   Military Stress Laboratory of the U.S. Army; Naval Medical Research Unit (Bethesda, MD); Stress and Hypertension Clinic of the Naval Gun Factory (Washington, DC); Neuropsychiatry section of the Walter Reed Army Medical Center (Washington, DC); Stress Medicine Division, Naval Health Research Center (San Diego, CA).

5.   Today it's even easier to measure stress hormones, because they can be measured in blood and saliva samples or even in hair. However, the measurement techniques used in scientific research cannot yet be applied in clinical settings.

Index

A

abdominal obesity, 36–37,
   105, 160
Abelson, James, 111
absolute stress, 28–29, 67, 69–70
ACTH (adrenocorticotropic
   hormone)
   in Cushing's syndrome, 38
   function of, 24
   in stress research, 173–174
acute stress
   effect of, 21
   importance of, 23–24
   physical response, 25–26
   recognition of, 105–106
   relevant information during,
      52–55
   survival and, 27–28
   transition to chronic stress,
      31–33
   vigilance with, 50
Addison, Thomas, 174

Addison's disease, 173, 177
adolescents
   belly breathing, 155–156
   effect of high allostatic load, 46
   effect of social status, 99–101
   effect of socioeconomic status,
      97–99
   intimidation, 101–104
   NUTS factors in, 13–15,
      119–125, 126
adrenal glands
   function of, 24
   reaction to stressors, 173
   research into, 174, 176–177
adrenaline
   allostatic load, 45
   discovery of, 174
   effect on cardiovascular
      system, 37
   function of, 24–25, 174–175, 182
   production of, 24
   research into, 176–177

adults
control of stress response, 68–69
NUTS factors in, 15–19
perception of stress in, 4
affiliation behavior, 81–84, 85–86
African dance class, 157
alcohol, 106–108
allostatic load, 43–48, 147
alternative plans, 110–111
altruism, 148–150
anger, 144
animals, 150–152
anxiety, 75–76, 135, 137–138
apple-shaped women, 36–37
athletes, 160
avoidance, 141–144

B
baboons, 89–90
belly breathing, 154–159
Berk, Lee, 163
Bernardi, Luciano, 157
biology of stress, 188–191
Björntorp, Per, 37
BlackBerry effect, 58–59
blood pressure, 45
body
allostatic load, 43–48
belly breathing, 154–159
exercise, 159–162
laughter, 162–163
response to demands on,
169–170, 171–172
response to stress, 153–154
stress inoculation, 163–165
books, self-help, 166–167
Borman, M.C., 180
brain
adolescent development, 13
distinguishing types of stress, 67
effect of acute stress, 25–26
effect of stress, 19, 29
function of, 7, 24

reaction to stress hormones,
180–182
stimulation of, 115–116
See also memory
breastfeeding, 85–86
breathing, 154–159
Brengden, Mara, 103
Brown-Séquard, Charles-Édouard,
174
Budde, Henning, 161
bullying, 101–104
burnout, 33–35, 63
Burns, John W., 75

C
Cacioppo, John T., 146
Canada, cost of stress, 127
Cannon, Walter, 79, 174, 175–176
carbohydrates, 67–68
cardiovascular disease, 37, 66,
72–75
cardiovascular system, 37, 66
central obesity, 36
Centre for Studies on Human
Stress, 119–120
Charney, Dennis, 149–150
children
with attention disorders, 52
diabetes, 39
effect of abuse, 64
effect of parental stress, 87–88
NUTS factors in, 11–13
overprotection of, 165
perception of stress in, 5–6
self-esteem, 77
cholesterol, 37–38, 44–48
chronic stress
body's response, 35–39, 66–68
cortisol concentrations in, 182
effect of, 22
effect on immune system,
39–42
measurement of, 43–48

recognition of, 106–108
relevant information during, 62–64
stages of, 33–42
stressor sensitivity and, 144
transition from acute stress, 31–33
Coates, John, 54
Cohen, Sheldon, 41–42
computer-based social networks, 147–148
contraceptive pills, 80
control, lack of, 9, 10–11, 69, 77
cortisol
    allostatic load, 44–48
    in burnout, 33–34
    in Cushing's syndrome, 38
    discovery of, 177, 178–179
    effect of stress on, 189–190
    function of, 24–25, 181–182
    gender-specific responses, 78–79
    in intimidation, 101–102
    production of, 24
    in stock traders, 54
cortisone
    side effects, 179–180
    synthesis of, 178–179
couples
    cynical hostility in, 73–74
    effect on stress response, 82–85
CRF (corticotrophin-releasing factor), 173–174
CRH (corticotrophin-releasing hormone), 24
Cushing's syndrome, 38, 180
cynical hostility, 73–74

D
Dallman, Mary, 144
dance, 162
David, Daryn H., 88

deconstructing source of stress, 109–110, 120–122
depression
    cardiovascular system and, 37
    childhood conditions and, 64
    cortisol levels in, 33
    increase in, 66
    stigma, 63
DeStress for Success program, 120–125, 126, 155–156
developmental disorders, 151–152
diabetes, 39, 105
diaphragmic breathing, 154–159
diseases, nonspecific responses, 169–170
distress, 29–30
Ditzen, Beate, 84
divided attention, 55–62
divorce, effect on children, 12–13
dominance in social hierarchies, 89–91, 93–97

E
eagles, 138–140
ego, 9, 10, 69
elderly
    control of stress response, 68–69
    effect of high allostatic load, 46
    NUTS factors in, 19–20
    perception of stress in, 5
    social support, 147–148
emotional support, 146
employees. See work environment
empowerment approach, 166
energy
    mobilization of, 154
    reduction of, 159–162
    reserves, 67–68
Epel, Elissa, 36
eustress, 29–30
Evans, Gary, 46
exercise, 159–162

F
females. *See* gender
fight-or-flight response
    choosing the right response,
        141–144
    development of theory, 175
    gender and, 81–84, 88
    hormones involved, 24–25
flight, 141–144
Flinn, Mark V., 87
flu vaccine, 41–42
Frasure-Smith, Nancy, 37
Freudenberger, Herbert, 34
Friedman, Meyer, 72, 185
Friedman, Stanford B., 69

G
gastric pain, 106
gender
    adolescents, 100
    effect of hormones, 80–81, 85–86
    parenting roles, 86–88
    physical activity, 161–162
    reduced workplace effectiveness,
        131
    response to intimidation,
        102–103
    stress response models, 81–84
    studies of, 78–79
    support of others, 84–85
Gerra, Gilberto, 158
glass of water stage, 108
glucocorticoids, 179
glucose, 38–39, 43–44
glycated hemoglobin, 45
Gruenewald, Tara L., 95
Guillemin, Roger, 173

H
Hansen, Åse Marie, 101
Harris, Geoffrey, 173
health problems, stress-related,
    65–66

heart, 37, 66
heart disease, 37, 66, 72–75
Hébert, Sylvie, 159
Hellhammer, Dirk, 94
Hench, Philip S., 178–179
Herbert, Joe, 54
hippocampus, 77, 180–181
Holmes, Thomas H., 183–184
homes, move from, 19–20
hormones, discovery of, 170–171
    See also specific hormones
hostility, 72–75, 76, 135–137, 138
hypothalamus, 24, 162, 173

I
immune system
    effect of altruism, 148–149
    effect of chronic stress, 39–42
individuals
    interpretation of situations, 69–70
    interpretation of stress, 29–30
    reaction to stressors, 186–188
information, seeking for
    control, 70–71
informational support, 146
instrumental support, 146
insulin resistance, 38–39
interleukin-6, 45
International Labour
    Organization (ILO), 127
Internet, 147–148
interpretation of situations,
    69–70
intimidation, 101–104

J
Jackson, Susan E., 34
Juster, Robert Paul, 46

K
Kendall, Edward C., 177, 178–179
Kiecolt-Glaser, Janice, 73–74
Kinnunen, Marja-Liisa, 46

Kirschbaum, Clemens, 77, 78, 80, 82
Kliewer, Wendy, 102
Korte, S. Mechiel, 138

L
laughter, 162–163
Lazarus, Richard, 186–188, 189, 191
Lespérance, François, 37
leukemia, 69–70
London Stock Exchange, 54
"looking sick," 169–170
low control, 9, 10–11, 69, 77
low self-esteem, 77, 135, 137–138
Lyons, David M., 164

M
MacArthur Study of Successful Aging, 43
Mai Thanh Tu, 85
males. *See* gender
Mammoth Magazine, 119–120
management of stress, 114–118
managers, 131–133, 134–135
Maslach, Christina, 34
Mason, John, 188–191
Mason, W.A, 69–71
Mayo Clinic, 177, 178
McClelland, David C., 148–149
McEwen, Bruce, 40, 43, 180–181
McGill Centre for Studies in Aging, 147–148
medical conditions, nonspecific responses, 169–170
meditation, 114
memory
    divided attention, 55–62
    relevant information, 52–55
    selective attention, 51–52
    social support and, 147
    vigilance and, 50
men. *See* gender
menopause, 36–37

menstrual cycle, effect on stress response, 80–81
Merck, 178
metabolic syndrome, 38, 47
military. *See* World War I; World War II
Milner, Brenda, 180–181
MIRA Foundation, 151–152
motor resources, 59
multitasking, 55–62
music, 59–60, 158–159

N
Nature, 172
nonsteroidal anti-inflammatory drugs, 181
norepinephrine, 45
novelty of situation, 9, 66, 69
NUTS factors
    about, 9–10
    in adolescents (SPIN), 119–125
    deconstructing source of stress, 110–112, 116, 120–122
    examples of, 11–20
    personality traits and, 135
    sensitivity to, 117, 122–123, 128–131
    source of in workplace, 132–133

O
obesity, 35–37
Odendaal, J.S., 151
O'Rourke, Norm, 74
Osler, William, 72, 185
oxytocin, 85

P
parasympathetic response, 155
parents, creating children's stress, 4–5
Parker, Karen, 164–165
pear-shaped women, 36–37
Penfield, Wilder, 180–181

Pepto-Bismol stage, 106
Peretz, Isabelle, 159
personality traits, 72–77, 134–135
pet therapy, 150–152
physical activity, 159–162
physical response to stress
    in adolescents, 13–14
    in adults, 15–16
    in children, 12
    in elderly, 19
    function of, 25–26
physiology, separation from
        psychological research, 168
pituitary gland, 24, 173
PMS (premenstrual syndrome),
    80–81
Pollak, Seth, 64
popularity, 101–104
post-traumatic stress disorder
    (PTSD), 101
poverty, 87
power, 95–96
prayer, 157–158
presenteeism, 131
Pruessner, Jens, 77
psychology
    separation from physiological
        research, 168
    stress research, 183–186

Q
questionnaires
    development of, 183–185, 188
    NUTS factors in workplace,
        132–133
    sensitivity to NUTS factors,
        128–131

R
Rahe, Richard H., 183–184
Rain Man, 51
reconstruction of source of stress,
    110–114, 121–125

recruitment of employees, 134,
    138–140
Reichstein, Tadeus, 179
relative stress, 29, 67, 69
relaxation, 110
repressed anger, 74–75
resilience, 110–112
resources, 59
response to stress.
    See stress responses
rheumatoid arthritis, 178
Rimmele, Ulrike, 160
Robert Half Group, 134
Rosenman, Ray, 72, 185
rum and Coke stage, 106–108
rumination, 76

S
Sapolsky, Robert, 89–90
schools
    bullying, 101–104
    change in, 14–15, 112–114
    exercise needs in, 160–161
Seeman, Teresa, 43, 147
selective attention, 51–52
self-esteem, 77, 135, 137–138
self-help books, 166–167
Selye, Hans, 169–174, 175–176,
    179, 189, 191
sensation seekers, 138
sense of low control, 9, 10–11, 69, 77
sensory deprivation, 115–116
shell shock, 175
singing, 156
situations. See stressors
Smith, A.M., 83
social hierarchies
    in adolescents, 97–101
    effect of dominance, 96–97
    perception of status, 95–96
    socioeconomic status, 91–93
    stability of, 89–91
    status in small groups, 93–94

social support, 145–148
Society for the Prevention of
    Cruelty to Animals (SPCA),
    152
socioeconomic status, 91–93, 97–99
source of stress. *See* stressors
SPIN characteristics, 121–125, 126
sports, 160, 161–162
Steptoe, Andrew, 92
steroid psychosis, 180
stress
    biology of, 188–191
    causes of, 7–8
    characteristics inducing, 8, 191.
        See also NUTS factors
    definition of, 175–176
    importance of, 163–165
    measurement of, 183–185
    origin of term, 171–172, 175–176
    perception of, 4–7
    recognition of, 105–108
    research of psychology of,
        183–186
stress, definition of, 176
stress hormones
    brain's reaction to, 180–182
    in delayed stress response,
        69–70
    discovery of, 174–178
    production of, 7
    research into, 189–191
    See also adrenaline; cortisol
Stress Inc., 127–128
stress inoculation, 163–165
stress recipes, examples of, 11–20
stress responses
    age specific, 12, 13–14, 15–16, 19
    control of, 68–69
    delay of, 69–70
    function of, 25–26
    gender specific, 78–88
    importance of, 21–22
    management of, 148–152

personality traits generating,
    72–77
research into, 171–173
stressors
    control of, 111
    deconstruction of, 109–110,
        120–122
    definition of, 176
    exposure to, 163–165
    individual reaction to, 69–70,
        186–188
    management of, 114–118
    physical, 189
    psychological, 189–191
    reconstruction of, 110–114,
        121–125
Stroud, Laura, 82
Suarez, Edward, 74
swans, 138–140

T
tantrums, 144
Taylor, Shelly, 82, 84, 86
tend-and-befriend model, 81–84,
    85–86, 88
Theorell, Tores, 156
threat to ego, 9, 10, 69
thymus, 172–173
time pressure
    as loss of control, 10–11
    stress as, 4–7
total obesity, 35–36
traumatic shock, 168, 183
Type 1 diabetes, 39
Type 2 diabetes, 39, 105
Type A personalities, 72–73, 185
Type B personalities, 185

U
United States, cost of stress, 127
U.S. Army, stress research, 183
unpredictability of situation, 9,
    66, 69

V
vacations, effect of chronic stress, 39–40
vaccines, 41–42
Vaillancourt, Tracy, 102
van Santen, Aafke, 76
verbal intimidation, 102
verbal resources, 59–62
Viau, Robert, 151
victimization approach, 166
vigilance, 50
viruses, 41–42
visual-spatial resources, 59
volunteerism, 148–150

W
waist/hip ratio, 35–37, 45
weight gain, 35–37
West, Jeremy, 157
West, Patrick, 99
Whitehall Study, 92–93
women. *See* gender
work environment
    anxious personality in, 137–138
    changes in, 16–19
        cost of stress, 126–127
        effect of stress, 131
        hostile personality in, 135–137
        origins of stress, 133–134
        recruitment, 134, 138–140
        role of management, 131–133
        sensitivity to NUTS factors, 128–131
        social hierarchy, 91–93
        stimuli in, 59–60
        understanding personalities, 134–135
World Health Organization, 66, 127
World War I, shell shock research, 175
World War II
    adrenal gland research, 177–178
    researchers, 168–169
    stress research, 183

Y
yoga, 114–115, 157